OXFORD LATIN READER

MAURICE BALME & JAMES MORWOOD

OXFORD UNIVERSITY PRESS

OXFORD
UNIVERSITY PRESS

Great Clarendon Street, Oxford OX2 6DP

Oxford University Press is a department of the University of Oxford.
It furthers the University's objective of excellence in research, scholarship,
and education by publishing worldwide in

Oxford New York

Auckland Cape Town Dar es Salaam Hong Kong Karachi
Kuala Lumpur Madrid Melbourne Mexico City Nairobi
New Delhi Shanghai Taipei Toronto

With offices in

Argentina Austria Brazil Chile Czech Republic France Greece
Guatemala Hungary Italy Japan South Korea Poland Portugal
Singapore Switzerland Thailand Turkey Ukraine Vietnam

Oxford is a registered trade mark of Oxford University Press
in the UK and in certain other countries

British Library Cataloguing in Publication Data

Data available

ISBN-13: 978 0 19 521209 9
ISBN-10: 0 19 521209 6

9 10

Printed and bound in Great Britain by Ashford Colour Press Ltd., Gosport

Contents

Acknowledgements

The publisher and authors would like to thank the many consultants
in the United Kingdom and the United States for comments and
suggestions that have contributed towards this second edition.
In particular: (UK) Julian Morgan, Deborah Bennett, David Cartwright,
Alison Doubleday, John Powell, Philip Powell, Jeremy Rider, Tim
Reader, F.R.Thorn, Andrew Wilson; (US) John Gruber-Miller, Carlos
Fandal, Dennis Herer, James Lowe, Diana Stone and Jeffrey Wills.

*The publishers would like to thank the following for permission to reproduce
photographs*:

J Allan Cash p. 190; Ancient Art & Architecture p. 63; Bibliothèque
Nationale p. 195; Bodleian Library p. 28; British Museum pp. 52,
62(top), 78(top), 110, 128, 131, 136, 146, 147, 160, 180, 187, 216; R L
Dalladay pp. 45, 89, 99, 150, 173, 188, 204; M Dixon pp. 60(top), 97,
98, 107, 148, 210, 218; Fitzwilliam Museum p. 186; Fototeca Unione of
the American Academy, Rome p. 62; Sonia Halliday pp. 38, 130(top),
169; A F Kersting p. 214; Mairani Grazia Neri pp. 10, 176, 185, 191;
Mansell Collection pp. 9, 21, 25, 39, 51, 58, 81, 88, 101, 104, 119, 140,
142, 154, 158, 168, 198, 208; James Morwood title page, pp. 11, 15, 17,
35, 48, 54, 61, 70, 72, 77, 78, 108, 111, 115, 118, 127, 130, 153, 166,
183, 194, 207, 211, 221; Museum of Fine Arts, Boston p. 148; National
Museum of Athens p. 112; National Museum of Wales p. 160; Fabrizio
Parisio p. 210; Octopus Books p. 162; Rhenisches Landesmuseum, Trier
p. 193; Roger-Viollet pp. 141, 172, 202; Scala pp. 12, 29, 150, 200;
E Smith p. 31; Somerset County Museum p. 157; Vatican Library pp.
143, 144, 146(bottom), 152; Werner Forman Archive p.54.

Cover photograph: Mansell Collection

The maps are by Tech Graphics, OUP

Introduction

The six authors included in this reader – Cicero, Caesar, Catullus, Virgil, Livy and Ovid – span what is called the Golden Age of Latin literature. The first three lived during the last years of the republic, the last three flourished under Augustus; Cicero, the eldest of these authors, was born in 106 BC, Ovid, the youngest died in about AD 17.

Although this period produced the greatest Latin writers, it was a time of rapid political decline and continual upheavals, in which the Romans, while they expanded their empire overseas, destroyed the old republic in a series of civil wars which were only ended when one man, Augustus, secured control of the state and became the first emperor.

By 150 BC the *nobiles** had a monopoly of political power, ruling the state through the senate, which controlled the magistrates and made decisions on all important matters by decrees of the senate (*senatus consulta*). In 133 BC the power of the senate was challenged by a tribune of the people called Tiberius Gracchus, who put a programme of land reform through the *concilium plebis* (assembly of the people); he then stood for a second term as tribune with a broader programme of reform, but while he was defending his decision before the people, the senators streamed out of the senate house to break up the assembly. In the ensuing riot, Gracchus himself and three hundred of his supporters were clubbed to death. This was the first blood spilt in political conflict for many hundreds of years.

Ten years later Tiberius' younger brother, Gaius, was elected tribune and put through a wide programme of reforms; he was elected for a second term and for a time he virtually controlled the republic from his position as tribune. But in 121 BC his popularity was waning and an attempt was made by a fellow tribune to repeal his legislation. A riot followed in which someone was killed. The senate promptly passed a decree authorizing the consuls to save the state. The consuls gathered forces and attacked Gracchus' men, who took refuge on the Aventine hill. Gracchus himself and many of his supporters were

---

*The *nobiles* were members of a small group of families from which the consuls were drawn; in the last hundred years of the republic only four 'new men', i.e. men whose families had not achieved the consulate, were admitted to this exclusive club.

killed; three thousand others were captured and put to death without trial.

The nobles had thus restored their power by force of arms and for a time the people were cowed into submission. But ten years later a military crisis turned the tables. Rome had become involved in a war in Africa which was not going well; an officer called Marius, who was on the staff of the general Metellus, thought he could manage things better and got permission to return to Rome and stand for the consulship. Although a *novus homo* (i.e. none of his family had ever been consul), he was elected consul and then, through the *concilium plebis*, had the African command transferred from the man appointed by the senate to himself (105 BC). He reorganized the army and brought the war to a successful conclusion.

Meanwhile Roman generals had suffered two devastating defeats in the north of Italy from invading German tribes. Marius, now a popular hero, was elected to a second consulship and was given command against the German invaders by the *concilium plebis*. He was elected to repeated consulships (104–101 BC) while he trained his army, and he eventually defeated the invaders in two great battles (Aquae Sextiae 102 BC, Vercellae 101 BC).

Back in Rome Marius was elected to a sixth consulship, but he was a military man and proved incapable of coping with the political situation. By now the state was riven by faction; the *optimates*, led by the more conservative *nobiles*, were opposed to the *populares*, who were continually agitating for reforms which would break the power of the *nobiles*; in between were the *equites*, who backed sometimes one faction, sometimes the other. Marius had been brought to power by the *populares* but now, when he considered their programme too extreme, he abandoned them and lost all influence himself. He left Rome and travelled in Asia, not returning to Rome until 90 BC.

At this time Rome's Italian allies (*socii*) were becoming increasingly restive. Excluded from the citizenship but required to serve in the army, they bore the burden of Rome's wars overseas without any compensating privileges or rewards. In 90 BC this smouldering discontent broke out into war (the so-called Social War); by 89 BC the Roman armies had broken the allies in a series of campaigns in which Sulla distinguished himself, and the senate ended the war by offering the allies the Roman citizenship for which they had fought. The towns of the allies who accepted this offer became self-governing *municipia*;

the allies themselves had full citizen rights in Rome. This was the beginning of the unification of Italy.

By now a new war was threatening in the East; Mithridates, king of Pontus (the Black Sea area), had attacked the Roman province of Asia, massacred Roman citizens and invaded Greece (88 BC). The senate assigned the command in this war to the consul for 88 BC, Sulla. A tribune transferred the command to Marius by a *plebiscitum*; Sulla then marched on Rome at the head of an army and Marius fled to Africa. Although little blood was spilt on this occasion, Sulla's march on Rome marked the end of the power struggle by constitutional means and anticipated future civil wars. Sulla had measures passed to reduce the power of the tribunes and left to take up his command in the East. Marius promptly returned to Italy, collected an army and marched on Rome. He took the city, massacred his opponents and had himself elected to a seventh consulship, but died a few days later (86 BC).

While Sulla was in the East, the *populares* controlled Rome under the leadership of Cornelius Cinna, whose daughter Caesar married. In 83 BC Sulla returned victorious from the East. Civil war ensued, culminating in a bloody battle at the gates of Rome (Battle of the Colline Gate, 1 November 82 BC). Reentering Rome, Sulla was appointed by the senate *dictator rei publicae constituendae* (dictator for reforming the constitution). He crushed all opposition ruthlessly, using proscriptions as one weapon to dispose of his enemies. He passed a series of measures intended to strengthen the power of the senate. In 79 BC he resigned his dictatorship and retired into private life, dying the following year.

Events following Sulla's death are explained in the running commentary on the extracts from Cicero, but we give below a chronological table which covers the period from the tribunate of Tiberius Gracchus to the death of Cicero. You may wish to refer to this from time to time as you read the passages of Cicero.

Chronological table

	Historical events	Caesar	Cicero
BC			
133	Tiberius Gracchus tribune		
123–122	C. Gracchus tribune		
111–105	War against Jugurtha		
107	Marius elected consul and given command in Africa		
106			Cicero born
105–100	Marius consul six years running		
102–101	Marius defeats Cimbri and Teutones		102 Quintus Cicero born
100		Caesar born	
90–89	Social War		89 He serves in Social War
88	Sulla marches on Rome		
87	Marius seizes Rome	His father dies	
87–83	Sulla in the East (first Mithridatic War)	He marries Cornelia	
82	Sulla returns to Italy (civil war)		
82–80	Sulla dictator		
81		81–78 Military service in Asia	First speech in law courts
78	Sulla dies		
76		He is captured by pirates	He marries Terentia
75			Tullia born
75–74			Quaestor in Sicily
70	Pompey and Crassus consuls		Speech in Verrem
68		Quaestor in Further Spain	
67	Pompey clears the seas of pirates		
66–63	Pompey's victories in the East (second Mithridatic War)		66 Praetor
65		Aedile	Marcus born
63	Catiline's conspiracy		Consul
62	Pompey returns from the East	Praetor	
61		Propraetor of Further Spain	
60	First Triumvirate (Caesar, Pompey, Crassus)		
59		Consul	
58–49		Governor of Gaul	58 Exiled
57	Conquest of Gaul		Recalled from exile
55		First expedition to Britain	
54		Second expedition to Britain	
53	Crassus killed at Carrhae	Revolt of Gaul	
51			Governor of Cilicia
50	Pompey joins nobles against Caesar		
49	Civil war	He invades Italy	He joins Pompey
48	Battle of Pharsalus	He defeats Pompey	
48–47		Caesar in Egypt – Cleopatra	
47			He is pardoned by Caesar
46		He defeats republican forces in Africa	He divorces Terentia
45			Death of Tullia
44		Elected dictator for life Assassinated (Brutus and Cassius)	He leads senators against Antony
43	Second Triumvirate (Antony, Octavian, Lepidus)		He is murdered

CICERO

By nature a thinker, a scholar and a literary man, Marcus Tullius Cicero (106–43 BC) was driven by ambition to a career in the law courts and the hurly-burly of Roman politics. His literary output is phenomenal. He wrote a good deal of poetry (perhaps rather poor stuff), seven works on rhetoric and seventeen on philosophy. Fifty-eight of his speeches survive from a career during which he dominated the Roman bar. Whenever events forced him to withdraw from Roman politics for a time, we find him writing. And in his writing he reshaped the Latin language; his influence remained incalculable throughout ancient times and right up to the last century.

Cicero

In this selection we use primarily his letters, which are perhaps the most interesting and attractive of all his works. These letters fall into three main collections: first, his letters to his closest friend Titus Pomponius Atticus, to whom he wrote sometimes two or three times a month; they were collected by Atticus and published after Cicero's death in sixteen books. Second, his letters to his other friends and family, collected by his secretary Tiro (who must have kept copies), and published again in sixteen books. Third, his letters to his brother Quintus, which form three books. They number in total over a thousand, mostly private letters, not intended for publication and written without reserve, in an easy, often colloquial, style.

This unique collection throws a vivid and fascinating light both on the politics of the time and on Cicero's own character. From them we get to know him better than any other man of ancient times. He was often anxious and self-critical; vain but well able to laugh at himself; full of self-doubts but in the last resort high principled and courageous; loyal and affectionate, impulsive and emotional. It is surprising that a man of so complex and humane a character should have survived so long and achieved so much in the last turbulent years of the republic.

The earliest letter from these collections was written in 68 BC, when Cicero was thirty-eight years old and had already made his mark in politics. From the earlier years of the correspondence only a few letters survive, but their numbers steadily increase (thirty letters from the period 68 to 60 BC, over six hundred from the last five years of his life). And so, in attempting to give a consecutive view of his life, we have used extracts from his speeches and his other works for the earlier years.

1 The young Cicero

Arpinum today

*Cicero was born in the town of Arpinum in the hills about sixty
miles south-east of Rome. His family had never taken part in
politics at Rome, but they were one of the leading families of the
district (*domi nobiles, *as the Romans put it). His father was a
scholarly man whose health was weak and whose principal love
was literature. The family home was large enough but not grand.
Cicero was devoted to his birthplace and often used to return there
in later life, as he told Atticus when he took him there on a visit
together with his brother Quintus. The following extract is taken
from Cicero's* de Legibus, *which is cast in the form of a dialogue.*

Atticus: antea mirabar (nihil enim esse his in locis nisi saxa et
montes cogitabam) te tam valde hoc loco delectari; nunc contra
miror te, cum Roma absis, usquam potius esse.
Cicero: ego vero, cum licet plures dies abesse, praesertim hoc
5   tempore anni, et amoenitatem et salubritatem hanc sequor; raro
autem licet. sed nimirum me alia quoque causa delectat, quae te
non attingit, Tite.
Atticus: quae tandem ista causa est?
Cicero: quia, si verum dicimus, haec est mea et huius fratris mei
10 germana patria; hic enim orti stirpe antiquissima sumus; hic sacra,
hic genus, hic maiorum multa vestigia. quid plura? hanc vides
villam, ut nunc quidem est, lautius aedificatam patris nostri studio,
qui cum esset infirma valetudine, hic fere aetatem egit in litteris,
sed hoc ipso in loco, cum avus viveret et antiquo more parva esset
15 villa, me scito esse natum. quare inest nescioquid et latet in animo
ac sensu meo, quo me plus hic locus fortasse delectet, si quidem
etiam ille sapientissimus vir, Ithacam ut videret, immortalitatem
scribitur repudiasse.

(*de Legibus* 2.1.2–3)

The sacra

1–2 **mirabar ... te ... delectari** 'I was surprised that you were delighted'.

2 **contra** 'on the other hand' (**contra** is here an adverb).

4 **abesse** 'to be away (from Rome)'.

6 **nimirum** 'certainly'.

8 **quae tandem ...?** 'whatever ...?' **tandem** is sometimes used to emphasize an interrogative.

9 **huius fratris mei** 'my brother here'; **huius** tells us that Quintus was with Cicero and Atticus on this occasion.

10 **germana patria** 'my true native country'. **sacra** 'sacred rites', i.e. the cult of the household gods worshipped at the hearth.

11 **quid plura?** 'why (should I say) more?', 'in short'.

12 **lautius** 'more grandly'.

15 **quare** 'for this reason'. **inest nescioquid et latet** 'there is something hidden deep in ...'; Cicero often uses doublets, two verbs or nouns with a similar meaning, to give emphasis.

16 **quo** 'because of which'. **si quidem** 'seeing that'.

17 **sapientissimus vir** Odysseus (= Ulysses); when the nymph Calypso offered him immortality if he would stay with her on her island, he refused, because he longed to return to his home, Ithaca, and his wife, Penelope.

18 **repudiasse = repudiavisse** 'to have rejected'.

When Cicero was about twelve years old, the family moved to Rome in order that he and his brother might have the best available education. By the time he left school, he had determined to achieve distinction in the law and had formed high ambitions.

In 91 BC, at the age of sixteen, he assumed the toga virilis, *and two years later he had to serve in the army for a short time in the Social War (the war in which the Romans fought their Italian allies – see Introduction); but he soon returned to the study of law in Rome. The usual way of embarking on a career in the law at this time was to be apprenticed to a leading lawyer, and when he was eighteen, Cicero began to study under Q. Mucius Scaevola, a famous jurist. It was then that he met his life-long friend Atticus, who was also a pupil of Scaevola. At the same time his interest in philosophy was aroused by the presence in Rome of teachers from Athens, who had fled to Italy when Greece was overrun by Mithridates, king of Pontus.*

A Roman orator

ego autem in iuris civilis studio multum operae dabam Q.
20   Scaevolae, qui quamquam nemini se ad docendum dabat, tamen
consulentibus respondendo studiosos audiendi docebat.
     eodemque tempore, cum princeps Academiae Philo cum
Atheniensium optimatibus Mithridatico bello domo profugisset
Romamque venisset, totum ei me tradidi admirabili quodam ad
25   philosophiam studio concitatus, in quo hoc etiam commorabar
attentius quod sublata iam esse in perpetuum ratio iudiciorum
videbatur. occiderat Sulpicius illo anno tresque proximo oratores
erant crudelissime interfecti, Q. Catulus, M. Antonius, C. Iulius.
eodem anno etiam Moloni Rhodio Romae dedimus operam et
30   actori summo causarum et magistro.

(*Brutus* 306)

19 **in iuris civilis studio** 'in my study of civil law'; the civil law was
an extremely elaborate system, built on precedent and continually
subject to revision. If you wished to bring a civil action, you
would first consult an expert in the law (*iurisconsultus*), who
would give you a *responsum*, telling you the legal formula under
which you should bring your action. Young men who were
training to be lawyers would be present and learn by listening to
the *iurisconsultus* giving his *responsa* and his reasons for them.
multum operae dabam 'I gave much (of) pains to', i.e. 'I studied
hard under'.

21 **consulentibus respondendo** 'by his answers to those who
consulted him'. **studiosos audiendi** 'those keen to listen'.

22–4 **Philo ... Romamque venisset** when Mithridates occupied Athens
in 87 BC (see Introduction), the philosophical schools were closed
and many of the leading philosophers fled to Rome, including
Philo who had been head of the Academy since 110 BC and taught
both philosophy and rhetoric. Cicero's devotion to philosophy
lasted throughout his life and he wrote many important
philosophical works, translating the Greek masters and adapting
them to Roman *mores*. **cum Atheniensium optimatibus** 'with
the leading men of the Athenians'.

25–6 **in quo ... commorabar attentius** 'I delayed in which (study)
more attentively', i.e. 'I extended this study more industriously'.
hoc ablative, 'for this reason'; **quod** 'because'; Cicero often uses
the demonstrative pronouns **id** and **hoc** to refer forwards to an **ut**
clause.

26 **sublata ... esse** 'to have been destroyed'. Under the regimes of
Marius and Sulla normal legal procedures had come to a halt;
their weapons were murder and proscriptions, not the processes of
law. **ratio iudiciorum** 'the system of the law courts', 'legal
practice'.

27 **Sulpicius** P. Sulpicius Rufus, statesman and orator; as tribune in
88 BC he had transferred the command in the East from Sulla to
Marius; when Sulla marched on Rome, Sulpicius was put to death.
illo anno 88 BC. **proximo** supply **anno**.

28 Catulus, Antonius and C. Iulius had all been executed by Marius
when he seized Rome after Sulla's departure to the East (87 BC).
Molon of Rhodes was the most famous teacher of rhetoric of this
period; in 87 BC he was in exile in Rome. Later Cicero studied
under him in Rhodes.

30 **actori summo causarum** 'a first rate pleader of (legal) cases'.

*It was not until 81 BC that Cicero felt ready to make his debut at the
bar in a civil law suit. The following year he successfully defended
Roscius against a freedman of Sulla, Chrysogonus, who brought
against Roscius a trumped up charge of murdering his father.
Cicero's decison to defend Roscius was extremely bold, since Sulla
was still dictator, and by his success he achieved instant fame. But
he thought it wise to retire from Rome until the excitement had died
down. He had also been advised that for the sake of his health he
should take a rest from the exertions of the law courts. He spent the
next two years travelling in Asia with his brother Quintus and
studied for some time under Molon.*

   *When he returned to Rome in 77 BC, he was in better health and
had achieved a more moderate style of rhetoric. Sulla was now
dead and constitutional government was more or less restored. In
76 BC he married Terentia, a woman of noble birth, and the
following year she bore him a daughter, Tullia. He had now
reached the age when he could stand for office; he was elected
quaestor for 75 BC and posted to Lilybaeum in the west of Sicily,
where he he performed his duties conscientiously and fairly,
winning the devotion of the Sicilian people. Many years later he
revealed in a speech in the law courts how he thought that
everyone at Rome must be praising his performance as quaestor.*

non vereor ne mihi aliquid, iudices, videar adrogare, si de quaestura
mea dixero. quamvis enim illa floruerit, tamen eum me postea
fuisse in maximis imperiis arbitror ut non ita multum mihi gloriae
ex quaesturae laude repetendum. sed tamen non vereor ne quis
35 audeat dicere ullius in Sicilia quaesturam aut clariorem aut
gratiorem fuisse. vere me Hercule hoc dicam: sic tum existimabam,
nihil homines aliud Romae nisi de quaestura mea loqui. frumenti in
summa caritate maximum numerum miseram; negotiatoribus
comis, mercatoribus iustus, mancipibus liberalis, sociis abstinens,
40 omnibus eram visus in omni officio diligentissimus; excogitati
quidam erant a Siculis honores in me inauditi. itaque hac spe
decedebam, ut mihi populum Romanum ultro omnia delaturum
putarem.
   at ego cum casu diebus eis itineris faciendi causa decedens e
45 provincia Puteolos forte venissem, cum plurimi et lautissimi in eis
locis solent esse, concidi paene, iudices, cum ex me quidam
quaesisset quo die Roma exiissem et num quid esset novi. cui cum
respondissem me e provincia decedere, 'etiam me Hercule,' inquit,
'ut opinor, ex Africa.' huic ego iam stomachans fastidiose, 'immo ex
50 Sicilia,' inquam. tum quidam, quasi qui omnia sciret, 'quid? tu
nescis' inquit 'hunc quaestorem Syracusis fuisse?' quid multa?
destiti stomachari et me unum ex eis feci qui ad aquas venissent.

(pro Plancio 65)

31 **mihi aliquid ... adrogare** 'to claim something for myself' = 'to boast'.

32 **quamvis ... illa floruerit** 'however much it (my quaestorship) flourished' = 'however successful it may have been'.

32–3 **eum ... ut** 'such ... that'. By the time he made this speech (54 BC) he had been consul and had saved the state from Catiline's conspiracy.

36 **me Hercule** 'by Hercules'; a common way of swearing the truth of what you are saying.

38 **caritate** 'dearness', 'high price', i.e. 'when the price of corn was very high (in Rome)', owing to shortage. **numerum** 'quantity'. **negotiatoribus** 'businessmen', i.e. bankers etc.

39 **mancipibus** 'contractors', especially tax-collectors. **sociis abstinens** 'honest (free from greed) towards the allies'; the *socii* were the native Sicilians, allies of the Roman people.

40–41 **excogitati ... erant** 'had been thought out, devised'.

41 **a Siculis** 'by the people of Sicily'.

42 **decedebam** 'I was leaving (my province)'. **ultro** 'of its own accord', 'unasked'. **delaturum** supply **esse**.

45 **Puteolos** Puteoli was not only an important port but a spa and a fashionable seaside resort; Cicero arrived there at the height of the season when the smartest (**lautissimi**) people were there.

47 **num quid esset novi** 'whether there was any news'.

48 **etiam me Hercule** 'yes, of course'.

49 **stomachans** 'getting annoyed'. **immo** 'no'.

50 **quasi qui omnia sciret** 'like a man who knew everything', 'a know-all'.

51 **Syracusis** there were two quaestors in Sicily, one posted at Syracuse, the other at Lilybaeum in the west of the island; Cicero had been at Lilybaeum.

52 **ad aquas** 'to (take) the waters'.

A peristylium

His performance as quaestor was to have important consequences, for a few years later the people of Sicily begged him to undertake the prosecution of Verres, the notorious governor who had pillaged Sicily for three years. He undertook this brief at great personal risk, for Verres was a noble supported by a strong following of the optimates; if he had failed, it would have been the end of his career. But his presentation of the case and the overwhelming evidence he collected was so devastating that Verres threw up the case and fled into exile before the verdict was reached. By this one success Cicero became the acknowledged leader of the Roman bar and his future success in politics was assured.

The following year (69 BC) he climbed the next rung of the political ladder, being elected aedile; the duties of aedile were mainly administrative and his tenure seems to have been uneventful.

His earliest surviving letter is dated November 68 BC, the year after he had been aedile. He writes to Atticus on domestic affairs. His brother Quintus had married Atticus' sister Pomponia and the marriage was in trouble; Pomponia was a difficult woman and Quintus had a quick temper.

quod ad me scribis de sorore tua, testis erit ipsa quantae mihi curae fuerit ut Quinti fratris animus in eam esset is qui deberet. quem
55 cum esse offensiorem arbitrarer, eas litteras ad eum misi quibus et placarem ut fratrem et monerem ut minorem et obiurgarem ut errantem. itaque ex iis quae postea saepe ab eo ad me scripta sunt confido ita esse omnia ut oporteat et velimus.

Epiroticam emptionem gaudeo tibi placere. Quintum fratrem
60 cottidie exspectamus. Terentia magnos articulorum dolores habet. et te et sororem tuam et matrem maxime diligit salutemque tibi plurimam adscribit et Tulliola, deliciae nostrae. cura ut valeas et nos ames et tibi persuade te a me fraterne amari.

(*ad Atticum* 1.5.2, 7–8)

Cicero's efforts to patch up things between Quintus and Pomponia were unsuccessful, as a letter written to Atticus many years later shows.

In 66 BC Cicero was elected to the praetorship, one of the two major magistracies; he would have been president of one of the standing courts in Rome. His first speech to the people as praetor was in support of a law to give Pompey a special command in the East against Mithridates; the previous year Pompey had held a command with exceptional powers which had enabled him to deal with the menace of the pirates who were dominating the

53 **quod ad me scribis** 'as for what you write to me'.

53–4 **quantae mihi curae fuerit ut** 'how anxious I have been that' (predicative dative).

54 **Quinti ... animus ... esset is qui ...** 'Quintus' feelings should be such as ...'.

55 **offensiorem** 'too resentful'.

55–6 **quibus ... placerem ... monerem ... obiurgarem** the relative with the subjunctive expresses purpose.

56 **minorem** 'younger'.

56–7 **obiurgarem ut errantem** 'scold him as doing wrong', i.e. 'rebuke his errors'.

59 **Epiroticam emptionem** Atticus had recently bought an estate in Epirus, on the mainland opposite Corfu, where he was to spend much of his time, free from the hurlyburly of Rome.

60 **articulorum** 'of the joints'; it sounds as if she was suffering from arthritis.

62 **et Tulliola** 'and (so does) little Tullia, my darling'. Cicero was always devoted to his daughter and often uses this affectionate diminutive.

63 **fraterne** 'like a brother'.

View over the bay at Puteoli

*Mediterranean; in three months he had swept them from the seas
and destroyed their strongholds on land. A tribune had now
proposed that Pompey's command should be extended to deal with
Mithridates who, despite his defeat by Sulla in 89 BC, had renewed
his war with Rome. In supporting this proposal Cicero offended the
nobiles, who were afraid that if Pompey were given such power, he
would become a dictator, as Sulla had. With Cicero's support
Pompey was given this command and not only finally defeated
Mithridates but spent the next two years reorganizing the whole of
the East, creating two new provinces, Bithynia and Pontus, and
Syria. Pompey now dominated the political scene and Cicero hoped
that by supporting him against the nobiles he would further his own
career.*

*It was usual for praetors to follow their year of office in Rome
by becoming governors of a province, but Cicero refused a
governorship, since he hated being absent from Rome and was
already beginning to prepare the ground for his election as consul,
for which he would become eligible in three years time. In 65 BC his
son Marcus was born. He wrote to Atticus in July to give him this
news, though the letter is more concerned with his election plans.*

Cicero Attico sal.

65   filiolo me auctum scito, salva Terentia.

    abs te iam diu nihil litterarum! ego de meis ad te rationibus
scripsi antea diligenter. hoc tempore Catilinam, competitorem
nostrum, defendere cogitamus. iudices habemus quos volumus,
summa accusatoris voluntate. spero, si absolutus erit,

70 coniunctiorem illum fore in ratione petitionis.

    tuo adventu nobis opus est maturo. nam prorsus summa opinio
est hominum tuos familiares, nobiles homines, adversarios honori
nostro fore. ad eorum voluntatem mihi conciliandam maximo te
mihi usui fore. quare Ianuario ineunte, ut constituisti, cura ut

75 Romae sis.

(*ad Atticum* 1.2)

65 **filiolo me auctum** 'that I have been blessed (literally, increased) by a little son'. **salva Terentia** 'Terentia being well' (ablative absolute).

66 **nihil litterarum** 'no letter!' (partitive genitive, compare **aliquid vini** = 'some (thing of) wine'). **rationibus** 'plans (for his election campaign)'.

67 **Catilinam** Catiline, the future conspirator, was being prosecuted for extortion while he was governor of Africa. Cicero says elsewhere that his guilt was as plain as daylight, but he now thought of defending him in order to have his cooperation in the elections of the following year; Catiline was standing for the consulship and, if they ran together, they might be able to exclude other candidates. **competitorem** 'my fellow candidate'.

68–9 **iudices ... voluntate** the composition of the jury was vital in a trial which had a strong political element. Both prosecuting and defending counsel could challenge members of the jury panel and have them removed. In this case the prosecuting counsel was colluding with the defence to produce a jury favourable to Catiline.

70 **coniunctiorem** 'more closely allied'.

71 **prorsus** 'certainly'.

72 **tuos familiares** Atticus had a number of close friends amongst the *nobiles* who might be persuaded to support Cicero, though the majority would certainly be opposed to the election of a *novus homo* (i.e. a man whose family had never held the consulship; it was thirty years since a *novus homo* was last elected).

2 Consulship, exile and return

In the event Cicero was elected consul in July 64 BC at the top of the poll. The nobiles *came round to supporting him at the last moment for fear of what Catiline might do, if elected. In his year as consul Cicero faced a major crisis when Catiline, rejected at the polls again in July 63 BC, resorted to revolution, planning, according to Cicero, to raise an army of malcontents, murder the consuls and seize power. Cicero learnt of the conspiracy from an informer but did not yet have enough evidence to take action. Catiline was still living openly in Rome and even attending the senate. The city was rife with rumour and panic was setting in. Cicero surrounded himself with a bodyguard and posted watches at key points in the city. The senate met and in a famous speech Cicero openly denounced him; this is how it begins.*

quo usque tandem abutere, Catilina, patientia nostra? quam diu etiam furor iste nos eludet? quem ad finem sese effrenata iactabit audacia? nihilne te nocturnum praesidium Palati, nihil urbis vigiliae, nihil timor populi, nihil concursus bonorum omnium, nihil
5 horum ora vultusque moverunt? patere tua consilia non sentis, constrictam iam horum omnium scientia teneri coniurationem tuam non vides? quid proxima, quid superiore nocte egeris, ubi fueris, quos convocaveris, quid consili ceperis quem nostrum ignorare arbitraris? o tempora, o mores! senatus haec intellegit, consul videt;
10 hic tamen vivit.

(*in Catilinam* 1.1)

This furious denunciation forced Catiline to flee from Rome to the army his lieutenants were trying to raise in Etruria. Cicero then arrested the ringleaders of the conspiracy who were still in Rome. He was hailed as parens patriae *and praised to the skies by men of all political persuasions. There followed a debate in the senate to decide what to do with the conspirators who had been arrested. Cicero put the question to the senate and one after another the senators voted for the death penalty until it came to Caesar's turn. He made a speech advocating that they should be imprisoned for life in separate towns. The feeling of the meeting swung towards his view until finally Cato made an impassioned speech for the immediate imposition of the death penalty, a plea which won the day. Cicero superintended their execution in the state prison and announced their death to the waiting crowd by one word,* vixere ('they have lived' = 'their life is over'). *This action, although performed on the advice of the senate, was to cost him dear when political enemies later prosecuted him for putting citizens to death without trial.*

1   **quo usque**? 'how long?' **abutere = abuteris** 'will you abuse?'
(Cicero prefers this form of the 2nd person singular of the future
passive).

2   **eludet** 'mock'. **sese ... iactabit** 'glory', 'strut around'.

2–3   **effrenata ... audacia** 'unbridled audacity'.

5   **horum ora vultusque** 'the faces and expression (= the expression
on the faces) of these men (the senators)'.

6   **constrictam** 'held fast'.

7–8   **quid ... ceperis** these indirect questions depend on **quem nostrum
ignorare arbitraris?**

Cicero denouncing Catiline in the senate

This crisis had temporarily united all parties and Cicero hoped to put an end to the political strife which had torn Rome apart for so many years, by a permanent alliance between the optimates *and the* equites, *a* concordia ordinum, *as he called it. For a short time it looked as if he might succeed, but the state was soon to be split by even worse divisions which led to civil war, while Cicero looked on helplessly.*

At the end of the following year (December 62 BC*) Pompey returned from the East and all held their breath; would he march on Rome, as Sulla had done on his return from the East, and make himself dictator? In the event he disbanded his army at Brundisium and all breathed a sigh of relief. The previous April Cicero had written to him offering to make a political alliance with him and expressing disappointment that Pompey did not recognize his own achievements as consul.*

illud non dubito quin, si te mea summa erga te studia parum mihi adiunxerint, respublica nos inter nos conciliatura coniuncturaque sit. ac ne ignores quid ego in tuis litteris desiderarim, scribam aperte, sicut et mea natura et nostra amicitia postulat. res eas gessi,
15 quarum aliquam in tuis litteris et nostrae necessitudinis et reipublicae causa gratulationem exspectavi; quam ego abs te praetermissam arbitror, quod verere ne cuius animum offenderes. sed scito ea, quae nos pro salute patriae gessimus, orbis terrae iudicio ac testimonio comprobari; quae, cum veneris, tanto
20 consilio tantaque animi magnitudine a me gesta esse cognosces, ut tibi multo maiori, quam Africanus fuit, me non multo minorem quam Laelium facile et in republica et in amicitia adiunctum esse patiare.

(*ad Familiares* 5.7.2–3)

When Pompey disbanded his army, the nobiles *were quick to move against him. They refused to confirm the arrangements he had made in the East and obstructed his attempts to secure land for his veterans.*

In 60 BC *Caesar returned from Spain to stand for the consulship; his election was strenuously resisted by the* nobiles *and he decided to make a secret pact with Pompey, whose eastern settlement was still being obstructed by the senate, and the millionaire M. Crassus (the First Triumvirate). They invited Cicero to join them, but after much heartsearching he refused to countenance such an illegal arrangement. He thereby lost all political influence.*

Caesar showed his hand as soon as he had entered his consulship, using a hired mob to overcome by violence all

11	**non dubito quin** 'I do not doubt that ...'. **mea summa erga te studia** 'my great devotion to you'; i.e. his consistent support for Pompey's cause.
11–12	**parum ... adiunxerint** 'has too little united ...', i.e. 'has failed to unite'.
12	**respublica** 'public affairs', i.e. 'public interest'. **nos inter nos** 'with each other'.
13	**desiderarim = desideraverim** 'I missed'.
15–16	**quarum aliquam ... gratulationem exspectavi** 'for which I expected some congratulation'. Pompey had evidently answered an earlier letter from Cicero without mentioning the latter's triumph in dealing with the conspiracy of Catiline. **et nostrae necessitudinis** ('friendship') **et reipublicae** both nouns depend on **causa** 'because of'.
17	**verere = vereris. ne cuius animum offenderes** 'in case you might offend someone's feelings', i.e. upset the *nobiles* who did not approve Cicero's actions as consul.
18–19	**orbis terrae iudicio** 'in the judgement of the whole world'.
20–23	**ut ... patiare** (= **patiaris**) 'that you will easily allow me, who am not much inferior to Laelius, to be united in politics and friendship with you, who are much greater than Africanus'. Laelius was the friend and adviser of the great Scipio Africanus Minor, who finally defeated and destroyed Carthage in 146 BC. Cicero hoped Pompey would accept himself in the role which Laelius had played to Scipio. His hopes were empty. Pompey treated him coldly and did not make a political alliance with him.

opposition to the measures he proposed and even chasing his fellow consul Bibulus out of the Forum to take refuge in his house. Cicero watched the deteriorating situation with despair. He wrote to Atticus in July 59 BC.

scito nihil umquam fuisse tam infame, tam turpe, tam peraeque
25 omnibus generibus, ordinibus, aetatibus offensum quam hunc
statum qui nunc est. Bibulus in caelo est nec quare scio, sed ita
laudatur quasi
    'unus homo nobis cunctando restituit rem'.
Pompeius, nostri amores, quod mihi summo dolori est, ipse se
30 adflixit. neminem tenet voluntate; ne metu necesse sit iis uti vereor.
populi sensus maxime theatro et spectaculis perspectus est; ludis
Apollinaribus Diphilus tragoedus in nostrum Pompeium petulanter
invectus est:
    'nostra miseria tu es magnus –'
35 miliens coactus est dicere. Caesar cum venisset mortuo plausu,
Curio filius est insecutus. huic ita plausum est ut salva republica
Pompeio plaudi solebat. tulit Caesar graviter.

                        (*ad Atticum* 2.19.2–3)

When Caesar departed to Gaul early in 58 BC, he left Publius Clodius in Rome to watch over his interests. Clodius was a bitter enemy of Cicero, who some years before had invalidated his alibi when he was being prosecuted for sacrilege. He now determined to have his revenge. Elected tribune for 58 BC he introduced a law banishing anyone who had put citizens to death without trial; Cicero was not named in this bill, but it was clearly aimed at him. Cicero panicked and, without attempting to defend himself, in March fled into exile from where he wrote despairing letters to his friends and family.

*   He fled first to southern Italy, but by the end of May had settled in the north-east of Greece (Thessalonica) from where he wrote a series of letters to Atticus, usually despairing, occasionally hopeful. By September he was desperate; still in Thessalonica he wrote this letter to Atticus.*

te oro et obsecro, T. Pomponi, si me omnibus amplissimis
carissimis iucundissimisque rebus hominum perfidia spoliatum, si
40 a meis consiliariis proditum et proiectum vides, si intellegis me
coactum ut ipse me et meos perderem, ut me tua misericordia iuves
et Quintum fratrem, qui potest esse salvus, sustentes, Terentiam
liberosque meos tueare, me, si putas te istic visurum, exspectes, si
minus, invisas, si potes, et pueros ad me cum litteris quam primum
45 et quam saepissime mittas. data xvi Kal. Oct.

                        (*ad Atticum* 3.19.3)

24–5 **peraeque ... offensum** 'equally offensive to'.

25 **generibus** 'classes'.

26 **Bibulus in caelo est** 'Bibulus is in heaven (= praised to the skies)'. Bibulus, Caesar's colleague in the consulship, tried to oppose Caesar but was silenced by his use of mob violence. But he is praised, says Cicero, as if 'he alone had restored the state by delaying' (a line quoted from the poet Ennius about the general Quintus Fabius Maximus, who saved Rome from Hannibal by avoiding battle with him).

29–30 **Pompeius, nostri amores ... ipse se adflixit** 'Pompey, my loved one ... has ruined his own self'; Cicero always wanted to ally himself with Pompey above all others. Now Pompey had given himself to Caesar with results which he found extremely unpleasant; instead of being the hero of the people, he was abominated by them.

31–2 **ludis Apollinaribus** the games in honour of Apollo, celebrated from 6 to 13 July, included dramatic performances. We do not know from what tragedy the line comes in which the tragic actor (**tragoedus**) Diphilus impudently (**petulanter**) attacked Pompey. Pompey was known as 'Pompeius Magnus', and so Diphilus was made to repeat a thousand times (**miliens**) the line 'It's through our misery that you are *magnus*'. Pompey found these demonstrations of popular feeling extremely distressing, whereas they simply made Caesar angry.

36 **Curio filius** he was a young noble who openly opposed the actions of the triumvirs. **huic ita plausum est** 'it was so clapped for him' (impersonal passive) = 'he was so applauded'. **salva republica** 'when the republic was safe', i.e. before the triumvirate took over, when Pompey was a popular idol.

tragoedus

38 **oro et obsecro** 'I pray and beseech'. **T. Pomponi** Atticus' full name was Titus Pomponius Atticus; this form of address is highly emotional. This paragraph consists of one long sentence, in which all the subsequent clauses depend on **te oro et obsecro**. Three conditional clauses (**si ... spoliatum (esse) (vides), si proditum et proiectum (esse) vides, si intellegis me coactum (esse) ut ... perderem**) are followed by three **ut** clauses expressing his prayer: **ut me ... iuves et Quintum ... sustentes, (ut) Terentiam ... tueare, (ut) me ... exspectes, si minus** (= 'if not') **invisas et pueros ... mittas**.

38–9 **me ... spoliatum (esse)** 'that I have been stripped of' (+ abl.).

39 **perfidia** ablative, 'by the treachery'.

40 **a meis consiliariis** 'by my advisers'.

41 **ut ... perderem** 'to ruin'.

42 **(ut) ... sustentes** 'to support'.

43 **te istic visurum (esse)** 'that you will see (me) there (i.e. in Italy)'. Cicero hopes that there is a chance he may be recalled soon and asks Atticus to wait for him in Italy rather than set out for his estate in Greece. Failing this, he asks him to visit (**invisas**) him in Greece.

44 **pueros** 'your slaves'; **puer** is often used to mean 'a slave'.

45 **data** 'posted'. **xvi Kal. Oct.** = 15 September.

In October he wrote an emotional letter to Terentia.

Tullius s.d. Terentiae suae et Tulliolae et Ciceroni suis.

noli putare me ad quemquam longiores epistulas scribere, nisi si
quis ad me plura scripsit, cui puto rescribi oportere. nec enim habeo
quid scribam nec hoc tempore quicquam difficilius facio. ad te vero et
50 ad nostram Tulliolam non queo sine plurimis lacrimis scribere. vos
enim video esse miserrimas, quas ego beatissimas semper esse volui
idque praestare debui, et, nisi timidi fuissemus, praestitissem.

a te quidem omnia fieri fortissime et amantissime video, nec miror,
sed maereo casum eius modi ut tantis tuis miseriis meae miseriae
55 subleventur. hem, mea lux, meum desiderium, unde omnes opem
petere solebant, te nunc, mea Terentia, sic vexari, sic iacere in
lacrimis et sordibus, idque fieri mea culpa, qui ceteros servavi ut nos
periremus!

ego ad quos scribam nescio, nisi ad eos qui ad me scribunt.
60 longius, quoniam ita vobis placet, non discedam; sed velim quam
saepissime litteras mittatis, praesertim si quid est firmius quod
speramus.

valete, mea desideria, valete. data a.d. iii Non. Oct. Thessalonica.

(*ad Familiares* 14.2.1, 2, 4)

This is perhaps the most affectionate letter Cicero wrote to Terentia,
who was doing all she could on his behalf.
The following year Pompey gradually became more and more
disillusioned with Clodius, who was running riot in Rome and causing
chaos with his gang of hired thugs; he even attacked Pompey himself,
who began to regret the exile of Cicero. At last a law was passed with
Pompey's support recalling Cicero. The latter had been kept in touch
with events by friends and had already prepared to return to Italy; he
sailed from Greece the very day the law was proposed (4 August 57 BC).
He landed at Brundisium and made a triumphant progress through
Italy, greeted everywhere by enthusiastic crowds. He describes his
return in a letter to Atticus, written from Rome in September.

nunc etsi omnia aut scripta esse a tuis arbitror aut etiam nuntiis ac
65 rumore perlata, tamen ea scribam brevi quae te puto potissimum ex
meis litteris velle cognoscere.

pridie Nonas Sextiles Dyrrachio profectus sum, ipso illo die quo
lex est lata de nobis. Brundisium veni Nonis Sextilibus. ibi mihi
praesto Tulliola mea fuit natali suo ipso die, qui casu idem natalis erat
70 et Brundisinae coloniae; quae res animadversa a multitudine summa
Brundisinorum gratulatione celebrata est. ante diem iii Idus Sextiles
cognovi, cum Brundisi essem, litteris Quinti fratris mirifico studio
omnium aetatum atque ordinum, incredibili concursu Italiae, legem
comitiis centuriatis esse perlatam. inde a Brundisinis honestissime
75 ornatus iter ita feci ut undique ad me cum gratulatione legati
convenerint. ad urbem ita veni ut nemo ullius ordinis nomenclatori
notus fuerit qui mihi obviam non venerit. cum venissem ad portam

46 **s.d. = salutem dat. Ciceroni** i.e. his son, Marcus.

52 **nisi timidi fuissemus** 'unless I had been timid', 'unless I had panicked'; Cicero frequently uses 'we' for 'I'; he refers to the fact that he fled into exile without attempting to defend himself.

54 **casum eius modi** 'a misfortune of such a kind that ...'.

55 **hem** 'alas!' This is followed by the accusative and infinitive of exclamation: **te nunc ... sic vexari** 'to think that you are so buffeted!' **mea lux** 'light of my life'. **meum desiderium** 'my darling'; **desiderium** = 'longing', 'desire', but it can be used of persons for whom you long or whom you desire.

57 **qui ceteros servavi** Cicero felt that he had saved Rome by executing the conspirators only to bring disaster on himself.

60 **longius ... non discedam** Terentia had evidently asked him not to distance himself further from Rome.

60–61 **velim ... mittatis** 'I should like you to send'.

61 **si quid est firmius** 'if there is anything firmer', i.e. if there is any more reliable news about his recall.

64 **a tuis** 'by your friends'.

65–6 **te ... potissimum ... velle** 'you would most like'.

67 **pridie Nonas Sextiles** = 4 August. **Dyrrachio** Dyrrachium on the west coast of Greece was the usual port of embarcation for Brundisium.

68 **lex est lata** 'the law was proposed'. **Nonis Sextilibus** = 5 August.

69 **praesto ... fuit** 'was there to meet me'; the adverb **praesto** = 'at hand', 'ready to help'. **(dies) natalis** by the 'birthday' of the colony of Brundisium he means the annual celebration of its foundation day, which was marked by a public holiday.

71 **ante diem iii Idus Sextiles** = 11 August.

72 **litteris Quinti** 'by a letter from Quintus'.

73 **incredibili concursu Italiae** 'by an incredible concourse of Italy', i.e. an incredible number of citizens from the *municipia* had swarmed to Rome to vote for the law recalling Cicero.

74 **comitiis centuriatis** 'the Centuriate Assembly'; this was the most important of the three assemblies in which the people met; its main function was to elect the senior magistrates but it could also pass laws.

75 **legati** 'envoys', i.e. deputations from the cities through which he passed on his way to Rome.

76–7 **nomenclatori notus** 'known to my name-caller'; the function of the *nomenclator* was to whisper to his master the name of anyone who approached him, but he could only know the names of the more prominent citizens, so that **nemo ... nomenclatori notus** means 'no one of any importance'.

77 **qui mihi obviam non venerit** they all streamed out of the city as Cicero approached the Porta Capena (the gate which led to the Via Appia) to greet him.

Capenam, gradus templorum ab infima plebe completi
erant; a qua plausu maximo cum esset mihi gratulatio
80 significata, similis et frequentia et plausus me usque
ad Capitolium celebravit in foroque et in ipso
Capitolio miranda multitudo fuit. postridie in senatu
senatui gratias egimus.

alterius vitae quoddam initium ordimur. iam
85 quidam qui nos absentis defenderunt incipiunt
praesentibus occulte irasci, aperte invidere.
vehementer te requirimus.

(*ad Atticum* 4.1.4–5, 8)

Cicero now attempted to break up the triumvirate by
detaching Pompey from Caesar and persuading him to
form an alliance with the senate. Caesar acted with
his usual decisiveness; he summoned Pompey and
Crassus to a meeting in April 56 BC; the triumvirate
was renewed and Cicero was told he must keep quiet.
From now on he was a frustrated observer of events,
recognizing that there was nothing he could do. He
spent most of his time in the country writing works on
philosophy and rhetoric.

While Cicero was in exile, Clodius' gangs had
destroyed not only his house in Rome but his two
favourite villas, one at Tusculum, the other at
Formiae. The senate voted that both his house in Rome
on the Palatine hill and the two villas should be
restored at public expense ('the consuls valued my
house at two million sesterces but the other properties
at very ungenerous figures – the Tusculan villa at 500,000, the
Formian at 250,000'). Rebuilding was started at once, but Clodius'
gangs were still running riot and tried to prevent the rebuilding and
even attacked Cicero, as he tells Atticus in a letter of 23 November 57
BC.

A fifteenth-century manuscript of
Cicero's letter to Atticus

armatis hominibus ante diem tertium Nonas Novembris expulsi sunt
fabri de area nostra, Quinti fratris domus primo fracta coniectu
90 lapidum ex area nostra, deinde inflammata iussu Clodi inspectante
urbe coniectis ignibus, magna querela et gemitu hominum omnium.
ille vel ante demens ruere, post hunc vero furorem nihil nisi caedem
inimicorum cogitare, vicatim ambire, servis aperte spem libertatis
ostendere.
95 itaque a.d. iii Id. Nov. cum Sacra via descenderem, insecutus est
me cum suis. clamor, lapides, fustes, gladii; et haec improvisa omnia.
discessi in vestibulum Tetti Damonis. qui erant mecum facile operas
aditu prohibuerunt. ipse occidi potuit; sed ego diaeta curare incipio,
chirurgiae taedet.

(*ad Atticum* 4.3.2–3)

78 **ab infima plebe** 'by the common people'.

84 **quoddam initium ordimur** 'I am starting a sort of beginning'; **quidam** is often used to soften a metaphor; Cicero was not literally beginning a second life.

86 **praesentibus occulte irasci** 'to become secretly angry at the present state of affairs.' His triumphant return and his immediate and successful resumption of politics in the following days was already beginning to arouse jealousy and opposition.

cum venissem ad Portam Capenam

88 **ante diem ... Novembris** = 3 November.

89 **de area nostra** 'from my building site'. **Quinti ... domus** his house was next door to Cicero's.

90–91 **inspectante urbe** 'while the city watched' = 'before the eyes of the whole city'.

92 **vel ante** 'even before this'.

92–4 **ruere ... cogitare ... ambire ... ostendere** historic infinitives, which are often used of successive actions in excited narrative; translate as though they were indicatives, 'he was rushing about' etc.

93 **vicatim ambire** 'going around the streets'.

93–4 **servis ... ostendere** Clodius was tempting slaves to serve in his gang by offering them liberty.

95 **a.d. iii Id. Nov.** = 11 November.

96 **fustes** 'clubs'.

97 **Tetti Damonis** we do not know who this was. **qui erant mecum** '(those) who were with me'; Cicero had no doubt taken the precaution of having an adequate escort in these dangerous times. **operas** 'gangs'.

98 **ipse** i.e. Clodius himself.

98–9 **sed ego ... taedet** 'but I'm beginning to practise cure by diet; I'm tired of surgery', i.e. 'I no longer wish to cure the troubles by violent measures' (ancient medicine was divided into three branches: dietetic, i.e. diet and general regime, pharmaceutic and surgery).

To meet the threats of Clodius, Titus Milo, who had been a strong supporter of Cicero's recall, raised a rival gang. All law and order were breaking down and gang fights were continually occurring. At the beginning of 56 BC Clodius had the audacity to prosecute Milo de vi, i.e. for using violence in politics. Cicero describes in a letter to Quintus what happened at the preliminary public hearing, which took place in the Forum.

100   a.d. viii Id. Febr. Milo adfuit. dixit Pompeius sive voluit; nam, ut
     surrexit, operae Clodianae clamorem sustulerunt, idque ei perpetua
     oratione contigit, non modo ut acclamatione sed ut convicio et
     maledictis impediretur. qui ut peroravit (nam in eo sane fortis fuit;
     non est deterritus; dixit omnia atque interdum etiam silentio, cum
105   auctoritate pervicerat) – sed ut peroravit, surrexit Clodius. ei tantus
     clamor a nostris (placuerat enim referre gratiam) ut neque mente
     nec lingua neque ore consisteret. ea res acta est, cum hora sexta vix
     Pompeius perorasset, usque ad horam octavam, cum omnia
     maledicta, versus denique obscenissimi in Clodium et Clodiam
110   dicerentur. ille furens et exsanguis interrogabat suos in clamore
     ipso quis esset qui plebem fame necaret; repondebant operae
     'Pompeius'. hora fere nona quasi signo dato Clodiani nostros
     consputare coeperunt; exarsit dolor. urgere illi ut loco nos
     moverent; factus est a nostris impetus; fuga operarum; eiectus e
115   rostris Clodius, ac nos quoque fugimus, ne quid in turba. senatus
     vocatus in curiam; Pompeius domum; neque ego tamen in senatum.

                                (*ad Quintum Fratrem* 2.3.2)

Cicero had been warned by the triumvirs to keep out of politics and his activities were now limited to pleading in the courts. But Caesar bore him no ill-will, and Cicero felt sufficiently confident in April 54 BC to write him a rather stilted letter recommending a rising young lawyer, who hoped to profit by serving on Caesar's staff in Gaul.

     Cicero Caesari imperatori salutem dat.
        vide quam mihi persuaserim te me esse alterum, non modo in
     eis rebus quae ad me ipsum sed etiam in iis quae ad meos pertinent.
120   mitto ad te Gaium Trebatium, de quo tibi haec spondeo, probiorem
     hominem, meliorem virum, pudentiorem esse neminem; accedit
     etiam quod familiam ducit in iure civili, vir singulari memoria,
     summa scientia. huic ego nec tribunatum neque praefecturam neque
     ullius beneficii certum nomen peto; totum hominem tibi trado. cura
125   ut valeas et me, ut amas, ama.

                            (*ad Familiares* 7.5, adapted)

100 **a.d. viii Id. Febr.** = 6 February. **adfuit** 'was present' = 'appeared in court'. **dixit Pompeius** i.e. spoke on behalf of Milo. **sive voluit** 'or rather, he wanted to'.

101–2 **perpetua oratione** 'throughout his whole speech'.

105–6 **tantus clamor a nostris** supply a verb, e.g. 'was raised'.

106 **referre gratiam** 'to return the compliment'.

106–7 **ut neque mente ... consisteret** 'so that he remained firm neither in mind ...' = 'could not control either his mind ...'.

108 **usque ad** 'right up to'.

109 **versus ... obscenissimi** Clodius and his notorious sister Clodia (who may have been the lover of Catullus) were said to have an incestuous relationship.

The Palatine hill

110 **exsanguis** 'bloodless', 'pale'.

111 **qui plebem fame necaret** there was an acute shortage of corn at this time and Pompey had been given a special commission to manage the corn supply.

112 **Clodiani** 'Clodius' gang'.

113 **consputare** 'to spit in unison'. **urgere** 'they shoved' (historic infinitive).

114 **fuga operarum** '(there was) a flight of the gangs', i.e. 'Clodius' gangs fled'; in this excited narrative Cicero adopts a telegraphic style, omitting verbs; so also in *l.* 115 **ne quid in turba** = 'in case something (should happen) in the confusion' etc.

118 **te me esse alterum** 'that you are my second self'.

120 **spondeo** 'I guarantee'.

121–2 **accedit etiam quod** 'added (to this) also is the fact that' = 'besides this ...'.

122 **familiam ducit** 'leads the field'.

123 **praefecturam** a prefect might perform various functions, both civil and military.

124 **ullius beneficii certum nomen** 'the specific name of any benefit' = 'any particular piece of patronage'.

Trebatius proved a disappointment; he did not answer Cicero's letters and was reluctant to follow Caesar to Britain because he was nervous of the sea-crossing.

Cicero wrote to him in the middle of June (54 BC), shortly before the second invasion commenced. Despite the light-hearted tone of the letter, he gives Trebatius a smart blow on the knuckles for not answering his letters and failing to take advantage of the opportunities for advancement that had been handed him on a plate.

ego te commendare non desisto, sed quid proficiam ex te scire cupio. spem maximam habeo in Balbo, ad quem diligentissime et saepissime scribo. illud soleo admirari, non me totiens accipere tuas litteras, quotiens a Quinto mihi fratre adferantur.

130   in Britannia nihil audio esse neque auri neque argenti. id si ita est, essedum aliquod capias suadeo et ad nos quam primum recurras. sin autem sine Britannia quod volumus, tamen adsequi possumus, perfice ut sis in familiaribus Caesaris. multum te in eo frater adiuvabit meus, multum Balbus, sed, mihi crede, tuus pudor

135 et labor plurimum. habes imperatorem liberalissimum, aetatem opportunissimam, commendationem certe singularem, ut tibi unum timendum sit, ne ipse tibi defuisse videaris.

(*ad Familiares* 7.7)

Caesar did in fact take Trebatius on as a iurisconsultus *(legal adviser) and he later had a distinguished career, becoming legal adviser to Augustus.*

Cicero's brother Quintus was serving on Caesar's staff and Cicero had been waiting anxiously to hear that he had landed safely in Britain. He wrote to him in August 54 BC. After giving him news of events in Rome, he continues thus.

venio nunc ad id quod nescio an primum esse debuerit. o iucundas mihi tuas de Britannia litteras! timebam Oceanum, timebam litus

140 insulae; reliqua quidem non contemno, sed plus habent tamen spei quam timoris magisque sum sollicitus exspectatione ea quam metu. te vero materiam scribendi egregiam habere video. quos tu situs, quas naturas rerum et locorum, quos mores, quas gentis, quas pugnas, quem vero ipsum imperatorem habes!

145   quomodonam, mi frater, de nostris versibus Caesar? nam primum librum se legisse scripsit ad me ante, et prima sic ut neget se ne Graeca quidem meliora legisse.

(*ad Quintum Fratrem* 2.15.4–5)

127   **in Balbo** Balbus was Caesar's private secretary and confidential agent, who watched over Caesar's interests in Rome when he was abroad; they communicated with each other in code.

128–9   **totiens ... quotiens** 'as often as ...'.

129   **tuas litteras** 'letters from you'.

130   **nihil ... neque auri neque argenti** before Caesar's invasions it had been believed that Britain was rich in minerals (gold, silver and tin); the truth was now emerging and this made the prospect of campaigning in Britain less attractive.

131   **essedum** the British war chariot was a novelty; the Gauls no longer used them, so Cicero suggests jocularly that Trebatius should capture a war chariot and taxi home in it – the only gain he would make from following Caesar to Britain.

132–3   **sin autem ... possumus** 'but if we can still (**tamen**) attain what we want without (your going to) Britain'.

138   **nescio an primum ... debuerit** 'I don't know whether which should have been first' = 'which perhaps should have been first', i.e. earlier in his letter.

139   **tuas ... litteras** 'your letter' (**litterae**, *pl.* = **epistola**), accusative of exclamation.

141   **exspectatione ea** i.e. by waiting to hear whether Quintus had arrived safely in Britain.

142   **materiam scribendi** 'material for writing'; Quintus Cicero was a voluminous writer of verse and had even composed tragedies while he was stationed in Gaul.

143   **quas naturas rerum et locorum** 'what natures of things and places' = 'what strange things and places'. Britain was completely unknown to the Roman world and was thought of as a land of uncouth, woad-painted barbarians, living in eternal mist and rain.

145   **quomodonam ... Caesar?** 'how does Caesar (feel) about ...?'

146   **primum librum** perhaps the poem which Caesar had praised so lavishly was Cicero's *de Temporibus Suis*, which deals with his exile. **prima** (*n. pl.*) 'the first part'.

It is remarkable that a letter written to his brother on active service overseas should be largely about their literary efforts and that what Cicero most wanted to hear was Caesar's opinion of his latest poem. Caesar was no mean critic of literature; perhaps there is a touch of irony in his judgement that he had never read anything better even in Greek. Although Cicero's prose works were generally acknowledged as masterly, his verse was second rate.

The fighting between the gangs of Clodius and Milo continued unabated; finally, in January 52 BC, the rival gangs met by chance on the Via Appia near Rome. In the ensuing fight Clodius was killed. The people, who regarded Clodius as their friend, rioted and burnt down the senate house. Milo was prosecuted, and Pompey, determined to put an end to this lawlessness and secure a condemnation, packed the court with soldiers. Cicero had undertaken the defence of his old ally but for once lost his nerve when he saw the soldiers packing the court; he threw up the case, though he published the brilliant speech which he would have made. Milo fled into exile in Marseilles.

The senate house

3 Governor of Cilicia

In 51 BC there was a shortage of eligible candidates for the governorship of the provinces and the senate decreed that anyone who was eligible and had not been a governor should now be assigned a province. Cicero was sent to Cilicia in southern Turkey. He went extremely reluctantly, but he did a good job when he got there, or so he himself tells Atticus in a letter written soon after he had reached his province; he writes on 31 July 51 BC while still hurrying towards his army, encamped near Tarsus, since there were rumours of an attack by the Parthians. He found the province ruined by the depredations of his predecessor, Appius Claudius.

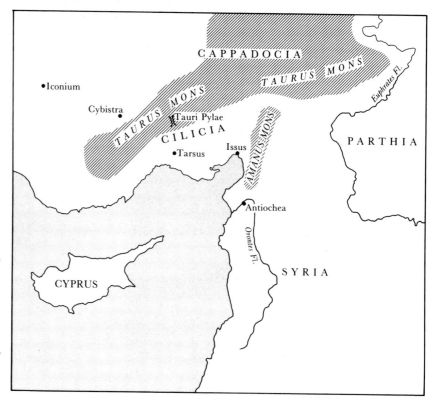

Cilicia

Cicero Attico salutem.

    etsi in ipso itinere et via discedebant publicanorum tabellarii et eramus in cursu, tamen surripiendum aliquid putavi spati, ne me immemorem mandati tui putares. itaque subsedi in ipsa via, dum
5 haec summatim tibi perscriberem.

    maxima exspectatione in perditam et plane eversam in perpetuum provinciam nos venisse scito pridie Kalendis Sextilis. audivimus nihil aliud nisi civitatum gemitus ploratus, monstra quaedam non hominis sed ferae nesciocuius immanis; quid quaeris? taedet omnino
10 eos vitae. levantur tamen miserae civitates quod nullus fit sumptus in nos neque in legatos neque in quaestorem neque in quemquam. itaque incredibilem in modum concursus fiunt ex agris, ex vicis, ex oppidis omnibus; et omnes mehercule etiam adventu nostro reviviscunt, iustitia abstinentia clementia tui Ciceronis cognita.
15 de Partho silentium est, sed tamen concisos equites nostros a barbaris nuntiabant ii qui veniebant. nos in castra properabamus, quae aberant bidui.

(ad Atticum 5.16)

1   **salutem** = **salutem dat**.

2–3   **etsi in cursu** 'although I am on my actual journey and on the road as the couriers of the publicans depart and I am continuing my march'. **discedebant ... eramus** the imperfect is used because the events will be past by the time the letter arrives; we should say 'are departing ... we are'. There are several more examples of this usage in the last paragraph of the letter. **publicanorum tabellarii** the publicans were the tax collectors; their headquarters were in Rome and they employed **tabellarii** ('letter carriers') to communicate with the provinces where their agents were actually collecting the taxes. This was the only form of regular post to and from the provinces, so Cicero could not afford to miss this opportunity of sending a letter to Atticus. **in cursu** 'on the march'.

3   **surripiendum aliquid ... spati** 'that I must snatch a moment (something of time)'.

4   **mandati tui** 'your instructions'; Atticus had asked him to write often.

7   **pridie Kalendis Sextiles** = 31 July.

8   **civitatum gemitus ploratus** 'the groans and laments of the states'; the province was divided into semi-automonous 'states'.

8–9   **monstra quaedam non hominis ... immanis** 'the monstrous deeds not of a human being but of some dreadful wild animal' (Appius Claudius, his predecessor).

9   **quid quaeris?** 'what do you expect?'

10   **eos** = the provincials.

10–11   **nullus fit sumptus in nos** 'no expense is made on me', i.e. he is not exacting any of the lavish entertainment and exactions often made by governors to line their pockets.

11   **legatos** 'deputies'; a governor was assigned by the senate a number of *legati*, who could be used for any function he chose, and one quaestor, in charge of finance.

15   **de Partho silentium est** 'not a sound from Parthia'; only two years earlier (53 BC) Crassus had been defeated by the Parthians at Carrhae with the loss of 44,000 men – the greatest military disaster the Romans had suffered since Hannibal's invasion of Italy. Since then the Romans had continually expected the Parthians to invade their eastern provinces. Cicero was proceeding to a post of real danger. **concisos equites nostros** 'that our cavalry had been cut up'.

17   **bidui: biduum** = 'two days'; supply e.g. **iter**.

Cicero reached his army base on 26 August and pressed on to meet the rumoured Parthian threat. Finding that the Parthians were nowhere near, he marched on to the eastern border of his province, where he engaged and defeated some hostile mountain tribes, a victory which earned him the title imperator. *He wrote to Atticus in December, giving an account of his campaign (see map, p. 36).*

in castra veni a.d. vii Kal. Septembres. a.d. iii exercitum lustravi
apud Iconium. ex his castris, cum graves de Parthis nuntii venirent,
20 perrexi in Ciliciam per Cappadociae partem eam quae Ciliciam
attingit, eo consilio, ut Parthi se Cappadocia excludi putarent. cum
dies quinque ad Cybistra Cappadociae castra habuissem, certior
sum factus Parthos ab illo aditu Cappadociae longe abesse, Ciliciae
magis imminere. itaque confestim iter in Ciliciam feci per Tauri
25 pylas. Tarsum veni a.d. iii Non. Octobres. inde ad Amanum
contendi, qui Syriam a Cilicia in aquarum divortio dividit; qui
mons erat hostium plenus sempiternorum. hic a.d. iii Id. Oct.
magnum numerum hostium occidimus. castella munitissima
nocturno Pomptini adventu, nostro matutino cepimus. imperatores
30 appellati sumus. castra paucos dies habuimus ea ipsa, quae contra
Darium habuerat apud Issum Alexander, imperator haud paulo
melior quam aut tu aut ego. ibi dies quinque morati, direpto et
vastato Amano inde discessimus. interim rumore adventus nostri et
Cassio, qui Antiochiae tenebatur, animus accessit et timor Parthis
35 iniectus est.

(*ad Atticum* 5.20.2–3)

Tauri pylae

18   **a.d. vii Kal. Septembres** = 26 August. **a.d. iii** = 30 August.
      lustravi 'I reviewed'.

21   **excludi** 'were shut out from'. The only way for an army to enter
      Cilicia from the north was through the pass in the Taurus mountains
      called the Cilician Gates (called by Cicero **Tauri pylas** = 'the gates
      of Taurus'). Cicero intended to block this route with his army.

23–4   **Parthos ... Ciliciae magis imminere** a glance at the map will
      show that any invasion from Parthia was more likely to come from
      south of the Taurus mountains.

25   **a.d. iii Non. Octobres** = 5 October. **Amanum** the Amanus
      mountains formed the border between Cilicia and Syria; Cicero did
      a good job if he cleared these mountains of hostile tribes.

26   **in aquarum divortio** 'on the watershed'.

27   **a.d. iii Id. Oct.** = 13 October.

29   **Pomptini** he was one of Cicero's *legati*. **nostro matutino
      (adventu)** 'by my arrival in the early morning'. Cicero made a
      two-pronged attack on these fortresses.

29–30 **imperatores appellati sumus** this title was only given to a general
      who had won a major victory, when he had been hailed *imperator*
      by his army on the battlefield. Cicero was extremely proud of the
      title and from now on heads his letters Cicero *imp*. It was up to the
      senate to decide whether such a victory merited a triumph in Rome;
      Cicero coveted this honour, but the civil war broke out before it
      was awarded.

31   **apud Issum** at Issus Alexander the Great had defeated Darius III,
      king of Persia, in 333 BC in one of the decisive battles of world
      history, which left the Persian empire open to his advance.

34   **Cassio** Cassius, who later with Brutus led the conspiracy to
      assassinate Julius Caesar, had been acting governor of Syria since
      Carrhae; Cicero implies that he was holed up in the capital,
      Antioch. Encouraged by Cicero's successes he attacked and routed
      a Parthian force which was threatening the frontier.

Alexander and Darius confront
each other at the Battle of Issus

Before Cicero had left Rome, he had asked a young friend Marcus
Caelius Rufus to keep him up to date on what was happening there.
In July 50 BC, a month before he was due to leave his province, he
wrote to Caelius asking for more news.

M. Cicero imp. s.d. M. Caelio aedili curuli.

    sollicitus equidem eram de rebus urbanis. ita tumultuosae
contiones, ita molestae Quinquatrus adferebantur; nam citeriora
nondum audieramus. sed tamen nihil me magis sollicitabat quam in
40 his molestiis non me, si quae ridenda essent, ridere tecum; sunt
enim multa, sed ea non audeo scribere. illud moleste fero, nihil me
adhuc de his rebus habere tuarum litterarum. qua re, etsi, cum haec
leges, ego iam annuum munus confecero, tamen obviae mihi velim
tuae litterae, quae me erudiant de omni republica, ne hospes plane
45 veniam. hoc melius quam tu facere nemo potest.

    urbem urbem, mi Rufe, cole et in ista luce vive! omnis
peregrinatio, quod ego ab adulescentia iudicavi, obscura et sordida
est iis quorum industria Romae potest illustris esse. quod cum
probe scirem, utinam in sententia permansissem! cum una
50 mehercule ambulatiuncula atque uno sermone nostro omnes fructus
provinciae non confero. sed, ut spero, propediem te videbo. tu mihi
obviam mitte epistulas te dignas.

(ad Familiares 2.12)

In October, Cicero received a letter from Caelius written in August,
presumably before he received Cicero's. It is partly light in tone,
partly very serious, since he predicts that civil war between
Pompey and Caesar is now inevitable.

Caelius Ciceroni s.

    tanti non fuit Arsacen capere et Seleuceam expugnare, ut earum
55 rerum quae hic gestae sunt spectaculo careres; numquam tibi oculi
doluissent, si in repulsa Domiti vultum vidisses. magna illa comitia
fuerunt et plane studia ex partium sensu apparuerunt.

    de summa republica saepe tibi scripsi me ad annum pacem non

36   **aedili curuli** Cicero rather pompously gives his own title (**imp.** = **imperator**) and the full title of Caelius who was aedile this year; the official title of an aedile was *aedilis curilis*. Caelius replies more informally: *Caelius Ciceroni s.* (= *salutem dat*).

37   **equidem** an emphatic form of **ego**. **eram** 'I am' (epistolary imperfect; 'I was anxious when I was writing this letter'); so also **adferebantur**, **audieramus**. **de rebus urbanis** 'about affairs at Rome'; **urbs** is regularly used of Rome without qualification.

38   **contiones** 'public meetings'. **Quinquatrus**, *nom. pl.* the festival of Minerva, from 19 to 23 March. Festivals were often the occasion of public demonstrations. **citeriora** 'more recent news' (literally, 'things nearer').

40   **non me ... ridere tecum** the accusative and infinitive depends on **nihil me magis sollicitabat** 'nothing upsets me more than (the fact) that ...'. **ridenda** 'to be laughed at'; Caelius was a high spirited young man who found the political junketings amusing, and he could be very funny about them, as his reply shows.

41   **ea non audeo scribere** Cicero is afraid his mail might be intercepted by political enemies.

43   **annuum munus** 'my year's duty'; Cicero stayed in Cilicia for precisely the year's tour allotted him, leaving even before his successor had arrived.

44   **hospes plane** 'an absolute foreigner' (guest in the city of Rome).

47   **peregrinatio** 'foreign service'.

49   **utinam ... permansissem** 'I wish I had stuck to this view'. But in fact he had been drafted to Cilicia and had had no option.

49–50   **cum una ... ambulatiuncula atque uno sermone nostro** 'with one little walk and one talk together' (**sermone nostro** 'our talk' = 'talk of us', 'talk together').

53   **s. = salutem dat.**

54–5   **tanti non fuit ... careres** 'it was not worth so much to take Arsace ... that you missed ... '; we should say, 'it was not worth taking ... to miss'. **Arsacen ... Seleuceam** Arsaces was the founder of the Parthian dynasty and his name was used of the current ruler, thus 'the king of Parthia'; Seleucea was near the Parthian royal capital of Ctesiphon. Caelius is ironically exaggerating Cicero's military successes.

56   **Domiti vultum** L. Domitius Ahenobarbus was one of the leaders of the *optimates*. In the recent elections for an augurship (priesthood) he had been rejected in favour of Antony, who was backed by Caesar. **magna** 'important'; the elections for the augurship were usually routine and unimportant, but in this case they had political significance.

57   **et plane studia ... apparuerunt** 'support (**studia**) was plainly based on party feelings'.

58   **de summa republica** 'on the political situation as a whole'.

videre, et quo propius ea contentio, quam fieri necesse est, accedit,
60 eo clarius periculum apparet. propositum hoc est de quo, qui rerum
potiuntur, sunt dimicaturi, quod Cn. Pompeius constituit non pati C.
Caesarem consulem aliter fieri, nisi exercitum et provincias
tradiderit, Caesari autem persuasum est se salvum esse non posse,
si ab exercitu recesserit; fert illam condicionem, ut ambo exercitus
65 traderent. sic illi amores et invidiosa coniunctio non ad occultam
recidit obtrectationem, sed ad bellum se erupit. in hac discordia
video Cn. Pompeium senatum quique res iudicant secum
habiturum, ad Caesarem omnes qui cum timore aut mala spe vivant
accessuros; exercitum conferendum non esse. omnino satis spatii
70 est ad considerandas copias et eligendam partem.

(ad Familiares 8.14.1–3)

*Cicero left his province the very day his annual tour of duty ended
and hurried back to Rome. On the way his secretary Tiro fell ill and
had to be left at Patrae on the Gulf of Corinth. Cicero wrote eleven
letters to him in the course of the next two months, showing a deep
concern and affection for him.*

*On 3 November (50 BC) Cicero wrote to Tiro en route from
Patrae to Dyrrachium, from where he would sail to Brundisium.*

Tullius Tironi suo s.d.p. et Cicero meus et frater et fratris filius.
  paulo facilius putavi posse me ferre desiderium tui, sed plane
non fero et, quamquam magni ad honorem nostrum interest quam
primum ad urbem me venire, tamen peccasse mihi videor qui a te
75 discesserim; sed quia tua voluntas ea videbatur esse, ut prorsus nisi
confirmato corpore nolles navigare, approbavi tuum consilium
neque nunc muto, si tu in eadem es sententia; sin autem, postea
quam cibum cepisti, videris tibi posse me consequi, tuum consilium
est. Marionem ad te eo misi, ut aut tecum ad me quam primum
80 veniret, aut, si morarere, statim ad me rediret. tu autem hoc tibi
persuade, si commodo valetudinis tuae fieri possit, nihil me malle
quam te esse mecum; si autem intelleges opus est te Patris
convalescendi causa paulum commorari, nihil me malle quam te
valere. si statim navigas, nos Leucade consequere; sin te
85 confirmare vis, et comites et tempestates et navem idoneam ut
habeas diligenter videbis. unum illud, mi Tiro, videto, si me amas,
ne te Marionis adventus et hae litterae moveant. cura ergo
potissimum ut valeas. de tuis innumerabilibus in me officiis est hoc
gratissimum.

(ad Familiares 16.1)

59–60   **quo propius ... eo clarius** 'the nearer ... the clearer'.

60–61   **propositum hoc est ... quod** 'the issue is this ... that'. Caelius puts the issue very clearly: Pompey would not allow Caesar to be elected consul until he had given up his command (**non pati ... aliter fieri, nisi ...**). Caesar would not give up his command until he had been elected to a second consulship, which would have given him immunity from prosecution by his enemies.

65   **illi amores et invidiosa coniunctio** 'their love for one another and their hateful alliance', i.e. the triumvirate.

65–6   **non ad occultam recidit obtrectationem** 'has not lapsed into secret bickering' **recidit** 'has fallen back into'; although the subject is grammatically plural, Caelius uses a singular verb.

67   **qui res iudicant** 'those who judge things' = 'those who form the juries'; the panel from which jurymen were selected consisted of the richest men in the state (under a law of Pompey of 55 BC).

68–9   **ad Caesarem ... accessuros** Caelius believes that Caesar's supporters will be a disreputable lot, motivated by self-interest.

69   **exercitum conferendum non esse** Caesar's army was incomparably better than Pompey's (as the event showed). Caelius considers that Pompey's cause is the more respectable but that Caesar is the stronger.

69–70   **omnino satis spatii est** 'in general, there's enough time'. Caelius in the event chose to support Caesar, the course of prudence, not honour. Cicero made the opposite choice.

71   **s.d.p. = salutem dat plurimam. et Cicero meus et frater et fratris filius** Cicero had with him his son (**Cicero meus**) and his brother Quintus (who had been one of his *legati* in Cilicia) and his nephew.

72   **desiderium tui** 'my longing for you', 'my missing you'; Tiro was quite indispensable to Cicero.

73   **magni ... interest** 'it is extremely important' (**magni** is genitive of value). **ad honorem nostrum** 'for the honour due to me', i.e. the triumph he hoped to celebrate in Rome.

74   **peccasse = peccavisse** 'to have done wrong'.

74–5   **qui ... discesserim** the relative + subjunctive expresses cause: 'because I left you'.

75–6   **prorsus ... nolles** 'you absolutely refused'.

78   **videris tibi posse** 'you seem to yourself to be able' = 'you feel that you are able'.

78–9   **tuum consilium est** 'it's your decision'.

79   **Marionem** a slave of Cicero. **eo ... ut** 'with the intention that'.

81   **commodo valetudinis tuae** 'with convenience to your health' = 'without damaging your health'.

84   **nos Leucade consequere** 'you will catch me up at Leucas' (**consequere = consequeris**); Leucas is the island to the south of Corfu.

85   **tempestates (idoneas)** 'suitable weather'.

86   **videbis** 'see that ...'; the future indicative is here equivalent to an imperative. **videto** 'see that ...' (archaic imperative; compare **scito, esto**).

88   **potissimum** 'above all'. **de tuis ... officiis** 'of all your innumerable services to me'.

4 Civil war and death

*Cicero arrived at Brundisium on 24 November 50 BC but did not
enter Rome at once because, if he did so, he would forfeit his
triumph. He wrote to Tiro on 4 January,* incidi in ipsam flammam
civilis discordiae vel potius belli *('I have fallen into the very flames
of civil discord, or rather civil war'). He was right: on 11 January
49 BC Caesar crossed the Rubicon, the border between his province
of Cisalpine Gaul and Italy, at the head of thirteen legions. The
civil war had begun. Pompey abandoned Rome before Caesar's
advance and marched with his army to Brundisium, from where he
sailed to Greece. On his march to Brundisium, Caesar wrote to
Cicero asking him for his support; this would have been valuable to
Caesar as it would have given his undertaking an air of
respectability and perhaps won over more moderate men to his
cause.*

Caesar imp. s.d. Ciceroni imp.
    cum Furnium nostrum tantum vidissem neque loqui neque
audire meo commodo potuissem, cum properarem atque essem in
itinere praemissis iam legionibus, praeterire tamen non potui quin
5   et scriberem ad te et illum mitterem gratiasque agerem, etsi hoc et
feci saepe et saepius mihi facturus videor; ita de me mereris. in
primis a te peto, quoniam confido me celeriter ad urbem venturum,
ut te ibi videam, ut tuo consilio, gratia, dignitate, ope omnium
rerum uti possim. festinationi meae brevitatique litterarum
10 ignosces. reliqua ex Furnio cognosces.

(ad Atticum 9.6a)

*Cicero considered Caesar a despot and would never have given
him help. He replied politely but firmly, offering himself as a
mediator.*

Cicero imp. s.d. Caesari imp.
    ut legi tuas litteras quas a Furnio nostro acceperam quibus
mecum agebas ut ad urbem essem, te velle uti 'consilio et dignitate
mea' minus sum admiratus; de 'gratia' et de 'ope' quid significares
15 mecum ipse quaerebam, spe tamen deducebar ad eam cogitationem,
ut te pro tua admirabili ac singulari sapientia de otio, de pace, de
concordia civium agi velle arbitrarer, et ad eam rationem
existimabam satis aptam esse et naturam et personam meam.

(ad Atticum 9.11a1)

1 **Ciceroni imp.** Cicero had not entered Rome and so was still technically *imperator*.

2 **Furnium** a tribune, now in Caesar's service, who had supported Cicero in the past.

3 **meo commodo** 'at my convenience'.

4 **praeterire ... non potui quin** 'I could not omit to'.

7 **ad urbem** i.e. Rome, as often.

8 **gratia** 'influence'.

8–9 **ope omnium rerum** 'assistance in all matters'.

Roman troops at a river

13 **mecum agebas** 'you negotiated with me', 'tried to persuade me'.
    te velle the accusative and infinitive depends on **minus sum admiratus**.

14 **de 'gratia' ... significares** this clause depends on **mecum ipse quaerebam** = 'I asked myself'.

16 **pro tua ... sapientia** 'in view of your wisdom'.

17 **agi velle** 'wanted it to be discussed' = 'wanted discussions'.

Hoping that he might remain neutral and effect a reconciliation, he hesitated some time before deciding to join Pompey in Greece. He eventually set sail on 7 June, writing to Terentia after boarding his ship together with young Marcus.

Tullius Terentiae suae salutem plurimam dat.

20   omnes molestias et sollicitudines quibus et te miserrimam habui et Tulliolam, quae nobis nostra vita dulcior est, deposui et eieci. quid causae autem fuerit postridie intellexi quam a vobis discessi. bilem plurimam noctu eieci. statim ita sum levatus ut mihi deus aliquis medicinam fecisse videatur.

25   navem spero nos valde bonam habere. in eam simul atque conscendi, haec scripsi. deinde conscribam ad nostros familiares multas epistulas, quibus te et Tulliolam nostram diligentissime commendabo. cohortarer vos quo animo fortiores essetis nisi vos fortiores cognossem quam quemquam virum. tu primum valetudinem

30 tuam velim cures; deinde, si tibi videbitur, villis iis utere quae longissime aberunt a militibus. fundo Arpinati bene poteris uti cum familia urbana si annona carior fuerit.

    Cicero bellissimus tibi salutem plurimam dicit. etiam atque etiam vale.

(*ad Familiares* 14.7)

Arriving at Pompey's camp at Dyrrachium, Cicero found himself neglected; his health was poor and he was given no work to do. Before pursuing Pompey to Greece, Caesar had to make an expedition to Spain to secure his rear. It was not until January 48 BC that he transported his legions to Greece and eventually defeated Pompey at Pharsalus on 7 August. Pompey fled to Egypt, where he was murdered. Cicero returned to Italy in October and stayed for nearly a year at Brundisium, in despair not only about the political situation and his own unhappy position, but also about his family (his brother Quintus had betrayed him and gone over to Caesar; Terentia had got into debt and tried to defraud him). Eventually he received a letter from Caesar, who was in Egypt, granting him pardon. When Caesar landed at Tarentum in September, Cicero went to meet him; he was kindly received and given leave to live where he liked. He at once went to his Tusculan villa and spent the rest of the year there or in Rome. On his way to his Tusculan villa, he wrote from Venusia on 1 October his last surviving letter to Terentia, an extraordinarily cold and almost insulting note.

35 Tullius s.d. Terentiae suae.

    in Tusculanum nos venturos putamus aut Nonis aut postridie. ibi sint omnia parata. plures enim fortasse nobiscum erunt et, ut arbitror, diutius ibi commorabimur. labrum si in balineo non est, ut sit; item cetera quae sunt ad victum et ad valetudinem necessaria. vale.

(*ad Familiares* 14.20)

20   **molestias** 'vexation'. **habui** 'I made'.

21–2 **quid causae ... fuerit** 'what was the reason (for my indisposition)'; **causae** is predicative dative.

22   **postridie ... quam** 'the day after ...'.

22–3 **bilem plurimam** 'a great deal of bile'; his wretchedness had been caused by an upset stomach and he felt a lot better after he had vomited up a great deal of bile.

25   **nos = me** (as often).

28   **cohortarer** 'I would be encouraging you'. **quo = ut** (as often when there is a comparative in the dependent clause).

29   **cognossem = cognovissem**.

30   **velim cures** 'I should like you to look after'; **volo** is sometimes followed by a subjunctive without any connecting conjunction. **si tibi videbitur** 'if it seems good to you', 'if you decide'. **utere** imperative.

31   **fundo Arpinati** 'our estate at Arpinum'.

32   **familia urbana** 'with our household from the city'; Terentia should take with her the servants from their house in Rome. **annona** 'the price of food'.

33   **Cicero bellissimus** 'our handsome young Cicero' (Marcus). **etiam atque etiam** 'again and again'. Cicero's anxiety is clear from this ending; would he ever see Italy and Terentia again?

36   **Nonis = 7** (October).

38   **labrum si ... ut sit** 'if there is no basin in the bathroom, see that there is'. **item** 'similarly'.

39   **ad victum** 'for subsistence'.

*He divorced Terentia before the end of the year and, excluded from
politics, he lived in retirement and devoted himself to writing on
rhetoric and philosophy. In February 45 BC he suffered yet another
blow when his beloved Tullia died in childbirth. He was inconsolable.
In March he wrote to Atticus from a lonely villa on the coast, which he
had recently bought.*

40   Cicero Attico sal.

in hac solitudine careo omnium colloquio, cumque mane me in
silvam abstrusi densam et asperam, non exeo inde ante vesperem.
secundum te nihil est mihi amicius solitudine. in ea mihi omnis sermo
est cum litteris. eum tamen interpellat fletus; cui repugno quoad
45   possum, sed adhuc pares non sumus. Bruto, ut suades, rescribam. eas
litteras cras habebis.

(*ad Atticum* 12.15)

*As he gradually recovered from the shock of
Tullia's death he resumed his writing;
between 46 and 44 BC he wrote two works
on rhetoric and eight on philosophy. In
December 45 BC he received a visit from
Caesar, who had now finally defeated the
last remnants of republican opposition and
had been elected dictator. He had always
admired Cicero and bore him no
resentment. Cicero received him in his villa
at Cumae and wrote to Atticus describing
this rather nerve-racking occasion.*

The citadel of Cumae

Cicero Attico sal.

o hospitem mihi tam gravem, ἀμεταμέλητον tamen! fuit enim
periucunde. sed cum secundis Saturnalibus ad Philippum vesperi
50   venisset, villa ita completa a militibus est ut vix triclinium ubi
cenaturus ipse Caesar esset vacaret; quippe hominum duo milia. sane
sum commotus quid futurum esset postridie; at mihi Barba Cassius
subvenit, custodes dedit. castra in agro, villa defensa est. ille tertiis
Saturnalibus apud Philippum ad horam vii, nec quemquam admisit;
55   rationes, ut opinor, cum Balbo. inde ambulavit in litore. post horam
viii in balneum. unctus est, accubuit. emeticam agebat; itaque et edit et
bibit sine cura et iucunde.

praeterea tribus tricliniis accepti comites eius valde copiose.
libertis minus lautis servisque nihil defuit. nam lautiores eleganter
60   accepi. quid multa? homines visi sumus. hospes tamen non is cui
diceres 'amabo te, eodem ad me cum revertere.' semel satis est. nihil
magni momenti in sermone, de litteris multa. quid quaeris? delectatus
est et libenter fuit. Puteolis se aiebat unum diem fore, alterum ad
Baias.

(*ad Atticum* 13.52, adapted)

41–2 **me ... abstrusi** 'I have hidden myself'.

43 **secundum te** 'second to you'. **amicius** 'dearer'.

44 **litteris** 'literature'.

44–5 **quoad possum** 'as far as I can'.

45 **adhuc pares non sumus** 'I am still not equal to it' = 'I still can't conquer it'. **Bruto ... rescribam** Brutus had written Cicero a letter of condolence.

48 **o hospitem ... tamen**! 'O, such an onerous guest, but one not to be regretted!'; Caesar's visit had given Cicero a great deal of worry but he did not regret it. ἀμεταμέλητον (*ametameleton*) 'not to be regretted'; Cicero often uses Greek when Latin did not supply him with just the right word.

48–9 **fuit enim periucunde** 'for he was very cheerful'. In colloquial Latin **esse** is often used with an adverb where you would expect an adjective as complement, e.g. **bene est** = 'it is well'.

49 **secundis Saturnalibus** 'on the second day of the Saturnalia' (18 December); the Saturnalia was the ancient midwinter festival which was taken over by Christmas in Christian times; it lasted for a week. **ad Philippum** i.e. to Philippus' villa; L. Marcius Philippus (consul 56 BC) had a villa near Cicero's and Caesar first payed a call on him. Cicero was alarmed to hear what a huge retinue Caesar was bringing with him on a private visit, including an escort of 2,000 soldiers. But one of Caesar's henchmen, Barba Cassius, arrived to make suitable arrangements.

51 **quippe** 'in fact (there were)'.

55 **rationes ... cum Balbo** '(he was doing) accounts with Balbus'; Balbus was his confidential agent and treasurer.

56 **in balneum (iit)** by now he had arrived at Cicero's house. **unctus est** 'he was anointed'; after a bath Romans were usually rubbed down with olive oil, which helped to keep their skin in good order in the dry Italian climate. **emeticam agebat** 'he was taking a course of emetics'; this was a common medical treatment at the time.

59 **lautis** 'grand'; Cicero entertained his guests with a careful distinction of their social status.

60 **quid multa?** 'why (say) much?' i.e. 'in short'. **homines visi sumus** 'I showed myself a man (of the world)'.

60–61 **hospes tamen non is (est) cui diceres** 'he is not the sort of guest to whom you would say'.

61 **amabo te, eodem ad me (veni) cum revertere** 'Please (literally, I shall love you), (come) to me the same way when you return', i.e. 'visit me on your return journey'.

61–2 **nihil magni momenti** 'nothing of great importance', i.e. nothing on politics.

63 **libenter fuit** 'he was cheerful' (see note on *ll.* 48–9 above).

64 **Baias** Baiae was a nearby seaside resort.

Caesar's behaviour was becoming steadily more authoritarian; he was even greeted as 'king' on one occasion but replied, non rex sum sed Caesar. *Early in 44* BC *he accepted the title* dictator perpetuus *('dictator for life'). This was one of the things which precipitated the conspiracy led by Brutus and Cassius. On 15 March he was struck down at a meeting of the senate in the theatre of Pompey and lay dead at the foot of the statue of his old enemy.*

On the very evening of the assassination, Cicero dashed off a note of congratulation to one of the conspirators.

65   Cicero Basilo sal.

tibi gratulor, mihi gaudeo; te amo, tua tueor; a te amari et quid agas quidque agatur certior fieri volo.

(*ad Familiares* 6.15)

Cicero hoped, perhaps rather naively, that the assassination of Caesar would be followed by the restoration of the republic and constitutional government. At a meeting of the senate on 17 March he took the lead in proposing a general amnesty; this was followed by a public reconciliation between Antony and the so-called Liberators. But at Caesar's funeral Antony stirred up the mob against Brutus and Cassius, who within a month were forced to flee from Rome. By May Antony was in command of the situation, and Cicero was in despair.

Caesar in his will had adopted his nearest male relative, his great nephew C. Octavius, and made him his heir. Octavian, as he was now called, was only nineteen, but as soon as he heard of Caesar's death he hurried to Italy from Apollonia, where he was doing military service, and claimed his inheritance, much of which Antony had already spent. There was at first no open breach between them while each manoeuvred for position. Octavian was friendly towards Cicero and Cicero thought he might be a useful tool to restrain Antony's growing power.

While the situation deteriorated, Cicero felt there was little he could do and decided to go to Athens to visit his son Marcus who was studying at the Lyceum. Cicero had heard reports of his extravagance and idleness and wanted to see for himself what he

66   **mihi gaudeo** 'I rejoice for myself' = 'I am delighted'. **tua tueor** 'I am watching over your interests'.

was up to. He set sail from Pompeii on 17 July but was driven back by contrary winds; when he landed in Italy, he heard that Antony was planning to be reconciled to the Liberators; he decided to return to Rome for a meeting of the senate which was to take place on 1 September. On his way he met Brutus who told him that far from any reconciliation there had been a final rupture between Antony and the Liberators. He and Cassius left Italy for the East. But Cicero decided to continue to Rome and arrived there just before the meeting of the senate.

The following day he made a speech before the senate strongly criticizing Antony. This speech and succeeding attacks on Antony before the people or senate precipitated Cicero to take the leadership in a last effort to contain Antony and restore the republic. Antony replied with a violent attack on Cicero and his whole career. He then left Rome to raise troops and intended to march on Rome and finally dispose of his enemies, but when some of his legions revolted to Octavian, he led his army out of Italy and marched into Cisalpine Gaul.

In February 43 BC Cicero found time to write a light-hearted letter to his philosopher friend Papirius Paetus, which ends on a more serious note, showing how active he was in promoting the cause of the senate against Antony.

sed cave, si me amas, existimes me, quod iocosius scribam,
abiecisse curam reipublicae. sic tibi, mi Paete, persuade, me dies et
70 noctes nihil aliud agere, nihil curare, nisi ut mei cives salvi
liberique sint. nullum locum praetermitto monendi, agendi,
providendi; hoc denique animo sum, ut, si in hac cura atque
administratione vita mihi ponenda est, praeclare actum mecum
putem. etiam atque etiam vale.

(*ad Familiares* 9.24.4)

Lepidus

*Led by Cicero, the senate declared war on Antony, despatched both
consuls to pursue him and gave a special command to Octavian to
lead a third army against him. In the battle which followed Antony
was defeated and retreated into Transalpine Gaul, but both consuls
were killed, leaving Octavian in command of the whole army
(battle of Mutina, April 43 BC). Octavian soon sent letters to the
senate, demanding that he be elected consul. He was not yet twenty
and had held no political office; his demand was entirely
unconstitutional. The senate refused. Thereupon he marched on
Rome and extorted what he wanted (August 43 BC).*

*Octavian then marched north, ostensibly to deal with Antony;
Antony came south to meet him with Lepidus, who had been
Caesar's 'Master of the cavalry' and was governor of Hither Spain.
They met at Bononia where instead of fighting they made a pact,
dividing the western provinces between them and agreeing to
prosecute the war against Brutus and Cassius in the East. In
November they arrived in Rome and the triumvirate was
established by law.*

*Proscriptions followed in which their enemies were outlawed or
murdered and their goods confiscated. Antony insisted on adding
Cicero to the list of the proscribed and Octavian did not demur.*

*Cicero had seen all that he had lived for and struggled for
finally destroyed. He did not fear death. The first book of the*
Tusculan Disputations, *a philosophical work he had completed
three years earlier, is devoted to 'the fear of death'; after quoting
examples of courage in the face of death, he concludes thus.*

Octavianus

75 quae cum ita sint, magna tamen eloquentia est utendum, ut
homines mortem vel optare incipiant vel certe timere desistant.
nam si supremus ille dies non exstinctionem, sed commutationem
affert loci, quid optabilius? sin autem perimit ac delet omnino,
quid melius quam in mediis vitae laboribus obdormiscere et ita
80 coniventem somno consopiri sempiterno?

(*Tusculan Disputations* 1.117)

Antonius

68 **cave ... existimes** 'beware of thinking' = 'don't think'. **iocosius** 'rather jokingly'.

71 **nullum locum** 'no occasion'.

72 **hoc ... animo sum** 'I am of this mind' = 'this is how I feel'.

73 **vita mihi ponenda est** 'my life must be spent'.

73–4 **praeclare actum mecum putem** 'I think it has been done very well with me', i.e. 'I think all is well with me'.

The rostra in Rome

75 **quae cum ita sint** 'although this is so'. **est utendum** '(we) must use'.

76 **vel ... vel certe** 'either ... or at least'.

77–8 **commutationem ... loci** 'a change of place', i.e. if the soul survives to go to a happier place. Cicero and most of the ancients reserved judgement on whether the soul survives the death of the body.

78 **optabilius** 'more desirable'. **sin** 'but if'. **perimit ac delet** 'it (death) annihilates and destroys' = 'utterly annihilates us'.

79 **laboribus** 'toils', 'sufferings'. **obdormiscere** 'to fall asleep'.

79–80 **ita coniventem** 'closing our eyes like this'.

When death came, he faced it with courage and resignation.

M. Cicero pro certe habens, id quod erat, non Antonio eripi se
posse, primum in Tusculanum fugit, inde in Formianum, ut ab
Caieta navem conscensurus, proficiscitur. unde aliquoties in altum
provectum cum modo venti adversi retulissent, modo ipse
85 iactationem navis pati non posset, taedium tandem eum et fugae et
vitae cepit, regressusque ad superiorem villam, 'moriar' inquit 'in
patria saepe servata.' satis constat servos fortiter fideliterque
paratos fuisse ad dimicandum; ipsum deponi lecticam et quietos
pati, quod fors iniqua cogeret, iussisse. prominenti ex lectica
90 praebentique immotam cervicem caput praecisum est. nec satis
stolidae crudelitati militum fuit; manus quoque, scripsisse aliquid
in Antonium exprobrantes, praeciderunt. ita relatum caput ad
Antonium, iussuque eius inter duas manus in rostris positum, ubi
ille consul, ubi consularis, ubi eo ipso anno adversus Antonium,
95 cum admiratione eloquentiae auditus fuerat. vix attollentes prae
lacrimis oculos homines intueri membra trucidati eius poterant.

(Livy fragment 50)

Cicero's tomb

81   **id quod erat** 'as was true'. **Antonio eripi** 'be rescued from Antony'.

82   **Tusculanum** Cicero's Tusculan villa was about 15 miles south of Rome; the house at Formiae was about 70 miles south of Rome near the harbour of Caieta.

82–3   **ut ... conscensurus** 'intending to board' (**ut** + future participle is occasionally used to express purpose). He had planned to sail to Greece and join Brutus and Cassius.

83–4   **in altum provectum** 'after putting out to sea'; the participle agrees with **eum** (*l.* 85).

86   **ad superiorem villam** i.e. the villa at Formiae.

88–9   **ipsum ... iussisse** accusative and infinitive still dependent on **satis constat** = 'it is generally agreed that he himself ordered ...'. **quietos** this agrees with **servos** (supplied).

89–90   **prominenti ... praecisum est** 'his head was cut off while he held his neck out of the litter ...' (literally, the head was cut off for him holding out ...). Cicero was being carried in a litter from the harbour of Caieta to his villa at Formiae when the soldiers appeared.

90–91   **nec satis ... fuit** 'nor was (this) enough for the brutish cruelty of the soldiers'.

91–2   **scripsisse ... exprobrantes** 'reproaching them (the hands) for having written'.

94   **consularis** 'as ex-consul'; the *consulares* were the senior statesmen of Rome.

95–6   **prae lacrimis** 'because of their tears'.

96   **trucidati** 'butchered'.

CAESAR

Caesar's family, the *gens Iulia*, belonged to the ancient patrician nobility, claiming descent from Iulus, son of Aeneas, and ultimately from Venus, Aeneas' mother. His uncle had been consul in 89 BC and his father praetor before his early death in 84 BC, when Caesar was sixteen years old. But the family was not wealthy and had dropped behind in the power struggle. His aunt Julia had been married to Marius, which suggests that the family's political sympathies lay with the *populares*. Caesar showed his own position as a very young man by marrying the daughter of Marius' successor Cornelius Cinna. When Sulla ordered him to divorce her, he refused to do so and was lucky to escape with his life. Sulla intended to get rid of him but friends begged for his life and Sulla reluctantly consented, saying to them, 'Have it your own way, but be warned that in that man there is many a Marius.' From then on the *nobiles* regarded him as a potential revolutionary and frustrated him whenever they could.

Before becoming governor of Gaul in 58 BC, Caesar had had limited experience as a soldier. As a young man he had served in Asia for several years as a military tribune and had been awarded the *corona civica* (a crown of oak leaves, given for saving a Roman's life in battle). He certainly lacked neither courage nor confidence, as an incident which took place a few years later shows. On his way to Rhodes to study rhetoric under one of the leading teachers of the time, he was captured by pirates and held to ransom; when the ransom had been paid and he was freed, he proceeded to Miletus where he raised a fleet on his own authority, pursued and captured the pirates, recovered his ransom and put them all to death by crucifixion, as he had threatened to do while he was in their hands.

He then continued his political career (see the chronological table, p. 8 above). Elected quaestor in 68 BC, he served in Further Spain. As aedile in 65, he performed administrative duties in Rome. He became praetor in 62 BC. He was now qualified for high command and was sent out to govern Further Spain as propraetor. Here he commanded an army and won a triumph for victories over some of the tribes of Spain. This was his first army command and his success must have made him confident of his skill as a general. From Spain he hurried back to Rome to stand for the consulship in the elections of 60 BC. Despite the opposition of the *optimates*, Caesar was elected consul for 59 BC and was given a province consisting of Cisalpine Gaul (i.e. North Italy) and Illyricum by a *plebiscitum* proposed by the tribune Vatinius, which overrode the senate's distribution of provinces. But this would have given Caesar little scope for military action and the senate added Transalpine Gaul.

Caesar was to hold this province for nine years, from 58 to 50 BC. In 58 BC when he proceeded to his province, the only part of Gaul controlled by Rome was Gallia Narbonensis, roughly equivalent to modern Provence, which formed a corridor between Italy and Spain. North of this were various fierce and independent Celtic tribes, who were often at war with each other. Soon after Caesar reached his province, the Helvetii, whose home was in the mountains of Switzerland, began a mass migration into Gaul. Caesar moved north, defeated them at Bibracte and forced them to return to Helvetia. He now found himself deeply involved in the affairs of the Gallic tribes of that area, the Sequani and the Aedui, who asked him to eject from their territory a German tribe which had settled there some years before. He defeated these Germans in a tough battle and forced them to withdraw across the Rhine. This action left him in virtual control of the lands of the Aedui and Sequani, and he stationed his troops in winter quarters at Vesontio, deep in the territory of the Sequani.

The following year (spring 57 BC) the tribes of the Belgae united in a great confederacy to resist further Roman enroachment. Caesar advanced to meet them; some tribes submitted, others resisted fiercely, but by the end of 57 BC he had overrun all northern Gaul while his lieutenant Publius Crassus had advanced through Normandy and Britanny without meeting serious opposition.

In 56 BC Caesar himself marched against the Veneti, a seafaring people of Britanny; after a tough struggle, in which he had to construct a fleet, he conquered them by sea. Meanwhile his lieutenants overran Aquitania and consolidated the conquest of Normandy. By the end of the year Caesar could claim that he had conquered all Gaul from the Rhine to the Pyrenees.

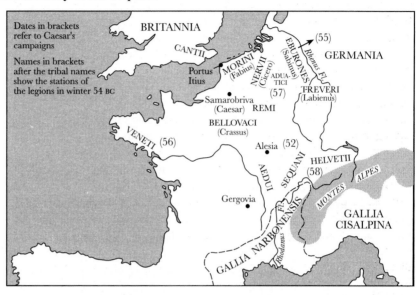

Gaul

In 55 BC he annihilated two German tribes which had crossed the Rhine into Gaul and made a foray into Germany. He next turned his attention to Britain, on the grounds that the southern tribes there, some of which had emigrated from Gaul to Britain, were supplying help and encouragement to the Gauls. We now take up the story in Caesar's own words.

Caesar's *Commentarii de Bello Gallico* (*Commentaries on the Gallic War*) are a sort of war diary in which he describes his campaigns in seven books, one for each year from 58 to 52 BC. He writes in the third person, calling himself Caesar, and appears to be giving a straightforward factual account of a patriotic Roman fighting necessary wars. The books actually contain an element of propaganda. Caesar writes for the public in Rome to justify the continual extension of his conquests and, according to his accounts, he never makes a mistake. In fact, as we shall see from his account of his invasions of Britain, he did make mistakes. But it is also clear that he was a brilliant general, and he writes extraordinarily clear and vivid accounts of his campaigns.

This section consists of extracts from Books 4 and 5. The first two chapters describe his two invasions of Britain (55 and 54 BC); the second two the rebellion in Gaul which followed.

I The first invasion of Britain

Caesar prepares to invade Britain.

exigua parte aetatis reliqua Caesar, etsi in his locis maturae sunt
hiemes, tamen in Britanniam proficisci contendit, quod omnibus
fere Gallicis bellis hostibus nostris inde sumministrata auxilia
intellegebat; et si tempus anni ad bellum gerendum deficeret, tamen
5 magno sibi usui fore arbitrabatur, si modo insulam adiisset et genus
hominum perspexisset, loca, portus, aditus cognovisset; quae omnia
fere Gallis erant incognita.

neque enim temere praeter mercatores illo adiit quisquam neque
eis ipsis quicquam praeter oram maritimam atque eas regiones quae
10 sunt contra Galliam notum est. itaque vocatis ad se undique
mercatoribus, neque quanta esset insulae magnitudo, neque quae
aut quantae nationes incolerent, neque quem usum belli haberent
aut quibus institutis uterentur, neque qui essent ad maiorum navium
multitudinem idonei portus reperire poterat.

15 ad haec cognoscenda C. Volusenum cum navi longa praemittit.
huic mandat ut exploratis omnibus ad se quam primum revertatur.
ipse cum omnibus copiis in Morinos proficiscitur, quod inde erat
brevissimus in Britanniam traiectus. huc navis undique ex finitimis
regionibus et quam superiore anno ad Veneticum bellum effecerat
20 classem convenire iubet. interim, consilio eius cognito et per
mercatores perlato ad Britannos, a compluribus insulae civitatibus
ad eum legati veniunt qui polliceantur obsides dare atque imperio
populi Romani obtemperare. quibus auditis, liberaliter pollicitus
hortatusque ut in ea sententia permanerent, eos domum remittit.
25 Volusenus, perspectis regionibus omnibus quantum potuit, quinto
die ad Caesarem revertitur, quaeque ibi perspexisset renuntiat.

navibus circiter LXXX onerariis coactis, quod satis esse ad duas
transportandas legiones existimabat, quod praeterea navium
longarum habebat quaestori, legatis, praefectisque distribuit. huc
30 accedebant XVIII onerariae naves, quae ex eo loco ab milibus
passuum octo vento tenebantur quominus in eundem portum venire
possent: has equitibus distribuit.

(*de Bello Gallico* 4.20–22)

Two long ships

2 **contendit** + infinitive 'hastened to'.

3 **summinstrata (esse) auxilia** 'help had been provided'.

5 **si modo** 'if only'; this sentence suggests that Caesar intended the expedition of 54 BC to be no more than a large-scale reconnaissance in preparation for a full-scale invasion later.

8 **temere** 'readily', 'without good reason'. **illo** 'to that place', 'there'; cf. **eo**.

9 **quicquam** is the subject of **notum est**.

11–14 **neque quanta esset ... portus** all these clauses are indirect questions depending on **reperire poterat**; it is characteristic of Caesar's style to postpone the main verb to the end of the sentence.

12 **usum** 'use' = 'method'.

13 **institutis** 'institutions', 'customs', 'way of life'.

15 **cum navi longa** 'a long ship', i.e. a war ship, as opposed to **navis oneraria** (a cargo or troop-carrying ship). **navi** Caesar regularly uses the alternative forms of the ablative singular in **-i** and the accusative plural in **-is** from 3rd declension nouns with **i-** stems (cf. **navis**, *l.* 18).

17 **Morinos** for the territory of the Morini, see map. The question of which port Caesar sailed from is debated; in the invasion of the following year, he says that he sailed from Portus Itius, tentatively identified with Boulogne, which has a harbour which could have held Caesar's fleet. The trouble with this identification is first that in later literature Boulogne is called Gesoriacum (the name Portus Itius occurs nowhere else); second, Boulogne to Dover is not the shortest crossing (it is 32 Roman miles from Britain; the shortest route is 24).

18 **traiectus, -us**, *m.* 'crossing'.

18–20 **navis ... et quam ... effecerat classem**: **navis** and **classem** are both objects of **iubet** (last word in the sentence). The previous year he had campaigned against the Veneti of Britanny, a seafaring people; he had had to build a fleet and fight a hard campaign to defeat them.

21 **civitatibus** 'states'; Caesar uses this word to describe the tribal groups into which Britain was divided at this time.

22 **legati** 'ambassadors'. *legatus* can mean a deputy of any kind (*legatus legionis* = a legionary commander); Caesar was allotted ten *legati* by the senate, whom he could employ as he chose.

23 **liberaliter pollicitus** 'making generous promises'.

25 **quantum potuit** 'as much as he could'. Volusenus' reconnaissance lasted four days; in this time he seems to have sailed along the coast eastwards until he found suitable landing beaches near Deal, but he did not venture inland.

28–9 **quod ... navium longarum** 'what of war ships' (partitive genitive) = 'all the war ships'. **praeterea** 'besides', i.e. in addition to the troop carriers.

29 **quaestori, legatis, praefectisque** these were the senior officers whom Caesar had with him on this expedition – one quaestor, two legionary commanders and various *praefecti*.

29–30 **huc accedebant** 'added to these were ...'; **accedo** is often used in this passive sense = 'am added to'.

31–2 **quominus ... possent** 'so that they could not ...'. These ships with the cavalry on board were ordered by Caesar to follow him as soon as they could, but they were driven back to port by adverse winds and never reached Britain.

The invasion fleet sails.

his constitutis rebus, nactus idoneam ad navigandum
tempestatem tertia fere vigilia solvit equitesque naves
35 conscendere et se sequi iussit. ipse hora circiter diei
quarta cum primis navibus Britanniam attigit atque
ibi in omnibus collibus expositas hostium copias
armatas conspexit. cuius loci haec erat natura, atque
ita montibus angustis mare continebatur, uti ex locis
40 superioribus in litus telum adigi posset. hunc ad
egrediendum nequaquam idoneum locum arbitratus,
dum reliquae naves eo convenirent ad horam nonam in ancoris
exspectavit. interim, legatis tribunisque militam convocatis, et
quae ex Voluseno cognosset et quae fieri vellet ostendit. his
45 dimissis, et ventum et aestum uno tempore nactus secundum,
dato signo et sublatis ancoris, circiter milia passuum septem ab
eo loco progressus aperto ac plano litore naves constituit.

(de Bello Gallico 4.23)

The cliffs of Dover

The landing.

at barbari, consilio Romanorum cognito, praemisso equitatu et
essedariis, quo plerumque genere in proeliis uti consuerunt, reliquis
50 copiis subsecuti nostros navibus egredi prohibebant. erat ob has
causas summa difficultas, quod naves propter magnitudinem nisi in
alto constitui non poterant, militibus autem, ignotis locis, impeditis
manibus, magno et gravi onere armorum oppressis, simul et de
navibus desiliendum et in fluctibus consistendum et cum hostibus
55 erat pugnandum, cum illi aut ex arido aut paulum in aquam
progressi, omnibus membris expeditis, notissimis locis, audacter
tela conicerent et equos insuefactos incitarent. quibus rebus nostri
perterriti atque huius generis pugnae omnino imperiti, non eadem
alacritate ac studio quo in pedestribus uti proeliis consuerant
60 utebantur.

A model of a British chariot

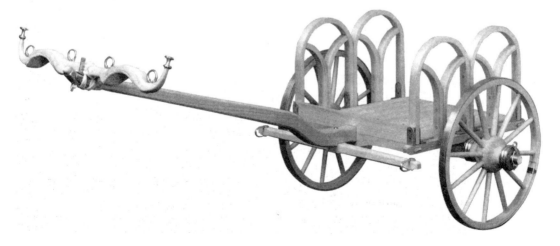

34 **tertia fere vigilia** the military day was divided into watches; there were four night watches between sunset and sunrise; the third watch lasted from midnight to 2.30 a.m.

35–6 **hora ... quarta** the fourth hour on 26 August, when Caesar sailed, would have been about 8.30 a.m.

36 **attigit** 'touched on', 'reached'.

37 **hostium copias** the Britons had evidently assembled a considerable army to meet the Roman invasion.

38 **haec erat natura** 'this was the nature' = 'such was ...' (looking forward to **uti = ut**). The description of the place makes it clear that Caesar's landfall was by the cliffs of Dover.

40 **telum** 'missile(s)'; the word is used of any weapon which could be thrown or shot.

41 **nequaquam idoneum** 'not at all suitable', 'quite unsuitable'.

42–3 **dum ... convenirent ... exspectavit** 'waited for them to gather' (subjunctive, because **dum** expresses purpose as well as time). He waited at anchor until the ninth hour (about 3.30 p.m.). Then with a following wind and tide he sailed about seven miles eastwards until he reached the open and level beach between Walmer and Deal.

44 **cognosset = cognovisset**.

49 **quo ... genere** 'which sort (of weapon)'; the Romans had not previously come across war chariots.

50 **prohibebant** 'were stopping' or 'tried to stop' (conative imperfect).

50ff. **has causas: has** looks forward to the long list of difficulties in the **quod** clause, which falls into two parts: first, the impossibility of bringing the ships close into shore; second, the difficulties faced by the Roman soldiers (**militibus ... desiliendum ... consistendum ... erat pugnandum**). Tacked onto this we have the advantages of the Britons; **cum illi ...** 'while they ...'.

The beach at Deal

57 **insuefactos** 'trained' (to enter the water etc.). Caesar makes it clear that the Britons put up a very stout resistance to the Romans and that unless he had taken quick action, the landing might have failed.

quod ubi Caesar animadvertit, navis longas paulum removeri ab
onerariis navibus et ad latus apertum hostium constitui atque inde
fundis, sagittis, tormentis hostes propelli ac summoveri iussit; quae
res magno usui nostris fuit. nam et navium figura et remorum motu
65 et inusitato genere tormentorum permoti barbari constiterunt ac
paulum pedem rettulerunt. atque nostris militibus cunctantibus,
maxime propter altitudinem maris, is qui decimae legionis aquilam
ferebat, contestatus deos, ut ea res legioni feliciter eveniret,
'desilite,' inquit, 'milites, nisi vultis aquilam hostibus prodere; ego
70 certe meum rei publicae atque imperatori officium praestitero.' hoc
cum magna voce dixisset, se ex navi proiecit atque in hostes
aquilam ferre coepit. tum nostri cohortati inter se ne tantum
dedecus admitteretur, universi ex navi desiluerunt. hos item ex
proximis navibus cum conspexissent, subsecuti hostibus
75 appropinquarunt.

pugnatum est ab utrisque acriter. nostri tamen, quod neque ordines
servare neque firmiter insistere neque signa subsequi poterant atque
alius alia ex navi quibuscumque signis occurrerat se aggregabat,
magnopere perturbabantur; hostes vero, notis omnibus vadis, ubi ex
80 litore aliquos singularis ex navi egredientis conspexerant, incitatis
equis impeditos adoriebantur, plures paucos circumsistebant, alii ab
latere aperto in universos tela coniciebant. quod cum animadvertisset
Caesar, scaphas longarum navium, item speculatoria navigia militibus
compleri iussit et, quos laborantis conspexerat, his subsidia
85 summittebat. nostri, simul in arido constiterant, suis omnibus
consecutis, in hostis impetum fecerunt atque eos in fugam dederunt;
neque longius prosequi potuerunt, quod equites cursum tenere atque
insulam capere non potuerant. hoc unum ad pristinam fortunam
Caesari defuit.

(*de Bello Gallico* 4.24–6)

essedum

A scapha

61 **navis** is governed by **iussit**.

63 **fundis, sagittis, tormentis** 'with slings, arrows, artillery'. The sling was an effective weapon which could fire stones or lead bullets up to a range of about 100 yards. Roman artillery consisted of massive catapults; the largest could fire a stone weighing 162 pounds up to 500 yards, but those mounted on warships were smaller. It is not surprising that the Britons should have wavered before such an onslaught.

64 **navium figura** 'by the form/the type of ships'; the Britons were unfamiliar with Roman warships.

65 **inusitato genere tormentorum** 'the unfamiliar type of artillery', but Caesar really means 'artillery, a type of weapon they were unfamiliar with'.

68 **contestatus deos** 'calling the gods to witness'.

69 **aquilam** the legionary standard was in the form of an eagle and was regarded with almost religious veneration; to lose the legion's standard was the ultimate disgrace.

70 **certe** 'at least'. **praestitero** 'I shall have performed' (future perfect indicative).

72 **inter se** 'each other'.

73 **hos** the object of **conspexissent**; you must supply as the subject ('they') e.g. 'men from the nearest ships'.

75 **appropinquarunt** = **appropinquaverunt**. Caesar regularly uses such shortened forms.

76 **pugnatum est** impersonal use of the passive, 'it was fought by both sides' = 'both sides fought'.

77 **signa** 'standards'; every section of the legion down to the century and maniple had its own distinctive standard; in battle you followed your standard-bearer, who could signal 'advance', 'withdraw', 'rally'. In this landing operation, in deep water and under fire, the soldiers could not keep ranks and order could not be maintained.

78 **alius alia ex navi ... se aggregabat** 'one from one ship, one from another ... gathered together/rallied'. **quibuscumque signis occurrerat** 'at whatever standards (each) had met', i.e. they were not keeping formation but joined up at random.

79–80 **ubi ... conspexerant** 'whenever they saw'.

80 **aliquos singularis**, *acc. pl.* 'any (Romans) singly (as opposed to in formation)'.

82 **in universos** 'against them altogether', i.e. against the Roman troops who were forming up.

83 **scaphas** 'dinghies'. **item speculatoria navigia** 'likewise (= and also) scouting boats'.

84 **quos ... his** the relative clause precedes the antecedent (a common word order in Caesar).

85 **simul** = **simul ac** 'as soon as'.

87 **equites** the cavalry had still not reached Britain, and Caesar had to make his landing without their support. In fact they never reached Britain (see p. 65 below).

aquila

The Britons sue for peace, but the Roman fleet is destroyed by storm.

90 hostes proelio superati, simul atque se ex fuga receperunt, statim ad
Caesarem legatos de pace miserunt; obsides daturos quaeque
imperasset sese facturos polliciti sunt. in petenda pace eius rei
culpam in multitudinem coiecerunt et propter imprudentiam ut
ignosceretur petiverunt. Caesar questus quod, cum ultro in
95 continentem legatis missis pacem a se petissent, bellum sine causa
intulissent, ignoscere imprudentiae dixit obsidesque imperavit;
quorum illi partem statim dederunt, partem ex longinquioribus
locis arcessitam paucis diebus sese daturos esse dixerunt. interea
suos remigrare in agros iusserunt, principesque undique convenire
100 et se civitatesque suas Caesari commendare coeperunt.
his rebus pace confirmata, post diem quartum quam est in
Britanniam ventum, naves XVIII quae equites sustulerant, ex portu
leni vento solverunt. quae cum appropinquarent Britanniae et ex
castris viderentur, tanta tempestas subito coorta est ut nulla earum
105 cursum tenere posset, sed aliae eodem unde erant profectae
referrentur, aliae ad inferiorem partem insulae, quae est propius
solis occasum, magno sui cum periculo deicerentur.
eadem nocte accidit ut esset luna plena, qui dies maritimos
aestus maximos in Oceano efficere consuevit, nostrisque id erat
110 incognitum. ita uno tempore et longas navis, quas Caesar in aridum
subduxerat, aestus compleverat, et onerarias, quae ad ancoras erant
deligatae, tempestas adflictabat, neque ulla nostris facultas
auxiliandi dabatur. compluribus navibus fractis, reliquae cum essent
funibus, ancoris, reliquisque armamentis amissis ad navigandum
115 inutiles, magna totius exercitus perturbatio facta est. neque enim
naves erant aliae quibus reportari possent, et omnia deerant quae ad
reficiendas navis erant usui et frumentum his in locis in hiemem
provisum non erat.

(*de Bello Gallico* 4.27–9)

The Britons renew the struggle.

quibus rebus cognitis, principes Britanniae, qui post proelium ad
120 Caesarem convenerant, inter se collocuti, cum equites et navis et
frumentum Romanis deesse intellegerent et paucitatem militum ex
castrorum exiguitate cognoscerent, optimum factu esse duxerunt,
rebellione facta, frumento commeatuque nostros prohibere et rem
in hiemem producere, quod eis superatis aut reditu interclusis
125 neminem postea belli inferendi causa in Britanniam transiturum
confidebant. itaque rursus coniuratione facta, paulatim ex castris
discedere ac suos clam ex agris deducere coeperunt.

91   **daturos (esse)** the accusative subject of the infinitive (**sese**) is placed with the second infinitive (**facturos**).

92   **imperasset = imperavisset. sese** an emphatic form of **se**.

92–3   **eius rei culpam ... coiecerunt** 'they threw the blame for this action on the mass (of the people)'. This excuse was plausible, since kingship was elective amongst the Celts, so that king and nobles had to pay attention to the views of the people.

94   **ultro** 'of their own accord'.

96   **ignoscere** supply **se**: 'he said that he pardoned their folly'. **obsides imperavit** 'he ordered (them to give) hostages'; **impero** can take the accusative of the thing ordered as well as the dative of the person, e.g. **hoc tibi impero** 'I order this to you' = 'I give you this order'.

97   **quorum ... partem** 'some of these (the hostages)'.

101   **post diem quartum quam = quarto die postquam** 'on the fourth day after'.

101–2   **est ... ventum** 'it was come' = 'we came' (impersonal use of the passive).

102   **sustulerant** 'had taken on board'.

105   **eodem** 'to the same place' (cf. **eo**).

107   **solis occasum** = 'west'. **sui cum periculo** 'with danger to themselves'; **sui** is genitive of **se**. **deicerentur** 'were thrown down (onto the shore)'; we should say 'were thrown up on the shore'.

109   **consuevit** 'is accustomed'.

09–10   **nostris id erat incognitum** Caesar had been fighting a naval war with the Veneti in Britanny the previous year and it is impossible to believe that he and his commanders did not know about the spring tides. The ensuing disaster seems to have resulted from serious incompetence and Caesar is here anxious to justify himself.

110   **longas navis** the object of (**aestus**) **compleverat**.

114   **armamentis** 'equipment'.
The soldiers panicked, seeing that they were cut off in a hostile island with no supplies and no means of returning to the continent.

121   **paucitatem** 'the small numbers'; Caesar had taken only two legions on this expedition and his cavalry had been blown back to France. A legion at full strength contained 6,000 men but they were usually below full strength. When Caesar led two legions to relieve Cicero (see chapter 3 below), he says that they numbered no more than 7,000 in total.

122   **optimum factu esse duxerunt** 'they judged that it was best to do ...' = 'they considered that their best course of action was ...' (**factu:** the supine in **-u** is used after adjectives, e.g. **mirabile dictu** = 'wonderful to relate').

123   **commeatu** 'from supplies'. **prohibere** 'to cut off'.

124   **eis** = the Romans. The Britons had a unique chance of destroying the invading force and were determined to make the most of it.

130

at Caesar, etsi nondum eorum consilia cognoverat, tamen fore id quod accidit suspicabatur. itaque ad omnis casus subsidia comparabat. nam et frumentum ex agris cotidie in castra conferebat et, quae gravissime adflictae erant naves, earum materia atque aere ad reliquas reficiendas utebatur et quae ad eas res erant usui ex continenti comportari iubebat. itaque, cum summo studio a militibus administraretur, XII navibus amissis, reliquis ut navigari

135

commode posset effecit.

dum ea geruntur, legione ex consuetudine una frumentatum missa, neque ulla ad id tempus belli suspicione interposita, cum pars hominum in agris remaneret, pars etiam in castra ventitaret, ei qui pro portis castrorum in statione erant Caesari nuntiaverunt

140

pulverem maiorem quam consuetudo ferret in ea parte videri quam in partem legio iter fecisset. Caesar id quod erat suspicatus, aliquid novi a barbaris initum consilii, cohortes quae in stationibus erant secum in eam partem proficisci, reliquas armari et confestim sese subsequi iussit. cum paulo longius a castris processisset, suos ab

145

hostibus premi atque aegre sustinere et ex omnibus partibus tela coici animadvertit. nam quod omni ex reliquis partibus demesso frumento pars una erat reliqua, suspicati hostes huc nostros esse venturos, noctu in silvis delituerant; tum dispersos, depositis armis, in metendo occupatos subito adorti, paucis interfectis reliquos

150

perturbaverant, simul equitatu atque essedis circumdederant.

quibus rebus perturbatis nostris novitate pugnae tempore opportunissimo Caesar auxilium tulit: namque eius adventu hostes constiterunt, nostri se ex timore receperunt. quo facto, ad lacessendum et ad committendum proelium alienum esse tempus

155

arbitratus suo loco se continuit et, brevi tempore intermisso, in castra legiones reduxit. dum haec geruntur, nostris omnibus occupatis, qui erant in agris reliqui discesserunt.

secutae sunt continuos compluris dies tempestates quae et nostros in castris continerent et hostem a pugna prohiberent.

160

interim barbari nuntios in omnis partis dimiserunt paucitatemque nostrorum militum suis praedicaverunt et quanta praedae faciendae atque in perpetuum sui liberandi facultas daretur, si Romanos castris expulissent, demonstraverunt. his rebus celeriter magna multitudine peditatus equitatusque coacta ad castra venerunt.

(*de Bello Gallico* 4.30–32, 34)

129   **ad omnis casus** 'for all eventualities'.

130   **frumentum** luckily for Caesar, at the end of August the corn would have been ripe.

131   **quae ... naves, earum materia** 'the material from those ships which ...' (literally, 'which ships had been most seriously damaged, the material from them').

134   **administraretur** 'it (the task) was managed'; impersonal use of the passive.

134–5   **reliquis ... effecit** 'he brought it about that it could be adequately sailed with the others', i.e. 'he saw that the others were seaworthy'. **navigari** impersonal use of the passive. Caesar's countermeasures show him at his best as a general, keeping a cool head in a crisis.

136   **ex consuetudine** 'according to custom', 'as usual'. **frumentatum** 'to forage'; supine in **-um** of **frumentari**, expressing purpose.

137   **interposita** 'having been put between', having arisen'. **cum** 'since'.

138   **pars hominum** i.e. some of the British chieftains. **ventitaret** 'were coming and going'.

139   **in statione** 'on guard duty'.

140   **pulverem maiorem** 'a larger dust cloud'. **quam consuetudo ferret** 'than custom brought' = 'than usual'.

141   **id quod erat** 'what was the truth'; this is explained by the accusative and infinitive: **aliquid ... initum (esse) = aliquid novi consilii a barbaris initum (esse)**.

148   **delituerant** 'had hidden'.

151   **quibus rebus ...** the succession of ablative phrases is confusing; it seems best to take **quibus rebus** as an ablative of cause referring to the whole situation, 'because of this situation' or 'because of these factors'; **novitate pugnae** then belongs to the ablative absolute **perturbatis nostris**. In a chapter omitted Caesar describes how the Britons used their war chariots, tactics which were quite unfamiliar to the Romans.

151–2   **tempore opportunissimo** goes with **Caesar auxilium tulit**.

152   **eius adventu** 'on his arrival' (ablative of cause).

153–5   **ad lacessendum ... alienum esse tempus arbitratus** 'thinking that the time was unsuitable for provoking/initiating'.

155   **brevi tempore intermisso** 'a short time having been let pass' = 'after a short interval'.

157   **reliqui** i.e. the rest of the Britons.

159   **continerent ... prohiberent** the subjunctives express consequence.

161–2   **praedae faciendae ... sui liberandi** the gerundives depend on **facultas** 'opportunity' (**sui** is the genitive of **se**, here plural in meaning, 'of freeing themselves').

Caesar beats off an attack on his camp and returns to France.

165   Caesar etsi idem quod superioribus diebus acciderat fore videbat, ut
si essent hostes pulsi, celeritate periculum effugerent, tamen
legiones in acie pro castris constituit. commisso proelio, diutius
nostrorum militum impetum hostes ferre non potuerunt ac terga
verterunt. quos tanto spatio secuti quantum cursu et viribus efficere
170   potuerunt, compluris ex eis occiderunt, deinde omnibus late
longeque aedificiis incensis se in castra receperunt.

    eodem die legati ab hostibus missi ad Caesarem de pace
venerunt. his Caesar numerum obsidum quem antea imperaverat
duplicavit eosque in continentem adduci iussit, quod propinqua die
175   aequinocti infirmis navibus hiemi navigationem subiciendam non
existimabat. ipse idoneam tempestatem nactus paulo post mediam
noctem navis solvit, quae omnes incolumes ad continentem
pervenerunt. his rebus gestis, ex litteris Caesaris dierum viginti
supplicatio a senatu decreta est.

(de Bello Gallico 4.35–8)

165 **idem ... acciderat** 'the same as had happened on previous days'. The **ut** clause explains what this was: as Caesar had no cavalry he could not catch and destroy the enemy when they were routed.

169–70 **tanto spatio ... quantum ... efficere potuerunt** 'for so great a distance as they could achieve ...', i.e. 'as far as they could ...'. **cursu et viribus** literally, 'by running and strength' = 'as far as speed and strength allowed'.

174 **propinqua die aequinocti** 'because the equinox (literally, the equinoctial day) was near'; the equinox is on 24 September; it is often the time of violent gales. Caesar's understanding of meteorology seems to have improved.

175 **hiemi** locative case, 'in the winter', 'under winter conditions'. Compare **ruri** 'in the country', **vesperi** 'in the evening'. **infirmis ... subiciendam (esse)** literally, 'that navigation should not be undergone by weak ships'. Caesar had had to make emergency repairs to his ships and he was afraid they were not fully seaworthy.

177 **navis solvit** Caesar seems to have sailed back to the continent on the very day of the battle.

178 **ex litteris Caesaris** 'on the strength of despatches from Caesar'.

178–9 **dierum viginti supplicatio** 'a thanksgiving of twenty days'. The senate decreed a *supplicatio* in times of crisis or as a thanksgiving for victory. Prayers and sacrifices were offered in the temples in Rome; a *supplicatio* could last for one or more days; twenty days is an extraordinarily long one. The senate had been consistently hostile to Caesar and one wonders what he had said in his despatches which inspired so long a celebration of an expedition which had been something of a fiasco.

2 The second invasion of Britain

Caesar was determined to return to Britain the following year. This time he made very thorough preparations; he intended to invade with overwhelming force, transporting five legions and 2,000 cavalry to Britain. For this purpose he needed a vast fleet and he gave orders for the construction of 600 transport ships of special design; they were to have a shallower draft than usual, for easier beaching, wider in the beam, for holding more troops, and a lower freeboard, for faster sailing. He left to spend the winter in Italy and returned to Gaul in the spring. After settling affairs in Gaul, he led his army to Portus Itius (Boulogne) where the invasion fleet had been ordered to assemble. This year he sailed in July, about a month earlier than the previous year.

The invasion fleet sails. The Romans make an unopposed landing and rout the Britons in their first engagement.

his rebus gestis, Labieno in continente cum tribus legionibus et equitum milibus duobus relicto, ut portus tueretur et rem frumentariam provideret quaeque in Gallia gererentur cognosceret, ipse cum quinque legionibus et pari numero equitum, quem in
5 continenti reliquerat, ad solis occasum navis solvit et leni Africo provectus media circiter nocte, vento intermisso, cursum non tenuit, et longius delatus aestu, orta luce, sub sinistra Britanniam relictam conspexit. tum rursus aestus commutationem secutus remis contendit ut eam partem insulae caperet qua optimum esse egressum superiore
10 aestate cognoverat. accessum est ad Britanniam omnibus navibus meridiano fere tempore, neque in eo loco hostis est visus; sed, ut postea Caesar ex captivis cognovit, cum magnae manus eo convenissent, multitudine navium perterritae, quae amplius octingentae uno erant visae tempore, litore discesserant ac se in
15 superiora loca abdiderant.
    Caesar, exposito exercitu et loco castris idoneo capto, ubi ex captivis cognovit quo in loco hostium copiae consedissent, cohortibus decem ad mare relictis
20 et equitibus trecentis qui praesidio navibus essent, de tertia vigilia ad hostis contendit, eo minus veritus navibus, quod in litore molli atque aperto deligatas ad ancoram
25 relinquebat, et praesidio navibus Q. Atrium praefecit. ipse noctu progressus milia circiter XII hostium copias conspicatus est. illi equitatu atque essedis ad flumen
30 progressi ex loco superiore

ad flumen progressi ex loco superiore
(the river Stour, near Canterbury)

1–8	**his rebus ... conspexit** this long sentence breaks up into a series of easily understood units: 1 **Labieno ... relicto** (ablative absolute), with the clause **ut ... cognosceret** dependent on it; 2 main clause (a) **ipse ... solvit**; (b) **et ... non tenuit**; (c) **et ... Britanniam relictam conspexit**.
1	**Labieno** when Caesar sailed for Britain, he was well aware of the danger of revolt in Gaul and left his most trusted lieutenant Labienus with what appeared adequate forces to watch the situation and act as necessary.
2–3	**rem frumentariam** 'his corn supply'.
4–5	**ipse ... solvit** Caesar sailed at the beginning of July at sunset (about 8 p.m.) with a gentle south-west wind (**Africus**), sailing against the tide; by midnight, when the wind dropped, the tide would have turned north-east, and the fleet drifted with it towards the North Sea. As soon as the tide turned in their favour, the fleet rowed hard to reach the beaches near Deal, where they had landed the previous year. They reached their landfall at midday, having left about 8 p.m. the previous day; the crossing had taken sixteen hours.
13–14	**amplius octingentae** 'more than 800' (in this strange idiom **quam** is omitted). The fleet of 600 new transports and twenty-eight warships was swelled by the addition of the ships he had used the previous summer and a number of private merchant ships. The whole sea must have seemed to the Britons to be covered by this vast invading force; it is no wonder that they panicked and allowed Caesar to make an unopposed landing.
21	**de tertia vigilia** the third watch of the night would be soon after midnight. And so in twelve hours (he had reached Britain about midday) he had supervised the disembarkation of an army of some 20,000 men and 2,000 cavalry, had organized a camp, had captured some of the enemy from whom he learnt the disposition of the Britons and then marched off with a force of some 15,000 legionaries and 1,700 cavalry in the middle of the night. Speed was one of the secrets of Caesar's military success.
22–3	**eo ... quod** 'for this reason ... that'. **veritus navibus** 'fearing for the ships'. The following **quod** clause is an attempt to excuse himself for the disaster which was to befall the fleet.
24	**deligatas** supply **eas** (i.e. the ships).
29	**ad flumen** the river Stour.

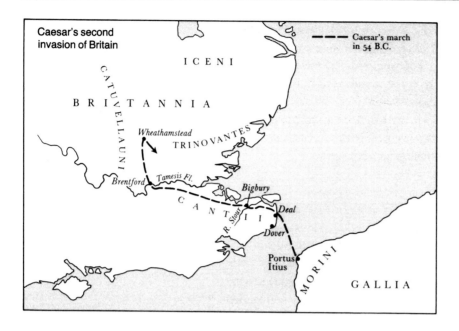

nostros prohibere et proelium committere coeperunt. repulsi ab
equitatu se in silvas abdiderunt, locum nacti egregie et natura et
opere munitum, quem domestici belli, ut videbatur, causa iam ante
praeparaverant; nam crebris arboribus succisis omnes introitus
35 erant praeclusi. ipsi ex silvis rari propugnabant nostrosque intra
munitiones ingredi prohibebant. at milites septimae legionis,
testudine facta et aggere ad munitiones adiecto, locum ceperunt
eosque ex silvis expulerunt paucis vulneribus acceptis. sed eos
fugientis longius Caesar prosequi vetuit et quod loci naturam
40 ignorabat et quod magna parte diei consumpta munitioni
castrorum tempus relinqui volebat.

(*de Bello Gallico* 5.8–9)

testudine facta

32–3 **locum ... munitum** this fortified position was probably Bigbury, which is on a wooded hill two miles west of Canterbury; built shortly before Caesar's invasion, it was the largest British fortress south of the Thames, protected by the slope of the hill (**natura**) and by a rampart and ditch (**opere**).

33 **domestici belli ... causa** 'for the sake of domestic/internal war'; tribal warfare was a common feature of Britain.

34 **praeparaverant** 'they had prepared in advance'.

34–5 **succisis** 'cut down' (from **sub-cido**); **praeclusi** 'shut in front'; **propugnabant** 'fought in front of': note how Caesar uses prepositional prefixes to give precision to the meaning of the verbs.

35 **rari** 'scattered', 'in small groups'.

37 **testudine facta** 'making a tortoise'; this was a formation commonly used in attacking a fortified position: the soldiers locked shields over their heads to ward off weapons hurled down at them. **aggere ... adiecto** 'piling a mound against the fortifications'; the fort was guarded by a ditch and rampart; the Romans filled in the ditch and piled up earth to the height of the rampart. Caesar describes these events concisely and without comment, but it must have been a lengthy and difficult operation which was not completed until most of the day had passed; he then broke off the action in order to have time to build a camp. A Roman army on the march in hostile territory always built a camp for the night; it was laid out on a set pattern, with a ditch and rampart. To build a camp for over 20,000 men would have taken some time. (Archaeologists have sometimes been able to trace the route taken by Roman armies from their 'marching camps', notably in Scotland.)

38–9 **eos fugientis**: **eos** = 'the enemy'; 'Caesar forbade (his men) to pursue their flight (them fleeing) too far'.

Caesar pursues the enemy but is recalled by news that the fleet has been badly damaged by a gale.

postridie eius diei mane tripertito milites equitesque in
expeditionem misit, ut eos qui fugerant persequerentur. his
aliquantum itineris progressis, cum iam extremi essent in
45 prospectu, equites a Q. Atrio ad Caesarem venerunt qui nuntiarent
superiore nocte maxima coorta tempestate prope omnis navis
adflictas atque in litore eiectas esse, quod neque ancorae funesque
subsisterent neque nautae gubernatoresque vim tempestatis pati
possent; itaque ex eo concursu navium magnum esse incommodum
50 acceptum.
    his rebus cognitis, Caesar legiones equitatumque revocari atque
in itinere resistere iubet, ipse ad navis revertitur: eadem fere quae
ex nuntiis litterisque cognoverat coram perspicit, sic ut amissis
circiter XL navibus reliquae tamen refici posse magno negotio
55 viderentur. itaque ex legionibus fabros deligit et ex continenti alios
arcessi iubet. ipse, etsi res erat multae operae et laboris, tamen
commodissimum esse statuit omnis navis subduci et cum castris
una munitione coniungi. in his rebus circiter dies X consumit, ne
nocturnis quidem temporibus ad laborem militum intermissis.
60 subductis navibus castrisque egregie munitis, easdem copias, quas
antea, praesidio navibus reliquit: ipse eodem unde redierat
proficiscitur.

(*de Bello Gallico* 5.10–11)

The Britons unite under Cassivellaunus. Caesar continues his advance, harried by larger British forces.

eo cum venisset, maiores iam undique in eum locum copiae
Britannorum convenerant, summa imperi bellique administrandi
65 communi consilio permissa Cassivellauno, cuius finis a maritimis
civitatibus flumen dividit quod appellatur Tamesis a mari circiter
milia passuum LXXX. huic superiore tempore cum reliquis
civitatibus continentia bella intercesserant; sed nostro adventu
permoti Britanni hunc toti bello imperioque praefecerant.
70   equites hostium essedariique acriter proelio cum equitatu nostro
in itinere conflixerunt, tamen ut nostri omnibus partibus superiores
fuerint atque eos in silvas collisque compulerint; sed compluribus

42 **postridie** this is only the second day after his landing. **tripertito** 'in three divisions'.

44 **aliquantum itineris** 'some part of the journey'. **extremi** 'the last (of the enemy forces)'.

46–7 **navis adflictas** in his desire to achieve surprise, Caesar had made the same mistake as in the previous year, in not taking adequate steps to secure the safety of the fleet. This mistake cost him dear, since while he was employed in repairing and securing the fleet the Britons gathered in larger numbers, united under one commander.

47ff. **quod ... subsisterent** ('held firm') **... possent** subjunctive, because they form part of what the messengers said; similarly **esse ... acceptum** is accusative and infinitive of indirect statement.

52 **resistere** 'to halt'. **eadem fere quae** 'pretty well the same as'.

53 **coram** 'in his presence', 'in person'.

55 **fabros** 'engineers'.

58–9 **ne nocturnis quidem ... intermissis** 'not even night time being interrupted for the work of the soldiers', i.e. 'the soldiers worked day and night without intermission'.

60–61 **easdem copias, quas antea** 'the same forces as before'.

64 **summa imperi bellique administrandi** 'the chief (of) command and (of) running the war'; we would say 'overall command in running the war'.

65 **Cassivellauno** king of the Catuvellauni, a powerful tribe in southern Britain, now settled in Hertfordshire, Casivellaunus was ambitious and continually trying to expand his territory beyond his boundary of the Thames (**Tamesis**), as the next sentence says.

67–8 **huic ... continentia bella intercesserant** 'continual wars occurred for this man', i.e 'this man (Cassivellaunus) was involved in continual wars'.

68–9 **sed nostro adventu ... praefecerant** the fact that the tribes of southern Britain now united under their old enemy shows how seriously they viewed the threat posed by the Romans.

70–71 **proelio ... conflixerunt** 'clashed in battle with ...'. Caesar's march from Canterbury to the Thames was seriously harried by the guerilla tactics employed by Cassivellaunus' men and he clearly suffered a setback when his army was suddenly attacked while they were building their camp for the night.

interfectis cupidius insecuti nonnullos ex suis amiserunt. at illi,
intermisso spatio, imprudentibus nostris atque occupatis in
75   munitione castrorum, subito se ex silvis eiecerunt impetuque in eos
facto qui in statione erant pro castris collocati, acriter pugnaverunt;
duabusque missis subsidio cohortibus a Caesare, atque eis primis
legionum duarum, cum haec perexiguo intermisso loci spatio inter
se constitissent, novo genere pugnae perterritis nostris, per medios
80   audacissime perruperunt seque inde incolumes receperunt. eo die
Q. Laberius, tribunus militum, interficitur. illi pluribus summissis
cohortibus repelluntur.

     postero die procul a castris hostes in collibus constiterunt,
rarique se ostendere et lenius quam pridie nostros equites proelio
85   lacessere coeperunt. sed meridie, cum Caesar pabulandi causa tris
legiones atque omnem equitatum cum C. Trebonio legato misisset,
repente ex omnibus partibus ad pabulatores advolaverunt, sic uti ab
signis legionibusque non absisterent. nostri acriter in eos impetu
facto reppulerunt neque finem sequendi fecerunt, quoad subsidio
90   confisi equites, cum post se legiones viderent, praecipites hostis
egerunt, magnoque eorum numero interfecto, neque sui colligendi
neque consistendi aut ex essedis desiliendi facultatem dederunt. ex
hac fuga protinus quae undique convenerant auxilia discesserunt,
neque post id tempus umquam summis nobiscum copiis hostes
95   contenderunt.

(de Bello Gallico 5.11, 15, 17)

*Caesar crosses the Thames despite fierce opposition and advances
into the territory of Cassivellaunus, whose fortress he captures.*

Caesar, cognito consilio eorum, ad flumen Tamesin in finis
Cassivellauni exercitum duxit; quod flumen uno omnino loco
pedibus, atque hoc aegre, transiri potest. eo cum venisset, animum
advertit ad alteram fluminis ripam magnas esse copias hostium
100   instructas. ripa autem erat acutis sudibus praefixisque munita,
eiusdemque generis sub aqua defixae sudes flumine tegebantur. eis
rebus cognitis a captivis perfugisque, Caesar praemisso equitatu
confestim legiones subsequi iussit. sed ea celeritate atque eo impetu
milites ierunt, cum capite solo ex aqua exstarent, ut hostes impetum
105   legionum atque equitum sustinere non possent ripasque dimitterent
ac se fugae mandarent.

77–8 **atque eis primis legionum duarum** 'and these the first cohorts of the two legions'. The first cohorts of every legion not only contained the best soldiers but were of double strength. It was a serious matter that they should be panic stricken (**perterritis nostris**, *l.* 79).

78 **haec = hae.**

78–9 **perexiguo ... inter se** 'a very small extent of place being left between them', i.e. 'at very close range'.

79 **novo genere pugnae** i.e. the use of chariots interspersed with cavalry. In a chapter omitted Caesar describes the tactics of the British war chariots, which were certainly a formidable force.

85 **pabulandi causa** 'to forage' (for corn and food for the horses). Caesar sent out over half his army on this foraging expedition, remembering how the year before one legion had been badly mauled in a similar situation. He seems to have had the legions drawn up in formation ready to repel a surprise attack; the enemy penetrated through the cavalry screen and right up to the legions.

87–8 **sic uti (= ut) ... non absisterent** 'so that they did not hold off from', i.e. they attacked the legions drawn up for battle.

89–90 **quoad subsidio confisi equites** 'until the cavalry trusting in the support (of the legions)'.

91–2 **sui colligendi ... facultatem** 'any opportunity of gathering themselves/rallying'.

92–3 **ex hac fuga** 'after this rout'.

93 **auxilia** 'the reinforcements' (the antecedent to **quae**).

94 **summis ... copiis** 'in full force'. Perhaps Caesar had tempted the enemy into a trap, anticipating what would happen in an action which proved the turning point in the war.

flumen uno loco pedibus transiri potest
(the Thames at Brentford)

97 **uno omnino loco** this place is generally held to be Brentford, where the Thames is fordable.

98–9 **animum advertit = animadvertit** 'he noticed/perceived'.

103 **ea celeritate atque eo impetu** 'with such speed and such dash'.

104 **cum ... exstarent** 'although they stood out of the water by the head alone' = 'although only their heads were above water'.

105 **dimitterent** 'abandoned'.

Cassivellaunus, ut supra demonstravimus, omni deposita spe
contentionis, dimissis amplioribus copiis, milibus circiter quattuor
essedariorum relictis, itinera nostra servabat paulumque ex via
110 excedebat locisque impeditis ac silvestribus sese occultabat, atque
eis regionibus quibus nos iter facturos cognoverat pecora atque
homines ex agris in silvas compellebat et, cum equitatus noster
liberius praedandi vastandique causa se in agros eiecerat, omnibus viis
semitisque essedarios ex silvis emittebat et magno cum periculo
115 nostrorum equitum cum eis confligebat atque hoc metu latius vagari
prohibebat. relinquebatur ut neque longius ab agmine legionum
discedi Caesar pateretur, et tantum in agris vastandis incendiisque
faciendis hostibus noceretur, quantum labore atque itinere legionarii
milites efficere poterant.

120 interim Trinobantes, prope firmissima earum regionum civitas,
legatos ad Caesarem mittunt pollicenturque sese ei dedituros atque
imperata facturos. Caesar imperat obsides XL frumentumque
exercitui. illi imperata celeriter fecerunt, obsides ad numerum
frumentumque miserunt. Trinobantibus defensis atque ab omni
125 militum iniuria prohibitis, Cenimagni, Segontiaci, Ancalites, Bibroci,
Cassi legationibus missis sese Caesari dedunt. ab eis cognoscit non
longe ab eo loco oppidum Cassivellauni abesse silvis paludibusuqe
munitum, quo satis magnus hominum pecorumque numerus convenit.
eo proficiscitur cum legionibus; locum reperit egregie natura et opere
130 munitum; tamen hunc duabus ex partibus oppugnare contendit. hostes
paulisper morati militum nostrorum impetum non tulerunt seseque
alia ex parte oppidi iecerunt. magnus ibi numerus pecoris repertus,
multique in fuga comprehensi sunt atque interfecti.

(*de Bello Gallico* 5.18–21)

Coin of the Catuvellauni

The river god of the Thames

108 **contentionis** 'of set battle'. Cassivellaunus now adopted classic guerilla tactics, which clearly made things very difficult for the Romans. **amplioribus copiis** he must have raised a huge army to resist the Romans if, after dismissing his larger forces, he still kept 4,000 charioteers.

113 **liberius** 'too freely'; compare **latius** 'too widely' (*l.* 115), **longius** 'too far' (*l.* 116).

116 **relinquebatur ut** 'it was left that ...' = 'the only course left was that ...'.

117 **discedi** impersonal use of passive, '(allowed) it to be departed' = '(allowed) them to depart'.

17–18 **tantum ... hostibus noceretur, quantum ...** 'so much damage was done to the enemy, as ...'. **hostibus noceretur** 'the enemy were damaged', impersonal use of the passive, **noceo** being a dative verb.

118 **labore atque itinere** 'by their exertions in marching'. As the cavalry had to keep close to the legions, the speed at which the legionaries marched determined how much damage the cavalry could do to the enemy.

120 **Trinobantes** these were, as Caesar says, perhaps the most powerful tribe in southern Britain, occupying Essex and Suffolk, with their capital at Camulodunum (Colchester). They had long been at war with Cassivellaunus and they now appealed to Caesar to protect them against him. Six other tribes then surrendered to Caesar, all perhaps afraid of the Catuvellauni. None of these tribes is known from other sources (the Cenimagni may be identified with the Iceni of Norfolk, whose queen Boudicca in the next century led a great rebellion against the Romans).

24–5 **ab omni ... prohibitis** 'protected from all abuses on the part of our soldiers'.

127 **oppidum** 'town'; but the word is used of any settlement and here means a fortified place of refuge. This *oppidum* is probably the large fortress on a hill top at Wheathampstead near St Albans; this covers over 100 acres and is protected by a ditch 40 feet deep with a high bank on each side (it was excavated in 1932 and the objects found there all date from about the time of Caesar's invasion).

The Kentish allies of Cassivellaunus make a surprise attack on the naval camp. When this is beaten off, Cassivellaunus surrenders and Caesar decides to return to Gaul.

dum haec in eis locis geruntur, Cassivellaunus ad Cantium, quod
135 esse ad mare supra demonstravimus, quibus regionibus quattuor
reges praeerant, nuntios mittit atque eis imperat uti coactis omnibus
copiis castra navalia de improviso adoriantur atque oppugnent. ei
cum ad castra venissent, nostri eruptione facta, multis eorum
interfectis, suos incolumes reduxerunt. Cassivellaunus, hoc proelio
140 nuntiato, tot detrimentis acceptis, vastatis finibus, maxime etiam
permotus defectione civitatum, legatos de deditione ad Caesarem
mittit. Caesar, cum constituisset hiemare in continenti propter
repentinos Galliae motus neque multum aetatis superesset, obsides
imperat et quid in annos singulos vectigalis populo Romano
145 Britannia penderet constituit.

(*de Bello Gallico* 5.22)

The failure of the surprise attack on the naval camp convinced Cassivellaunus that he must sue for peace and he had to accept the terms dictated by Caesar. Caesar not only followed the usual procedure of taking hostages but imposed a tax on 'Britain', as if it had been reduced to the status of a province. But Caesar had already decided that he must return to Gaul at once because of the incipient rebellions there and he never had a chance to return to Britain. We do not know whether or for how long the Britons paid tax. Within a short time the tribes of Britain were again quite independent of Rome and Augustus firmly resolved not to get involved there; a hundred years passed before the Romans again invaded Britain under Claudius (AD 43).

Tacitus gives a fair summary of what Caesar had achieved:

primus omnium Romanorum divus Iulius cum exercitu
Britanniam ingressus, quamquam prospera pugna terruerit
incolas et litore potitus sit, potest videri ostendisse posteris, non
tradidisse.

(*Agricola* 13.2)

The first of all the Romans to invade Britain with an army was
the divine Julius, and although he terrified the inhabitants by
some victories and won possession of the coast, he may seem to
have shown Britain to posterity, not to have handed it over to
them.

Coin commemorating
the conquest of Britain

134 **Cantium** 'Kent'. That there were four separate kingdoms in Kent
shows how small some of the tribal units in Britain were.

144–5 **quid in annos singulos vectigalis ... penderet** 'what of tax (=
what taxes) it (Britain) should pay each year'.

3 Revolt in Gaul 1: The ambush of Sabinus and Cotta

Caesar had left Britain earlier than he had intended because of
reports that some of the Gallic tribes were restless. On arrival in Gaul
he decided to distribute his legions singly amongst various tribal
territories instead of concentrating the army in one large camp (see
map, p. 57). He did this, he says, because the harvest had failed and
he thought this arrangement would put less strain on the
commissariat, but it proved a serious error of judgement.

Instead of returning at once, to Italy, where he usually spent the
winter, he waited until he knew that the legions were all settled in their
winter quarters and the camps fortified (autumn 54 BC).

Ambiorix, king of the Eburones, makes a sudden attack on the camp of
Sabinus and Cotta. After failing to take it, he offers the Romans safe
conduct, if they leave their camp to join Cicero or Labienus.

diebus circiter quindecim quibus in hiberna ventum est initium
repentini tumultus ac defectionis ortum est ab Ambiorige et
Catuvolco; qui, cum ad finis regni sui Sabino Cottaeque praesto
fuissent frumentumque in hiberna comportavissent, Indutiomari
5   Treveri nuntiis impulsi suos concitaverunt subitoque oppressis
lignatoribus magna manu ad castra oppugnatum venerunt. cum
celeriter nostri arma cepissent vallumque ascendissent atque una ex
parte equitibus emissis equestri proelio superiores fuissent, desperata
re hostes suos ab oppugnatione reduxerunt. tum suo more
10   conclamaverunt uti aliqui ex nostris ad colloquium prodiret: habere
sese quae de re communi dicere vellent, quibus rebus controversias
minui posse sperarent.

mittitur ad eos colloquendi causa C. Arpineius et Q. Iunius; apud
quos Ambiorix ad hunc modum locutus est: sese pro Caesaris in se
15   beneficiis plurimum ei confiteri debere, quod eius opera stipendio
liberatus esset quod Aduaticis finitimis suis pendere consuesset,
quodque ei et filius et fratris filius ab Caesare remissi essent; neque id
quod fecerit de oppugnatione castrorum, aut iudicio aut voluntate sua
fecisse, sed coactu civitatis, quod repentinae Gallorum coniurationi
20   resistere non potuerit. esse Galliae commune consilium: omnibus
hibernis Caesaris oppugnandis hunc esse dictum diem, ne qua legio
alterae legioni subsidio venire posset. monere, orare Sabinum ut suae
ac militum saluti consulat. magnam manum Germanorum conductam
Rhenum transisse: hanc adfore biduo. ipsorum esse consilium,
25   velintne priusquam finitimi sentiant eductos esse ex hibernis milites
aut ad Ciceronem aut ad Labienum deducere, quorum alter milia
passuum circiter quinquaginta, alter paulo amplius ab eis absit. illud se
polliceri et iure iurando confirmare, tutum iter per finis daturum.

(de Bello Gallico 5.26–7)

1   **diebus ... ventum est** 'within about fifteen days after their arrival (within which it was come) in winter quarters'.

2–3   **Ambiorige et Catuvolco** these were joint kings of the Eburones, whose territory lay between the Meuse and the Rhine. Ambiorix was the moving spirit in this rebellion and fought on longer than any other Gallic chieftain.

3   **praesto** this adverb means 'at hand' 'ready'; with **esse** + dative of the person concerned it means 'to help'. Sabinus and Cotta held joint command of one and a half legions in the territory of the Eburones.

4–5   **Indutiomari Treveri nuntiis** 'by messages from Indutiomarus of the Treveri'; Indutiomarus was king of the Treveri; their territory adjoined that of the Eburones to the south-east.

6   **oppugnatum** 'to attack'; supine in **-um**, expressing purpose.

9   **suo more** 'in their usual way', i.e. shouting instead of sending an envoy under truce.

10   **uti ... prodiret**: **uti = ut**, introducing indirect command; the sentence continues in indirect statement '(they said) that they had things which ...'. **aliqui = aliquis** 'someone'.

14   **ad hunc modum** 'to this effect'. The speech which follows is all in indirect form – mostly accusative and infinitive of indirect statement.

14–15   **pro ... beneficiis** 'in view of the kindnesses ...'.

15   **confiteri debere** 'he confessed that he owed'. **eius opera** 'by his (Caesar's) efforts'. **stipendio** 'from the tax'.

16   **pendere consuesset** 'he had been accustomed to pay'.

19   **coactu civitatis** 'through the compulsion of the citizen body', i.e. 'compelled by his fellow citizens'.

21   **hunc esse dictum diem** 'this had been declared the day'. **ne qua legio** 'lest any legion', 'so that no legion'.

22   **monere, orare** 'he begged and prayed'.

22–3   **ut ... consulat** (+ dat.) 'to take thought for'.

23   **conductam** 'hired', i.e. they were mercenaries hired by the Gauls.

24   **biduo** 'in two days'. **ipsorum esse consilium** 'it was the plan/decision of (the Romans) themselves', i.e. 'the Romans must decide for themselves'.

25–6   **velintne ... deducere** 'whether they wanted to lead'.

26   **Ciceronem** = Quintus Cicero, Cicero's younger brother; he was commanding a legion in winter quarters in the territory of the Nervii, about 50 miles to the north; Labienus was on the borders of the Treviri, about 50 miles or more to the south. Cicero will prove to be the hero of the hour.

28   **iure iurando** 'by swearing an oath'. **daturum = se daturum esse**.

*The Roman commanders hold a council of war to decide whether
to accept the proposal of Ambiorix.*

Arpineius et Iunius ea quae audierunt ad legatos deferunt. illi
30 repentina re perturbati, etsi ab hoste ea dicebantur, tamen non
neglegenda esse existimabant. itaque ad consilium rem deferunt
magnaque inter eos exsistit controversia. complures tribuni
militum et primorum ordinum centuriones nihil temere agendum
neque ex hibernis iniussu Caesaris discedendum existimabant.
35 quantasvis magnas etiam copias Germanorum sustineri posse
munitis hibernis docebant; re frumentaria non premi; interea et ex
proximis hibernis et a Caesare conventura subsidia.

   contra ea Sabinus sero facturos clamitabat, cum maiores manus
hostium adiunctis Germanis convenissent aut cum aliquid
40 calamitatis in proximis hibernis esset acceptum. brevem
consulendi esse occasionem. suam sententiam in utramque partem
esse tutam: si nihil esset durius, nullo cum periculo ad proximam
legionem perventuros: si Gallia omnis cum Germanis consentiret,
unam esse in celeritate positam salutem.

45   hac in utramque partem disputatione habita, cum a Cotta
primisque ordinibus acriter resisteretur, 'vincite,' inquit, 'si ita
vultis,' Sabinus, et id clariore voce, ut magna pars militum
exaudiret 'neque is sum,' inquit, 'qui gravissime ex vobis mortis
periculo terrear: hi sapient; si gravius quid acciderit, abs te
50 rationem reposcent qui, si per te liceat, perendino die cum
proximis hibernis coniuncti communem cum reliquis belli casum
sustineant, non reiecti et relegati longe ab ceteris aut ferro aut
fame intereant.'

(de Bello Gallico 5.28–30)

*Eventually Sabinus' view is accepted and the Romans leave their
camp.*

consurgitur ex consilio; comprehendunt utrumque et orant ne sua
55 dissensione et pertinacia rem in summum periculum deducant. res
disputatione ad mediam noctem perducitur. tandem dat Cotta
permotus manus: superat sententia Sabini. pronuntiatur prima luce
ituros. prima luce sic ex castris proficiscuntur ut quibus esset
persuasum non ab hoste sed ab homine amicissimo Ambiorige
60 consilium datum, longissimo agmine maximisque impedimentis.

(de Bello Gallico 5.31)

31   **consilium** 'a council of war'; we find that there were present at
      this, besides the commanding officers, all the tribunes and the
      senior centurions; the **primorum ordinum centuriones** are
      probably the six centurions of the first cohort.

33–4 **agendum ... discedendum** supply **esse**.

35   **quantasvis magnas** 'as large as you like', 'however large'.

38   **sero facturos = se sero facturos esse** 'they would act too late'.

41   **suam sententiam** his own opinion was that they should take the
      advice of Ambiorix and march to the next legion.

46   **primis ordinibus** 'the senior centurions'. **acriter resisteretur** 'it
      was being fiercely resisted by' = 'he was being strongly opposed
      by' (impersonal use of passive).

47–8 **ut magna pars militum exaudiret** the soldiers must have been
      crowding around the doors of the council hall and listening. It was
      disgraceful of Sabinus to make this emotional appeal to the
      soldiers when he was engaged in a council of war with the senior
      officers.

48   **neque is sum qui ... terrear** 'nor am I the sort of man to be
      terrified': the subjunctive in this relative clause is 'generic'.

49   **hi sapient** 'these men (the soldiers) will understand'.

50   **rationem reposcent** 'they will demand a reason/justification'. **si
      per te liceat** 'if it were lawful through you (Cotta)' = 'if you
      allowed them'. **perendino die** 'the day after tomorrow'.

50   **relegati** 'cut off'.

54   **consurgitur ab consilio** 'they get up from the council of war'
      (impersonal passive). **comprehendunt utrumque** 'they (= the
      other officers) seize hold of each (Cotta and Sabinus)'.

55   **dissensione et pertinacia** 'by their disagreement and obstinacy' =
      'by their obstinate disagreement'.

56–7 **dat ... manus** 'gives hands' = 'gives in', 'surrenders'. **permotus**
      '(though) much disturbed'.

58–9 **ut quibus esset persuasum** 'like men to whom it had been
      persuaded' = 'like men who were convinced'.

60   **consilium datum (esse)** 'that the advice had been given'.
      longissimo agmine maximisque impedimentis there is an
      implied criticism here; they should have marched in close
      formation and lightly equipped, but the soldiers would not abandon
      their possessions. If the legion and a half were up to full strength
      they would have numbered about 9,000 men, which could have
      formed an extremely long column, almost impossible to control in
      any action.

Sabinus and Cotta are ambushed and their forces annihilated.

at hostes, posteaquam ex nocturno fremitu vigiliisque de
profectione eorum senserunt, collocatis insidiis bipertito in silvis
opportuno atque occulto loco a milibus passuum circiter duobus
Romanorum adventum exspectabant et, cum se maior pars agminis
65   in magnam convallem demisisset, ex utraque parte eius vallis subito
se ostenderunt, novissimosque premere et primos prohibere
ascensu atque iniquissimo nostris loco proelium committere
coeperunt.

     tum demum Sabinus, qui nihil ante providisset, trepidare et
70   concursare cohortisque disponere, haec tamen ipsa timide atque ut
eum omnia deficere viderentur; quod plerumque eis accidere
consuevit qui in ipso negotio consilium capere coguntur. at Cotta,
qui cogitasset haec posse in itinere accidere atque ob eam causam
profectionis auctor non fuisset, nulla in re communi saluti deerat et
75   in appellandis cohortandisque militibus imperatoris et in pugna
militis officia praestabat. cum propter longitudinem agminis minus
facile omnia per se obire et quid quoque loco faciendum esset
providere possent, iusserunt pronuntiare ut impedimenta
relinquerent atque in orbem consisterent.

80   at barbaris consilium non defuit. nam duces eorum tota acie
pronuntiare iusserunt, ne quis ab loco discederet: illorum esse
praedam atque illis reservari quaecumque Romani reliquissent:
proinde omnia in victoria posita existimarent. nostri, tametsi ab
duce et a fortuna deserebantur, tamen omnem spem salutis in
85   virtute ponebant, et quotiens quaeque cohors praecurrerat, ab ea
parte magnus numerus hostium cadebat. qua re animadversa,
Ambiorix pronuntiari iubet ut procul tela coiciant neu propius
accedant et quam in partem Romani impetum fecerint cedant.
nostri tamen tot incommodis conflictati, multis vulneribus acceptis,
90   resistebant et magna parte diei consumpta, cum a prima luce ad
horam octavam pugnaretur, nihil quod ipsis esset indignum
committebant. tum Q. Lucanius fortissime pugnans, dum
circumvento filio subvenit, interficitur; L. Cotta legatus omnis
cohortis ordinesque adhortans in adversum os funda vulneratur.

95   his rebus permotus Sabinus, cum procul Ambiorigem suos
cohortantem conspexisset, interpretem suum ad eum mittit rogatum
ut sibi militibusque parcat. ille appellatus respondit: si vellet secum
colloqui, licere. ille cum Cotta saucio communicat, si videatur,
pugna ut excedant et cum Ambiorige una colloquantur. sperare ab
100   eo de sua ac militum salute impetrari posse. Cotta se ad armatum
hostem iturum negat atque in eo perseverat.

     Sabinus quos tribunos militum circum se habebat se sequi iubet
et, cum propius Ambiorigem accessisset, iussus arma abicere
imperatum facit suisque ut idem faciant imperat. interim, dum de

62   **bipertito** 'in two places' (at either end of the valley).

66   **novissimos** 'the rearguard'.

69   **qui ... providisset** 'because he had foreseen'; the relative with the subjunctive can express cause.

69–70   **trepidare ... concursare ... disponere** historic infinitives; translate as indicatives, 'he panicked, ran about' etc.

70   **haec ... ipsa** supply **faciebat**.

70–71   **ut ... viderentur** 'as though everything seemed to fail him' = 'as though he thought everything was hopeless'.

73   **cogitasset = cogitavisset**.

74   **profectionis auctor non fuisset** 'had not been the adviser of the departure', i.e. 'he had not supported the plan to depart'.

75   **imperatoris** supply **officia praestabat**.

77   **omnia per se obire** 'to meet (i.e. to see to) everything in person'.

78   **possent, iusserunt** 'they' = 'the generals'. **iusserunt pronuntiare** 'they ordered (their officers) to announce'.

79   **in orbem consisterent** 'should form a circle', i.e. a hollow square.

81   **pronuntiare iusserunt** we would say 'ordered it to be proclaimed'; compare **Ambiorix pronuntiari iubet** below (*l.* 87). **ne quis** 'that no one should ...'. The purpose of this order was to discourage their men from abandoning the attack in order to seize the Roman baggage.

83   **proinde ... existimarent** 'accordingly ... they must think' (subjunctive of indirect command).

87   **neu** 'and not'.

88   **quam in partem** 'into what part' = 'wherever'.

92   **Q. Lucanius** was a senior centurion.

94   **in adversum os** 'full in the face'. **funda** 'by a sling stone'.

96   **rogatum** 'to ask' (supine in **-um** expressing purpose).

98–9   **communicat ... ut** 'communicates, suggesting that (**ut**), if he agreed (if it seemed good to him)'.

99   **sperare** 'he hoped' (indirect statement).

9–100   **ab eo** i.e. from Ambiorix.

100   **impetrari posse** 'it could be effected'; the whole sentence means, 'he hoped he could secure from Ambiorix the safety of himself and his soldiers'.

105 condicionibus inter se agunt, paulatim circumventus interficitur.
tum vero suo more victoriam conclamant ululatumque tollunt
impetuque in nostros facto ordines perturbant. ibi L. Cotta pugnans
interficitur cum maxima parte militum. reliqui se in castra recipiunt
unde erant egressi. aegre ad noctem oppugnationem sustinent:
110 noctu ad unum omnes desperata salute se ipsi interficiunt. pauci ex
proelio elapsi incertis itineribus per silvas ad T. Labienum in
hiberna perveniunt atque eum de rebus gestis certiorem faciunt.

(*de Bello Gallico* 5.32–7)

*The loss of a legion and a half, perhaps 7,500 men, was the most
serious setback Caesar received in Gaul. Suetonius says that on
receiving the news of this disaster, Caesar let his hair and beard
grow until he had avenged it. Caesar put the blame fairly and
squarely on Sabinus. List the places where Caesar criticizes
Sabinus; how fair is his condemnation?*

hiberna

106 **suo more victoriam conclamant** 'according to their custom raise the victory shout'. **ululatum** 'shrieking'.

110 **ad unum** 'to a man'.

1–12 **in hiberna** Labienus' winter quarters were in the territory of the Treveri, probably at Mouzon, on the Meuse, about 50 miles to the south-west of the quarters of Cotta and Sabinus.

lignatores

4 Revolt in Gaul 2: The siege of Cicero's camp

Ambiorix rouses the Aduatici and the Nervii and falls on Cicero's camp with huge forces

hac victoria sublatus Ambiorix statim cum equitatu in Aduaticos,
qui erant eius regno finitimi, proficiscitur; neque noctem neque
diem intermittit peditatumque sese subsequi iubet. re demonstrata
Aduaticisque concitatis, postero die in Nervios pervenit hortaturque
5   ne sui in perpetuum liberandi atque ulciscendi Romanos pro eis
quas acceperint iniuriis occasionem dimittant: interfectos esse
legatos duo magnamque partem exercitus interisse demonstrat;
nihil esse negoti subito oppressam legionem quae cum Cicerone
hiemet interfici. facile hac oratione Nerviis persuadet.
10   itaque confestim dimissis nuntiis ad Ceutrones, Grudios,
Levacos, Pleumoxios, Geidumnos, qui omnes sub eorum imperio
sunt, quam maximas manus possunt cogunt et de improviso ad
Ciceronis hiberna advolant, nondum ad eum fama de Sabini morte
perlata. huic quoque accidit ut nonnulli milites qui ligationis causa
15   in silvas discessissent repentino equitum adventu interciperentur.
eis circumventis, magna manu Eburones, Nervii, Aduatici atque
horum omnium socii et clientes legionem oppugnare incipiunt.
nostri celeriter ad arma concurrunt, vallum conscendunt. aegre is
dies sustentatur, quod omnem spem hostes in celeritate ponebant
20   atque hanc adepti victoriam in perpetuum se fore victores
confidebant.

(de Bello Gallico 5.38–9)

Cicero fails to get messages to Caesar but gallantly holds out against the attacks of the Gauls.

mittuntur ad Caesarem confestim ab Cicerone litterae, magnis
propositis praemiis, si pertulissent: obsessis omnibus viis missi
intercipiuntur. noctu ex materia quam munitionis causa
25   comportaverant turres admodum centum XX excitantur incredibili
celeritate; quae deesse operi videbantur perficiuntur. hostes postero
die multo maioribus coactis copiis castra oppugnant, fossam
complent. eadem ratione, qua pridie, ab nostris resistitur. hoc idem
reliquis deinceps fit diebus. nulla pars nocturni temporis ad
30   laborem intermittitur; non aegris, non vulneratis facultas quietis
datur. quaecumque ad proximi diei oppugnationem opus sunt noctu
comparantur. ipse Cicero, cum tenuissima valetudine esset, ne
nocturnum quidem sibi tempus ad quietem relinquebat, ut ultro
militum concursu ac vocibus sibi parcere cogeretur.

1   **sublatus** 'elated' (perfect passive participle of **tollo**).   **Aduaticos** their territory lay between that of the Eburones and the Nervii.

3   **intermittit** 'let pass', i.e. he marched day and night.

7   **interisse** = **interiisse**.

8–9   **nihi esse negoti ... interfici** 'it was nothing of business that the legion should be killed', i.e. 'there was no difficulty in killing ...'.

12   **cogunt** 'they collect'.

13   **Ciceronis hiberna** Cicero's winter quarters were in the territory of the Nervii, perhaps at Binche on the river Sambre, over 100 miles east of Caesar, who was at Samarobriva (Amiens).

14   **huic quoque accidit** 'it happened to him (Cicero) too'; the attack on the camp of Cotta and Sabinus had also begun when the enemy fell on soldiers gathering wood for fuel.

18–19   **aegre is dies sustentatur** 'that day is endured with difficulty', i.e. 'they hardly survived that day'.

20   **adepti** one would expect **adeptos**, agreeing with **se** ('they were confident that if they won victory ...').

22–3   **magnis propositis praemiis** 'great rewards being offered (to the messengers)'.

23   **missi** 'those sent'.

25   **turres admodum centum XX excitantur** 'at least 120 towers were erected'; these towers, built of wood, were several storeys high and enabled the defenders to rain down missiles on attackers. The camp for one legion would have been about 50 acres in area and if there really were 120 towers they must have been built very close together; perhaps the figure is wrong.

26   **quae deesse ... perficiuntur** 'what seemed to be lacking to the fortifications (**operi**) was made good'.

29   **deinceps** 'in succession'.

31   **opus** 'necessary'; the word is here used as if it were an indeclinable adjective = **necessaria**.

32   **cum** 'although'.   **tenuissima valetudine** 'in very weak health'.

33–4   **ut ultro ... cogeretur** 'so that he was actually compelled' (**ultro** = 'beyond'; used idiomatically it = 'beyond what you would expect'; here 'beyond the normal duties of the soldiers').

35   tunc duces principesque Nerviorum cum Cicerone colloqui sese
velle dicunt. facta potestate, eadem quae Ambiorix cum Sabino
egerat commemorant: omnem esse in armis Galliam; Germanos
Rhenum transisse; Caesaris reliquorumque hiberna oppugnari.
addunt etiam de Sabini morte: licere illis incolumibus per se ex
40   hibernis discedere et quascumque in partis velint sine metu
proficisci. Cicero ad haec unum modo respondit: non esse
consuetudinem populi Romani accipere ab hoste armato
condicionem; si ab armis discedere velint, se adiutore utantur
legatosque ad Caesarem mittant.

45   ab hac spe repulsi Nervii vallo pedum IX et fossa pedum XV
hiberna cingunt, reliquisque diebus turris ad altitudinem valli,
falces testudinesque parare et facere coeperunt. septimo
oppugnationis die, maximo coorto vento, fervefacta iacula in casas,
quae more Gallico stramentis erant tectae, iacere coeperunt. hae
50   celeriter ignem comprehenderunt et venti magnitudine in omnem
locum castrorum distulerunt. hostes maximo clamore, sicuti parta
iam victoria, turris testudinesque agere et scalis vallum ascendere
coeperunt. at tanta militum virtus atque ea praesentia animi fuit ut,
cum ubique flamma torrerentur maximaque telorum multitudine
55   premerentur suaque omnia impedimenta atque omnis fortunas
conflagrare intellegerent, non modo de vallo decederet nemo sed
paene ne respiceret quidem quisquam, ac tum omnes acerrime
fortissimeque pugnarent. hic dies nostris longe gravissimus fuit, sed
tamen hunc habuit eventum, ut eo die maximus numerus hostium
60   vulneraretur atque interficeretur, ut se sub ipso vallo constipaverunt
recessumque primis ultimi non dabant. paulum quidem intermissa
flamma et quodam loco turri adacta et contingente vallum, tertiae
cohortis centuriones ex quo stabant loco recesserunt suosque omnis
removerunt; nutu vocibusque hostis, si introire vellent, vocare
65   coeperunt: quorum progredi ausus est nemo. tum ex omni parte
lapidibus coniectis deturbati, turrisque succensa est.

                      (*de Bello Gallico* 5.40–43)

The courage of the centurions Pullo and Vorenus.

erant in ea legione fortissimi viri, centuriones T. Pullo et L.
Vorenus. hi perpetuas inter se controversias habebant quinam
anteferretur, omnibusque annis de locis summis simultatibus
70   contendebant. ex his Pullo, cum acerrime ad munitiones
pugnaretur, 'quid dubitas,' inquit, 'Vorene? aut quem locum tuae pro
laude virtutis spectas? hic dies de nostris controversiis iudicabit.'
haec cum dixisset, procedit extra munitiones, quaeque pars hostium

35ff. The Gauls attempt the same tactics which they had used so
successfully with Sabinus, but Cicero was made of sterner stuff.

39 **licere illis ... per se** 'they were allowed through him' = 'they had
his permission'.

43 **se adiutore utantur** 'let them use him as their helper', i.e. he
would intercede for them with Caesar.

45 **vallo pedum IX et fossa pedum XV** 'with a rampart nine feet
high and a ditch fifteen feet wide'. Caesar says in a sentence
omitted that the Gauls had learnt the Roman methods of siege
warfare from captives and that one could judge the vast numbers of
the enemy from the speed with which this operation was
completed.

46 **turris ad altitudinem valli** 'siege towers up to the height of the
(Roman) rampart'.

47 **falces** 'grappling hooks'.

48 **fervefacta iacula** 'burning javelins'.

49 **stramentis ... tectae** 'covered with straw' = 'thatched'.

51-2 **sicuti parta iam victoria** 'as though they had already won the
victory'.

52 **turris testudinesque agere** 'to bring up their towers and shelters';
the towers and **testudines** (here mobile shelters) were on wheels
and could be hauled up to the rampart of the defending fortress.
scalis 'with scaling ladders'.

54 **cum ... torrerentur** 'although they were being scorched'.

60 **ut se ... constipaverunt** 'as they packed themselves (were packed)
together'.

61 **recessum** 'chance of retreat'.

64 **nutu vocibusque** 'by signs and shouts'.

66 **deturbati (sunt)** 'they (the Gauls) were dislodged'.

68-9 **quinam anteferretur** 'which should be preferred'; **quinam?** is an
emphatic form of **quis?**; **anteferretur** is indirect deliberative
subjunctive; direct words: **quinam anteferatur?** 'who is to be
preferred?'.

69 **de locis summis** 'about the highest places/positions', i.e. 'about
promotion'.

69-70 **simultatibus contendebant** 'competed with rivalry'.

71-2 **quem locum ... spectas?** a very difficult phrase which appears to
mean 'what chance (place) are you looking for for praise of your
courage?' Some editors emend **pro laude** to **probandae** = 'what
chance of proving your courage?'

73-4 **quaeque pars ... irrumpit = in eam partem hostium quae
confertissima est visa irrumpit** 'burst into the part of the enemy
which seemed densest'.

confertissima est visa irrumpit. ne Vorenus quidem sese vallo
75 continet sed omnium veritus existimationem subsequitur. tum
mediocri spatio relicto Pullo pilum in hostis immittit, atque unum e
multitudine procurrentem traicit; quo percusso et exanimato, hunc
scutis protegunt, in hostem tela universi coiciunt neque dant
regrediendi facultatem. transfigitur scutum Pulloni et verutum in
80 balteo defigitur. avertit hic casus vaginam et gladium educere
conanti dextram moratur manum, impeditumque hostes
circumsistunt. succurrit inimicus illi Vorenus et laboranti subvenit.
ad hunc se confestim a Pullone omnis multitudo convertit; illum
veruto arbitrantur occisum. gladio comminus rem gerit Vorenus,
85 atque uno interfecto reliquos paulum propellit: dum cupidius instat,
in locum deiectus inferiorem concidit. huic rursus circumvento fert
subsidium Pullo, atque ambo incolumes compluribus interfectis
summa cum laude sese intra munitiones recipiunt. sic fortuna in
contentione et certamine utrumque versavit, ut alter alteri inimicus
90 auxilio salutique esset neque iudicari posset uter utri virtute
anteferendus videretur.

(de Bello Gallico 5.44)

*Cicero gets a message through to Caesar, who marches to relieve
him.*

quanto erat in dies gravior atque asperior oppugnatio, tanto
crebriores litterae nuntiique ad Caesarem mittebantur; quorum pars
deprehensa in conspectu nostrorum militum cum cruciatu
95 necabatur. erat unus intus Nervius, nomine Vertico, qui a prima
obsidione ad Ciceronem perfugerat, suamque ei fidem praestiterat.
hic servo spe libertatis magnisque persuadet praemiis ut litteras ad
Caesarem deferat. has ille in iaculo inligatas effert, et Gallus inter
Gallos sine ulla suspicione versatus ad Caesarem pervenit. ab eo de
100 periculis Ciceronis legionisque cognoscitur.
Caesar acceptis litteris hora circiter undecima diei, statim
nuntium in Bellovacos ad M. Crassum mittit, cuius hiberna aberant
ab eo milia passuum XXV; iubet media nocte legionem proficisci
celeriterque ad se venire. exit cum nuntio Crassus. alterum ad
105 C.Fabium mittit, ut in Atrebatum finis legionem adducat, qua sibi
iter faciendum sciebat. scribit Labieno, si rei publicae commodo
facere posset, cum legione ad finis Nerviorum veniat. reliquam
partem exercitus, quod paulo aberat longius, non putat
exspectandam; eqaites circiter quadringentos ex proximis hibernis
110 colligit.

(de Bello Gallico 5.45–6)

75 **omnium existimationem** 'the opinion of all' = 'what all his comrades would think of him'.

76 **mediocri spatio relicto** 'when a small space was left (between him and the enemy)', i.e. 'when he was close'.

77 **quo percusso ... hunc**: **quo** and **hunc** both refer to the wounded Gaul; one would expect **quem percussum** and no **hunc**. The effect of this irregularity is to separate off the ablative absolute phrase 'he fainted from his wound (struck and fainting) and they (the Gauls) protected him'.

78 **in hostem** i.e. Pullo.

79 **scutum Pulloni** 'the shield for Pullo' = 'Pullo's shield'.

'9–80 **verutum in balteo defigitur** 'a javelin stuck in his sword-belt'.

80 **avertit hic casus vaginam** 'this chance knocked his sheath sideways'.

81 **moratur** here used transitively: 'slowed up the hand for him trying ...', i.e. 'slowed up his hand as he tried ...'.

84 **comminus** 'at close quarters', i.e. 'hand to hand'.

85 **cupidius** 'too eagerly'; he did not see where he was going and fell into a hollow in the ground.

88–9 **sic fortuna ... versavit** 'Fortune so played each of them in their bitter rivalry (contention and rivalry) that ...'; **versavit** literally means 'turned'; Fortune first turned them one way, then another.

0–91 **uter utri ... videretur** 'which seemed to be preferred in courage to the other', i.e. 'which of them seemed the more courageous'.

92–3 **quanto ... gravior ... tanto crebriores** 'the more serious ... the more frequent'.

94 **cum cruciatu** 'with crucifixion'.

95–6 **a prima obsidione** 'from the beginning of the siege'.

98 **in iaculo inligatas** 'bound in his javelin'.

99 **versatus** 'moving about'.

–100 **ab eo ... cognoscitur** 'it is learnt from him'. Caesar was at Samarobriva with one legion. For the disposition of the other legions see map, p. 57 above.

104 **exit cum nuntio Crassus** i.e. Crassus marched as soon as he got the message.

106 **rei publicae commodo** 'with advantage to the public interest', i.e. 'without damaging the public interest'.

*Caesar's plan was to march to the relief of Cicero, picking up
Fabius on the way; Crassus (the son of M. Crassus killed at
Carrhae) was to meet him* en route. *Labienus was to make an
independent attack on the Nervii from the south-east, if he could;
in the event he could not move, because his camp was being
attacked by the victorious Treviri.*

*Caesar received Cicero's letter at about 5 p.m. and acted with
his usual decision and speed, and his officers were equally prompt
in carrying out his orders.*

hora circiter tertia ab antecursoribus de Crassi adventu certior
factus, eo die milia passuum XX procedit. Crassum Samobrivae
praefecit legionemque attribuit, quod ibi impedimenta exercitus,
obsides civitatum, litteras publicas, frumentum omne quod

115 tolerandae hiemis causa devexerat relinquebat. Fabius, ut
imperatum est, non ita multum moratus in itinere cum legione
occurrit. Labienus, interitu Sabini et caede cohortium cognita,
cum omnes ad eum Treveri copiae venissent, veritus ne, si ex
hibernis fugae similem profectionem fecisset, hostium impetum

120 sustinere non posset, litteras Caesari remittit: quanto cum periculo
legiones ex hibernis educturus esset; docet omnis equitatus
peditatusque copias Treverorum tria milia passuum longe ab suis
castris consedisse.

Caesar, consilio eius probato, etsi opinione trium legionum

125 deiectus ad duas redierat, tamen unum communis salutis auxilium
in celeritate ponebat. venit magnis itineribus in Nerviorum finis.
ibi ex captivis cognoscit quae apud Ciceronem gerantur quantoque
in periculo res sit. tum cuidam ex equitibus Gallis magnis
praemiis persuadet uti ad Ciceronem epistolam deferat. hanc

130 Graecis conscriptam litteris mittit, ne intercepta epistola nostra ab
hostibus consilia cognoscantur. si adire non possit, monet ut
tragulam cum epistola ad ammentum deligata intra munitionem
castrorum abiciat. in litteris scribit se cum legionibus profectum
celeriter adfore; hortatur ut pristinam virtutem retineat. Gallus

135 periculum veritus, ut erat praeceptum, tragulam mittit. haec casu
ad turrim adhaesit neque ab nostris biduo animadversa tertio die a
quodam milite conspicitur, dempta ad Ciceronem defertur. ille
perlectam in conventu militum recitat, maximaque omnis laetitia
adficit. tum fumi incendiorum procul videbantur, quae res omnem

140 dubitationem adventus legionum expulit.

(*de Bello Gallico* 5.47–8)

A Gallic prisoner

111	**hora ... tertia** about 8.30 a.m. **antecursoribus** 'advance guard'.
120–21	**quanto cum periculo ... educturus esset** '(he explained) with what great danger he would lead'.
124	**consilio eius probato** 'having accepted his (Labienus') decision (not to leave his camp)'.
124–5	**opinione trium legionum deiectus** 'disappointed of his expectation of three legions'; of the four legions available, he had had to leave one to guard Samarobriva; he had now heard that Labienus could not make it. He was therefore reduced to two legions (**ad duas redierat**). Moreover the legions were seriously under strength; Caesar says they numbered about 7,000 men. With his small force, his only hope was to take the enemy by surprise.
131	**monet (eum)** 'he advised him, if he could not get into (the camp), to ...'.
132	**tragulam ... deligata** 'a javelin with the letter tied to the thong'.
137	**dempta** 'taken down'.
139	**fumi incendiorum** 'smoke from their camp fires'.

The Gauls abandon the siege of Cicero's camp and march to meet Caesar.

Galli re cognita per exploratores obsidionem relinquunt, ad
Caesarem omnibus copiis contendunt. haec erant armatae circiter
milia LX. Cicero data facultate Gallum ab eodem Vericone, quem
supra demonstravimus, repetit qui litteras ad Caesarem deferat. hunc
145   admonet iter caute diligenterque faciat. perscribit in litteris hostis ab
se discessisse omnemque ad eum multitudinem convertisse. quibus
litteris circiter media nocte Caesar allatis suos facit certiores eosque
ad dimicandum animo confirmat. postero die luce prima movet
castra et circiter milia passuum quattuor progressus trans vallem et
150   rivum multitudinem hostium conspicatur. erat magni periculi res
tantulis copiis iniquo loco dimicare; tum, quoniam obsidione
liberatum Ciceronem sciebat, aequo animo remittendum de
celeritate existimabat. consedit et quam aequissimo loco potest
castra communit, atque haec, etsi erant exigua per se, vix hominum
155   milium septem, angustiis viarum quam maxime potest contrahi eo
consilio, ut in summam contemptionem hostibus veniat.

(de Bello Gallico 5.49)

Caesar routs the Gallic forces and relieves Cicero.

eo die parvulis equestribus proeliis ad aquam factis, utrique sese suo
loco continent: Galli, quod ampliores copias, quae nondum
convenerant, exspectabant; Caesar, si forte timoris simulatione
160   hostis in suum locum elicere posset, ut citra vallem pro castris
proelio contenderet. prima luce hostium equitatus ad
castra accedit proeliumque cum nostris equitibus
committit. Caesar consulto equites cedere seque in castra
recipere iubet; simul ex omnibus partibus castra altiore
165   vallo muniri portasque obstrui atque in his administrandis
rebus quam maxime concursari et cum simulatione agi
timoris iubet.

    quibus omnibus rebus hostes invitati copias traducunt
aciemque iniquo loco constituunt, nostris vero etiam de
170   vallo deductis propius accedunt et tela intra munitionem
ex omnibus partibus coiciunt, praeconibusque
circummissis pronuntiari iubent, seu quis Gallus seu
Romanus velit ante tertiam horam ad se transire, sine
periculo licere; ac sic nostros contempserunt, ut alli
175   vallum manu scindere, alii fossas complere inciperent.
tum Caesar omnibus portis eruptione facta equitatuque
emisso celeriter hostes in fugam dat, sic uti omnino
resisteret nemo, magnumque ex eis numerum occidit
atque omnis armis exuit.

Caesar legionem collaudat

144 **hunc** i.e. Caesar.

150 **erat magni periculi res** 'it was a very dangerous situation'.

151 **tantulis** 'such small'. Caesar had scarcely 7,000 men, the Gauls 60,000.

152 **aequo animo** 'with calm mind', i.e. 'without worrying'.

152–3 **remittendum (esse) de celeritate** 'that he should slacken (from) his speed'.

154–5 **haec (castra) ... exigua per se, vix ... septem** 'this was small in itself, consisting of scarcely 7,000 men'. Caesar made his forces appear even smaller, reducing the size of the camp by narrowing the roads that ran between the lines of tents.

156 **ut ... veniat** 'so that he should come into the greatest contempt to the enemy', i.e. 'to incur the greatest contempt of the enemy'. His tactics are made clear in the next chapter.

The enemy attack

157 **ad aquam** i.e. near the stream mentioned above.

158 **Galli** supply **haec fecerunt**.

159 **Caesar, si forte ...** 'Caesar (did this), if by chance ...' = 'in the hope that ...'.

165 **obstrui** 'to be blocked'.

166–7 **concursari ... agi iubet** literally, 'he ordered it to be rushed about and to be done'; translate these impersonal passives as actives.

168 **traducunt** 'lead their forces across (the stream)'.

169–70 **nostris ... deductis** Caesar tempted the enemy on by withdrawing his men from the rampart, as though they were giving up.

172–3 **seu quis Gallus seu Romanus** 'if any Gaul or Roman'.

180   longius prosequi veritus, quod silvae paludesque intercedebant,
omnibus suis incolumibus copiis eodem die ad Ciceronem pervenit.
legione producta cognoscit non decimum quemque esse reliquum
militem sine vulnere. ex eis omnibus iudicat rebus quanto cum
periculo et quanta cum virtute res sint administratae. Ciceronem
185 pro eius merito legionemque collaudat; centuriones singillatim
tribunosque militum appellat, quorum egregiam fuisse virtutem
testimonio Ciceronis cognoverat. de casu Sabini et Cottae certius ex
captivis cognoscit. postero die contione habita rem gestam
proponit; milites consolatur et confirmat: quod detrimentum culpa
190 et temeritate legati sit acceptum, hoc aequiore animo ferendum
docet, quod beneficio deorum immortalium et virtute eorum
expiato incommodo neque hostibus diutina laetitia neque ipsis
longior dolor relinquantur.

(de Bello Gallico 5.50–52)

*Meanwhile Labienus had suppressed the revolt of the Treveri, but
Gaul remained extremely restless; Caesar spent the rest of the
winter in Gaul and raised his army to ten legions. In 53 BC he had
to put down several smaller revolts and claimed to have pacified
Gaul, but there was seething discontent; this broke out into a major
rebellion in 52 BC when all Gaul united under the Avernian chief
Vercingetorix. This culminated when Vercingetorix was defeated
and forced to take refuge in the hill town of Alesia. Caesar besieged
this with a double ring of earthworks; after he had beaten off the
army of Gauls, 250,000 strong, which came to relieve
Vercingetorix, the latter surrendered and was held captive until
Caesar's triumph of 46 BC. Other tribes fought on, including the
Eburones led by Ambiorix, who had started the original rebellion.
Caesar defeated the last coalition of Gallic tribes at Uxellodunum
in 51 BC and spent the rest of this year and the following year
settling the province by conciliatory measures. When he finally left
Gaul at the end of 50 BC, he could fairly claim to have pacified all
Gaul.*

*Whatever intentions Caesar had when he embarked on the
conquest of Gaul, its historical consequences were extremely
important. The Gauls had fought hard for their liberty, but if they
had succeeded in throwing off the Roman yoke, they would
probably have continued to fight amongst themselves and would
perhaps have fallen to incursions of the German tribes from beyond
the Rhine. Caesar's conquests opened up central Europe to
Mediterranean civilization, and as long as the Rhine frontier was
held, the Gauls lived in peace and developed a Latin culture based
on a Celtic foundation.*

182 **legione producta** 'when (Cicero's) legion was paraded'. **non decimum quemque** 'not every tenth man' = 'not one in ten'.

185 **pro eius merito** 'in accordance with his deserts'. **singillatim** 'individually'.

188 **contione habita** 'holding a meeting'.

38–9 **rem gestam proponit** 'he put before them the thing done', i.e. 'assessed the situation'.

189 **quod detrimentum** 'the loss which ...'; the antecedent (**detrimentum**) is placed inside the relative clause.

190 **legati** i.e. Sabinus.

)–91 **hoc ... quod** 'for this reason ... that ...' (**hoc** is ablative and anticipates **quod**).

192 **expiato incommodo** 'the reverse having been atoned for/repaired'.

The Dying Gaul

CATULLUS

Gaius Valerius Catullus was born at Verona in North Italy about 84 BC and died about 54 BC at the age of thirty. He came from a wealthy family which owned a villa on Lake Sirmio besides their town house. When Julius Caesar was governor of Gaul and was making his assize circuit in Cisalpine Gaul, he used to stay with them, which suggests that they were one of the leading families of the district. He had one beloved brother. Otherwise we know nothing of his family or boyhood.

Sirmio

When he was about twenty he came to Rome and soon became a member of a literary group which was attempting a new sort of poetry. These young poets, the *poetae novi*, as Cicero contemptuously called them, rejected the traditional genres of Roman poetry, epic and drama, and used poetry as a vehicle for expressing their own emotions on any subject which occurred to them, from the trivial to the profound; they have much more in common with modern poets than any of their predecessors. In form, their poetry was strongly influenced by the Greek poets who had lived in Alexandria two hundred years before, especially by Callimachus, who rejected epic and wrote poems which were short, light and original.

Catullus was the first Roman love poet. Our selection contains some of the poems that he wrote about his passionate and unhappy affair with Clodia, the sister of Cicero's enemy Clodius, who was stolen from him by Caelius, his friend and Cicero's.

Catullus is a poet who uses the language and rhythms of everyday speech with splendid effect; indeed, many of his poems are studded with colloquialisms. You will find that most of the poems seem to be the natural expression of universal emotions, but beneath their apparent spontaneity there lies a great deal of poetic art, seen most clearly in their careful construction.

He wrote in a variety of metres. Apart from the metres

traditionally used by Roman poets, dactylic hexameters, used for epic, and elegiac couplets, used for epigrams, he first introduced many metres used by the Greek lyric poets. We give the name of the metre used in each poem in parentheses after the text; they are explained in the metrical appendix. You may not wish to study the technical side of ancient metre but you should learn with the help of your teacher to read the poems rhythmically, since sound is of paramount importance in ancient poetry. You will find that Catullus' favourite metre is 'hendecasyllables', which simply means 'lines of eleven syllables'. Of the twenty-six poems in this selection thirteen are written in this metre; it has a lilting rhythm which is easily felt.

Catullus' total output was confined to one slim volume. He preceded the first part with a dedication to his friend, the historian Cornelius Nepos.

cui dono lepidum novum libellum
arida modo pumice expolitum?
Corneli, tibi: namque tu solebas
meas esse aliquid putare nugas
5 iam tum, cum ausus es unus Italorum
omne aevum tribus explicare cartis
doctis, Iuppiter, et laboriosis.
quare habe tibi quidquid hoc libelli
qualecumque; quod, o patrona virgo,
10 plus uno maneat perenne saeclo.

(1; metre: hendecasyllables)

1 **cui dono** 'to whom do I give?' = 'to whom am I to give?' **lepidum** 'elegant, witty'.

2 **arida ... expolitum** '(just) polished by the dry pumicestone'. Pumice was used to smooth the surface of the ends of the papyrus roll (*volumen*).

4 **meas ... nugas** 'that my nonsense was (worth) something'.

5 **iam tum, cum** 'already, at the time when ...'. **unus Italorum** 'the only one of the Italians'; Cornelius was the only Italian to have dared to write a universal history (**omne aevum explicare**).

6 **cartis** 'volumes'; **carta** properly means a sheet of papyrus but is here equivalent to *volumen*.

8–9 **quidquid hoc libelli qualecumque** literally, 'whatever this (is) of a little book, of whatever kind', i.e. 'this little book, such as it is, for what it's worth'.

9 **o patrona virgo** 'my maiden patron', i.e. the Muse which protects me.

10 **uno ... saeclo** 'than one generation'.

1 **lepidum novum libellum**: these words describe the appearance of the book but also hint at the nature of the contents. What sort of poems is Cornelius to expect?

2 How does Catullus denigrate his own poetry? How does he show that he really values it?

All the poems we include in this selection are concerned with Catullus' own feelings occasioned by various experiences. And so we arrange them around three themes: Catullus and his friends, Catullus in love, the sequel.

1 Catullus and his friends

Several poems are written to or about Licinius Calvus, an almost exact contemporary of Catullus, an orator and poet who belonged to his set.

The morning after he had spent the day with Calvus, when they were amusing themselves by writing verses for each other, he sent him this poem to say how much he had enjoyed himself.

hesterno, Licini, die otiosi
multum lusimus in meis tabellis,
ut convenerat esse delicatos:
scribens versiculos uterque nostrum
5 ludebat numero modo hoc modo illoc,
reddens mutua per iocum atque vinum.
atque illinc abii tuo lepore
incensus, Licini, facetiisque,
ut nec me miserum cibus iuvaret
10 nec somnus tegeret quiete ocellos,
sed toto indomitus furore lecto
versarer, cupiens videre lucem,
ut tecum loquerer simulque ut essem.
at defessa labore membra postquam
15 semimortua lectulo iacebant,
hoc, iucunde, tibi poema feci,
ex quo perspiceres meum dolorem.
nunc audax cave sis, precesque nostras,
oramus, cave despuas, ocelle,
20 ne poenas Nemesis reposcat a te.
est vemens dea: laedere hanc caveto.

(50; metre: hendecasyllables)

puella tabellas tenet

1 **hesterno ... die** 'yesterday'.

2 **tabellis** 'tablets', 'notebook'. **tabella** is a diminutive form of
tabula. Catullus is very fond of diminutives; they can express
smallness, affection, pity, contempt, according to the context. In
this poem we have **versiculos** (*l.* 4) 'little verses', 'scraps of verse';
ocellos (*l.* 10) 'little eyes', 'poor eyes', and **ocelle** (*l.* 19), which has
a metaphorical meaning, 'my darling'; **lectulo** (*l.* 15) 'my little bed'.

3 **ut convenerat esse delicatos** 'as it had been agreed (= we had
agreed) to be smart'.

5 **numero modo hoc modo illoc** 'now in this metre, now in that';
illoc the suffix **-c** or **-ce**, found in **hic, haec, hoc, huc, illinc** etc.,
could be attached to any demonstrative in early Latin.

6 **reddens mutua** literally, 'giving back things in exchange', i.e.
'taking it in turns'. They would agree on a metre and subject and
then compose an epigram *ex tempore* alternately.

7–8 **tuo lepore/incensus ... facetiisque** 'fired by your charm and wit'.

9 **iuvaret** 'pleased', i.e. I took no pleasure in food.

11 **indomitus furore** 'ungovernable in my frenzy', i.e. 'in an
uncontrollable frenzy'.

12 **versarer** 'I tossed and turned'.

17 **perspiceres** the subjunctive expresses purpose, 'so that you might
see from it'.

18 **audax cave sis** 'beware of being rash', 'beware of asking for
trouble'.

19 **oramus** 'I beg'. **cave despuas** 'beware of spitting out', 'rejecting'.

20 **Nemesis** the goddess of Justice, who punishes men for arrogance
and pride.

21 **vemens = vehemens**. **caveto** alternative imperative form
(compare **esto, scito**), introducing a note of mock solemnity.

---

1 Explain in your own words how Catullus and Calvus had
spent the day.

2 How did Catullus feel the next day?

3 **preces nostras** (*l.* 18): what do you suppose these prayers
were?

4 The second half of the poem is filled with the language of
love, e.g. **miser** is often used of the unhappy lover. What
other words or phrases suggest that Catullus has fallen in love
with Calvus? How serious is Catullus in his declaration of
love? Calvus was not attractive (he was short and fat); if it
wasn't his beauty Catullus had fallen for, what else might it
have been?

*One day Catullus heard Calvus perform in court when he was prosecuting Caesar's hated henchman Vatinius. Trials were held in the basilicas in the Forum and there was usually a crowd of spectators (*corona*) surrounding the court and listening eagerly to the eloquence of the advocates. During his speech Vatinius is said to have jumped up and cried,* rogo vos, iudices, num, si iste est disertus, ideo me damnari oportet *('I ask you, members of the jury, whether, because he is eloquent, I should therefore be found guilty').*

    Catullus tells the following anecdote.

> risi nescioquem modo e corona
> qui, cum mirifice Vatiniana
> meus crimina Calvus explicasset,
> admirans ait haec manusque tollens,
> 5 'di magni, salaputium disertum!'

        (53; metre: hendecasyllables)

Cicero may have been defending Vatinius on this occasion. Catullus knew and admired Cicero, as the following epigram shows; he had evidently done Catullus some favour for which he thanks him.

> disertissime Romuli nepotum,
> quot sunt quotque fuere, Marce Tulli,
> quotque post aliis erunt in annis,
> gratias tibi maximas Catullus
> 5 agit pessimus omnium poeta,
> tanto pessimus omnium poeta,
> quanto tu optimus omnium patronus.

        (49; metre: hendecasyllables)

Catullus also knew Caesar, who was a friend of his family, but did not care for him. He wrote several offensive poems about him, but Caesar is said to have forgiven him and asked him to dinner. The following epigram suggests that Caesar had made overtures of friendship, but Catullus has no wish to be in his good books.

> nil nimium studeo, Caesar, tibi velle placere,
>   nec scire utrum sis albus an ater homo.

        (93; metre: elegiac couplet)

The Forum at Rome

2 **mirifice** 'wonderfully'.
3 **explicasset = explicavisset** 'had explained'.
5 **salaputium disertum** 'what an eloquent little cock!'

What did Catullus find amusing about this incident?

1 **disertissime ... nepotum** 'most eloquent of the descendants of Romulus'.
2 **quot sunt** 'as many as' = 'all who'. **Marce Tulli** Cicero's full name was Marcus Tullius Cicero.
7 **patronus** 'advocate', 'pleader'.

It has been suggested that there is a note of irony in Catullus' praise of Cicero. What do you find to support this view? (Did Catullus really suppose himself the 'worst of poets'?)

1 **nil nimium studeo** 'I am not really keen'.
2 **albus an ater** 'white or black', i.e. 'good or bad' (a proverbial phrase).

The three other poems Catullus wrote to Caesar are obscenely offensive, but this one may have struck home equally hard; why?

*At one Saturnalia (the ancient equivalent of Christmas, when
friends sent each other presents), Calvus sent Catullus a collection
of bad poetry. Catullus replied with a poem of furious indignation.*

ni te plus oculis meis amarem,
iucundissime Calve, munere isto
odissem te odio Vatiniano:
nam quid feci ego quidve sum locutus
5   cur me tot male perderes poetis?
isti di mala multa dent clienti,
qui tantum tibi misit impiorum.
quod si, ut suspicor, hoc novum ac repertum
munus dat tibi Sulla litterator,
10 non mi est male, sed bene ac beate,
quod non dispereunt tui labores.
di magni, horribilem et sacrum libellum!
quem tu scilicet ad tuum Catullum
misti, continuo ut die periret,
15 Saturnalibus, optimo dierum!
non non hoc tibi, salse, sic abibit.
nam, si luxerit, ad librariorum
curram scrinia, Caesios, Aquinos,
Suffenum, omnia colligam venena,
20 ac his suppliciis remunerabor.
vos hinc interea valete abite
illuc, unde malum pedem attulistis,
saecli incommoda, pessimi poetae.

(14; metre: hendecasyllables)

Sulla litterator

1   Do you think Calvus hoped his present would be well
received? What evidence is there that he sent it as a joke?
2   Was Catullus really angry with Calvus?

*Catullus wrote an emotional poem of welcome to his friend
Veranius when he returned to Rome from serving on the staff of the
governor of Spain.*

Verani, omnibus e meis amicis
antistans mihi milibus trecentis,
venistine domum ad tuos penates
fratresque unanimos anumque matrem?
5   venisti. o mihi nuntii beati!
visam te incolumem audiamque Hiberum

1   **ni = nisi**.
2   **munere isto** 'because of this gift'.
3   **odio Vatiniano** 'Vatinian hatred' = 'the hatred Vatinius feels for you' (because Calvus had prosecuted Vatinius, see poem 53 above).
4   **quidve** 'or what'.
6   **clienti** here an advocate's client, someone Calvus had been defending in court.
7   **tantum ... impiorum** 'such a pack of sinners'.
8   **quod si** 'but if'. **repertum** 'recherché'.
9   **litterator** 'schoolmaster'; a *litterator* was the master of an elementary school.
10 **non mi est male ... beate**: literally, 'it is not badly for me but well and happily', i.e. 'I'm not upset but very pleased'.
11 **tui labores** Calvus had evidently been defending Sulla in court; an advocate might not receive fees but usually expected to receive a handsome present. **dispereunt** 'perish' = 'are wasted'.
12 **sacrum** 'cursed'.
13 **scilicet** 'surely'.
14 **misti = misisti**.
15 **Saturnalibus** the first day of the Saturnalia was 17 December.
16 **non ... sic abibit** 'it won't end like this'. **salse** 'my witty friend'.
17 **si luxerit** 'as soon as it is light'.
7–18 **ad librariorum ... scrinia** 'to the shelves of the booksellers'; we know little about the book trade in Catullus' time but in the time of Augustus there were certainly several bookshops in Rome.
8–19 **Caesios, Aquinos, Suffenum** 'poets like Caesius, Aquinus and Suffenus'; we know nothing of Caesius and Aquinus, who were evidently bad poets; Catullus attacks Suffenus as a writer of endless bad verses in poem 22.
21 **vos** 'you' are the bad poets Calvus has sent him.
22 **malum pedem** 'your bad feet', a pun, since it means both 'Go back to where you came from' and 'Go back to where you brought your bad verse from' (**pes** = 'a metrical foot').
23 **saecli incommoda** 'curses of our time'.

2   **antistans ... trecentis** 'worth more to me (excelling for me) than three hundred thousand friends': Veranius is worth all the friends in the world.
4   **unanimos** 'of one mind', 'loving'. **anum** 'old'.
5   **o ... nuntii beati** 'O happy news' (probably a genitive of exclamation, which is common in Greek).
6   **Hiberum** genitive plural, 'of the Spaniards'.

narrantem loca, facta, nationes,
ut mos est tuus, applicansque collum
iucundum os oculosque suaviabor.
10   o quantum est hominum beatiorum,
quid me laetius est beatiusve?

(9; metre: hendecasyllables)

*Although Catullus came from a wealthy family, he often seems to
have been hard up in Rome. He invites his friend Fabullus to dinner
but says Fabullus will have to provide the dinner, since he is broke.
Fabullus had served with Veranius in Spain; perhaps the dinner
party was to welcome him back to Rome.*

cenabis bene, mi Fabulle, apud me
paucis, si tibi di favent, diebus,
si tecum attuleris bonam atque magnam
cenam, non sine candida puella
5   et vino et sale et omnibus cachinnis.
haec si, inquam, attuleris, venuste noster,
cenabis bene; nam tui Catulli
plenus saculus est aranearum.
sed contra accipies meros amores,
10   seu quid suavius elegantiusve est:
nam unguentum dabo, quod meae puellae
donarunt Veneres Cupidinesque,
quod tu cum olfacies, deos rogabis
totum ut te faciant, Fabulle, nasum.

(13; metre: hendecasyllables)

*As Fabullus is told to bring a pretty girl with him, perhaps the party
is to be a foursome and Catullus' girl is to be there too; and so the
reference to the precious scent she has given him is a compliment to
her.*

cenabis bene

8   **applicans** 'drawing back'.

9   **suaviabor** 'I shall kiss'. Modern Italians and ancient Romans could be extremely demonstrative in their affection; so Cicero's brother Quintus writes to Tiro: *ego vos a.d. iii Kal. videbo tuosque oculos ... dissuaviabor* ('I shall see you on the 28th and shall kiss your eyes') (*ad Fam.* 16.27.2).

10   **o ... beatiorum** 'O, whatever there is of happier men' = 'of all the happy men there are'.

11   **quid** though neuter this refers to Catullus, 'who?'

5   **sale** properly 'salt', but it then comes to mean 'wit'; it is ambivalent here but **cachinnis** (= 'laughter') shows that the second meaning is intended.

6   **venuste noster** 'my charming friend'.

8   **plenus saculus est aranearum** 'my purse is full – of cobwebs'.

9   **contra** 'in return' (**contra** is here an adverb). **meros amores** 'sheer love'; or it may mean 'something you will really love', i.e. the scent (**unguentum**) referred to in *l.* 11.

10   **seu quid ... est** 'or something even more delightful and elegant'.

11   **unguentum** an essential accompaniment of Roman dinner parties; the guests anointed themselves lavishly with sweet-smelling perfumes.

12   **donarunt** = **donaverun**t. **Veneres Cupidinesque** 'all the loves and Cupids', i.e. 'all the powers of love; the perfume had a very erotic scent, like those on television advertisements.

13   **quod tu cum olfacies** 'when you smell it'.

14   **nasum** 'nose'.

Stone carving showing fruit and nuts

Compare the following translations of this poem and say which you prefer.

Now please the gods, Fabullus, you
Shall dine here well in a day or two;
But bring a good big dinner, mind.
Likewise a pretty girl and wine
And wit and jokes of every kind.
Bring these, I say, good man, and dine
Right well: for your Catullus' purse
Is full – but only cobwebs bears.
But you with love itself I'll dose,
Or what still sweeter, finer is,
An essence to my lady given
By all the Loves and Venuses;
Once sniff it, you'll petition heaven
To make you nose and only nose.

(William Marris, 1924)

unguentum dabo

say Fabullus

you'll get a swell dinner at my house

a couple three days from now (if your luck holds out)

all you gotta do is bring the dinner

    and make it good and be sure there's plenty

Oh yes don't forget a girl (I like blondes)

and a bottle of wine maybe

    and any good jokes and stories you've heard

just do that like I tell you ol' pal ol' pal

you'll get swell dinner

    ?

    what,

        about,

            ME?

well;

    well here take a look in my wallet,

        yeah those're cobwebs

but here,

    I'll give you something too

    I CAN'T GIVE YOU ANYTHING BUT

        LOVE BABY

no?

well here's something nicer and a little more cherce maybe

I got a perfume see

it was a gift to HER

    straight from VENUS and CUPID LTD.

when you get a whiff of that you'll pray the gods

to make you (yes you will, Fabullus)

    ALL

        NOSE

                (Frank Copley, 1957)

2 Catullus in love

Catullus was a man of strong emotions, who was equally violent in his likes and dislikes and had many hated enemies as well as devoted friends. It was inevitable that when he fell in love, it would be no ordinary passion. Unfortunately the woman for whom he fell was Clodia, usually identified with the sister of Cicero's enemy Publius Clodius; she came from one of the noblest families in Rome and was married, unhappily, to Quintus Metellus Celer, a member of another of the great noble families, who was consul in 60 BC and died the following year, poisoned by Clodia, according to Cicero. Clodia was beautiful and notoriously immoral; Cicero says she was a shameless whore.

When Catullus fell in love with Clodia, at first he did not dare declare his love. Instead he sent her a free translation of a famous poem by the Greek lyric poet Sappho. 'It was intended as a test, a feeler. If she were in love with him, she would understand what he meant; if not – after all it was only a translation' (L. P. Wilkinson).

Notice that he does not address the poem to Clodia but to Lesbia. This did not disguise the fact that it was intended for Clodia, since there was a convention that that poets did not give the girl whom they were addressing her real name but a name with the same metrical value.

>   ille mi par esse deo videtur,
>   ille, si fas est, superare divos,
>   qui sedens adversus identidem te
>   spectat et audit
> 5   dulce ridentem, misero quod omnis
>   eripit sensus mihi: nam simul te,
>   Lesbia, aspexi, nihil est super mi
>   vocis in ore,
>   lingua sed torpet, tenuis sub artus
> 10 flamma demanat, sonitu suopte
>   tintinant aures, gemina teguntur
>   lumina nocte.

>   (51; metre: sapphic stanzas)

Catullus expressed his love for Clodia obliquely in a poem about her pet sparrow, perhaps challenging Clodia to admit her love for him.

>   passer, deliciae meae puellae,
>   quocum ludere, quem in sinu tenere,
>   cui primum digitum dare appetenti
>   et acres solet incitare morsus,
> 5   cum desiderio meo nitenti

1   **ille** Catullus watches Clodia sitting and laughing with some unknown man (her husband? a lover?). The sight of her beauty robs him of all his faculties.

2   **si fas est** 'if it is right (to say so)'.

3   **adversus** 'opposite (you)'. **identidem** 'again and again'; this privileged man can enjoy Clodia's company repeatedly.

5   **quod** 'a thing which'.

5–6   **misero ... mihi** 'from me in my unhappiness': **miser** is often used of the unhappy lover.

6   **simul = simul atque** 'as soon as'.

7–8   **nihil ... vocis** 'there is no voice (nothing of voice) left for me ...'; **est super = superest** 'is left'.

9   **torpet** 'is numb'.

10   **demanat** 'flows', 'creeps'.

10–11   **sonitu suopte/tintinant aures** 'my ears ring with their own sound'.

11–12   **gemina ... nocte** 'my eyes (**lumina**) are covered by a double night', i.e. 'my two eyes are covered in darkness'.

> Describe in your own words the symptoms which Catullus says affect him as he watches Clodia. Do you think these symptoms are occasioned only by his passion for her or does jealousy play a part in them?

2   **in sinu** 'on her lap'.

3   **primum digitum** 'her finger-tip'.

4   **morsus** 'bites', 'nips'.

5   **desiderio meo nitenti** 'my radiant darling'; **desiderium** = 'longing', 'desire', but it can be used of the person you long for (so Cicero ends a letter written to his family when he was in exile: *valete, mea desideria, valete*).

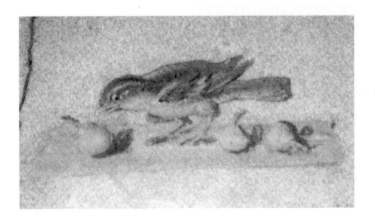

passer

cārum nescīoquid lūbet iocāri,
et sōlāciolum suī dōloris,
crēdō, ūt tūm grāvis ācquiescat ārdor;
tēcum ludere sīcut ipsa possēm
10   et tristes animi levare cūras!

(2; metre: hendecasyllables)

When the sparrow died, he wrote a lament for it.

lugete, o Veneres Cupidinesque,
et quantum est hominum venustiorum;
passer mortuus est meae puellae,
passer, deliciae meae puellae,
5   quem plus illa oculis suis amabat;
nam mellitus erat suamque norat
ipsam tam bene quam puella matrem,
nec sese e gremio illius movebat,
sed circumsiliens modo huc modo illuc
10   ad solam dominam usque pipiabat:
qui nunc it per iter tenebricosum
illud, unde negant redire quemquam.
at vobis male sit, malae tenebrae
Orci, quae omnia bella devoratis.
15   tam bellum mihi passerem abstulistis.
o factum male! o miselle passer!
tua nunc opera meae puellae
flendo turgiduli rubent ocelli.

(3; metre: hendecasyllables)

1   How did the sparrow show its affection for its mistress?
2   Read *l.* 11 several times aloud. How does the sound help to give
    a picture of the sparrow's journey?
3   The poem takes the form of a lament. How does Catullus inflate
    the death of the sparrow to make into a tragedy?
4   How does the focus of the poem change in the last two lines and
    how does this affect the meaning of the whole poem?

Soon Clodia had accepted him as her lover and he is deliriously happy.

vivamus, mea Lesbia, atque amemus,
rūmoresque senum severiorum
ōmnes unīus aestimemus āssis!
sōles occidere et redire possūnt;
5   nobis cum semel occidit brevis lux,
nox est perpetua una dormienda.
da mi basia mille, deinde centum,

5–6 **cum ... iocari** 'when my radiant darling pleases to play some sweet game'; **lubet** + dative 'it pleases'.

7 **et solaciolum sui doloris** 'and the comfort to her pain'; this seems to be a second vocative; the sparrow is addressed first as **deliciae meae puellae**, then as **solaciolum sui doloris** (but the use of **sui** for **eius** is very odd).

9 **possem** 'I wish I could'.

1 How does Catullus' girl play with the sparrow?
2 Why, according to Catullus, does she play with it?
3 **sui doloris** (*l.* 7): what pain is Catullus referring to? What is meant by **gravis ardor** (*l.* 8)?
4 **credo** (*l.* 8): what is the significance of this aside?
5 What does Catullus wish? Why does he wish this?
6 Describe the scene Catullus envisages in this poem and the emotions which he feels and which he imagines his girl feels.

2 **quantum est ... venustiorum** 'whatever there is of men of finer feeling', i.e. 'all men of finer feeling'; **venustus** (formed from **Venus**) = 'lovely', 'attractive', used first of physical characteristics, then of mental; here its associations with Venus predominate – only those who know love can appreciate the tragedy of the death of his girl's pet sparrow.

6 **mellitus** 'honey-sweet', 'a honey'.   **norat = noverat** 'he knew'.

8 **e gremio** 'from her lap'.

9 **circumsiliens** 'hopping around'.

10 **usque pipiabat** 'used to chirp continually'.

11 **tenebricosum** 'shadowy', 'dark'.

13 **at vobis male sit** 'but may it be bad for you' = 'but curse on you!'

14 **Orci** 'of Hell'.

17 **tua ... opera** 'through your fault', 'because of you'.

18 **turgiduli** 'swollen'.

2 **rumores** 'gossip'.

3 **unius aestimemus assis** 'let us value at one *as*' i.e. 'let us think not worth a penny' (an *as* was a coin of very low value).

7 **basia**, *n. pl.* 'kisses'.

dein mille altera, dein secunda centum;
deinde usque altera mille, deinde centum.
10   dein, cum milia multa fecerimus,
conturbabimus illa, ne sciamus,
aut ne quis malus invidere possit,
cum tantum sciat esse basiorum.

(5; metre: hendecasyllables)

> Compare the following translations of the first six lines. Which do you think better conveys the feelings of Catullus' poem and why?

My sweetest Lesbia, let us live and love;
And though the sager sort our deeds reprove,
Let us not weigh them. Heaven's great lamps do dive
Into their west, and straight again revive.
But soon as once is set our little light,
Then must we sleep one ever-during night.

(Thomas Campion, 1601)

Clodia

I said to her, darling, I said
let's LIVE and
let's LOVE and
what do we care what those old
purveyors of joylessness say?
(they can go to hell, all of them)
the Sun dies every night
in the morning he's here again
you and I, now,
when our briefly tiny light flicks out,
it's night for us, one single
everlasting
Night.

(Frank Copley, 1957)

*To him Clodia is incomparably beautiful; he dismisses
contemptuously a girl said to rival Clodia in beauty.*

salve, nec minimo puella naso
nec bello pede nec nigris ocellis
nec longis digitis nec ore sicco
nec sane nimis elegante lingua,
5   decoctoris amica Formiani.
ten provincia narrat esse bellam?
tecum Lesbia nostra comparatur?
o saeclum insapiens et infacetum!

(43; metre: hendecasyllables)

9   **usque** 'continually', 'without stop'.

11   **conturbabimus illa** 'we'll muddle the count of them'.

12   **invidere** 'to cast an evil eye on us'. It was believed that evil men could cast a spell on you by their evil eye. This was particularly liable to happen if you were too happy. If Catullus and Clodia lost count of their kisses, they were less likely to suffer from the evil eye than if they knew they had kissed 3,300 times.

da mi basia mille

1   **naso** 'nose'.

4   **nec sane ... lingua** 'and a tongue which is certainly not very refined'; this seems to refer to the girl's speech rather than to her appearance; she has no wit.

5   **decoctoris ... Formiani** 'the girlfriend of the bankrupt from Formiae'. The bankrupt from Formiae was an upstart called Mamurra, who had made a fortune in the service of Caesar in Gaul and Britain, as we learn from another poem (29), in which Catullus attacks him savagely. From yet another poem (41) we learn that the girl was called Ameana and that she made exorbitant demands for her sexual services.

6   **ten = tene. provincia** 'the province' is Catullus' homeland, Gallia Cisalpina; the implication is that though the 'provincials' may consider Ameana beautiful, she would not be thought much of in Rome.

8   **o saeclum ... infacetum** 'What a stupid and tasteless generation!'

What does the catalogue of Ameana's defects enable you to say about the attractions of Clodia?

But Catullus was filled with agonizing doubts about Clodia's constancy; he could not believe her love would last.

> iucundum, mea vita, mihi proponis amorem
> hunc nostrum inter nos perpetuumque fore.
> di magni, facite ut vere promittere possit
> atque id sincere dicat et ex animo,
> 5 ut liceat nobis tota perducere vita
> aeternum hoc sanctae foedus amicitiae.

(109; metre: elegiac couplets)

He hoped she might leave her husband and marry him, but knew that her promises were not to be relied on.

> nulli se dicit mulier mea nubere malle
> quam mihi, non si se Iuppiter ipse petat.
> dicit: sed mulier cupido quod dicit amanti
> in vento et rapida scribere oportet aqua.

(70; metre: elegiac couplets)

When she proved unfaithful, he was finally disillusioned but loved her even more violently.

> dicebas quondam solum te nosse Catullum,
> Lesbia, nec prae me velle tenere Iovem.
> dilexi tum te non tantum ut vulgus amicam,
> sed pater ut gnatos diligit et generos.
> 5 nunc te cognovi: quare etsi impensius uror,
> multo mi tamen es vilior et levior.
> qui potis est, inquis? quod amantem iniuria talis
> cogit amare magis, sed bene velle minus.

(72; metre: elegiac couplets)

He expresses the same feelings, perhaps more forcibly, in two short lines.

> odi et amo. quare id faciam, fortasse requiris.
> nescio, sed fieri sentio, et excrucior.

(85; metre: elegiac couplet)

What makes these two lines so powerful?

1 **proponis** 'you offer, promise', followed by the accusative and infinitive; subject **amorem hunc nostrum**.

2 **inter nos** 'between ourselves', i.e. their love will be mutual.

5 **tota ... vita = totam vitam** (as often in inscriptions). **perducere** 'to prolong'.

---

1 **proponis** (*l.* 1), **possit** (*l.* 3): what significance do you find in the change of person?

2 What sort of love does the last line suggest?

---

1 What is the effect of the first **dicit** in *l.* 3?

2 *ll.* 3 and 4, compare:

> Woman's faith and woman's trust –
> Write the characters in dust,
> Stamp them on the running stream,
> Print them on the moonlight's beam.

> (Walter Scott)

Both poets have the same message; which, in your view, conveys it more effectively?

---

1 **nosse = novisse**.

2 **prae me** 'before me', 'rather than me'.

3 **dilexi: diligo** means 'I love' without any connotations of sexual passion. **vulgus** 'the crowd', 'the common man'.

4 **gnatos = natos**, 'sons'. **generos** = 'sons-in-law'.

5 **impensius** 'more violently'. **uror** 'I am burning'.

6 **mi = mihi** 'to me', 'in my eyes'. **vilior** 'cheaper', 'more worthless'.

7 **qui potis est** 'how is this possible?' **qui** is an old form of the ablative ('in what way?'). **potis** ('possible') is an indeclinable adjective.

---

1 In *ll.* 3–4 what sort of love does Catullus say he felt for Clodia? How realistic do you think he is being about his love?

2 What is a paradox? How are *ll.* 6–8 paradoxical?

3 How psychologically convincing do you find the poet's state of mind?

---

2 **excrucior** 'I am in torture'.

He tried to cast out Clodia from his heart, but could not.

     miser Catulle, desinas ineptire,
     et quod vides perisse perditum ducas.
     fulsere quondam candidi tibi soles,
     cum ventitabas quo puella ducebat
5   amata nobis quantum amabitur nulla;
     ibi illa multa cum iocosa fiebant
     quae tu volebas nec puella nolebat,
     fulsere vere candidi tibi soles.
     nunc iam illa non volt; tu quoque impotens noli,
10   nec quae fugit sectare, nec miser vive,
     sed obstinata mente perfer, obdura.
     vale, puella. iam Catullus obdurat,
     nec te requiret nec rogabit invitam.
     at tu dolebis, cum rogaberis nulla.
15   scelesta, vae te, quae tibi manet vita?
     quis nunc te adibit? cui videberis bella?
     quem nunc amabis? cuius esse diceris?
     quem basiabis? cui labella mordebis?
     at tu, Catulle, destinatus obdura.

              (8; metre: limping iambics)

*Finally, the love in which he had rejoiced has become a foul disease
of the mind. He prays the gods to rid him of this plague.*

     si qua recordanti benefacta priora voluptas
       est homini, cum se cogitat esse pium,
     nec sanctam violasse fidem, nec foedere nullo
       divum ad fallendos numine abusum homines,
5   multa parata manent in longa aetate, Catulle,
       ex hoc ingrato gaudia amore tibi.
     nam quaecumque homines bene cuiquam aut dicere possunt
       aut facere, haec a te dictaque factaque sunt.
     omnia quae ingratae perierunt credita menti.
10   quare iam te cur amplius excrucies?
     quin tu animo offirmas atque istinc te ipse reducis,
       et dis invitis desinis esse miser?
     difficile est longum subito deponere amorem.
       difficile est, verum hoc qua lubet efficias;
15   una salus haec est, hoc est tibi pervicendum,
       hoc facias, sive id non pote sive pote.
     o di, si vestrum est misereri, aut si quibus umquam
       extremam iam ipsa in morte tulistis opem,
     me miserum aspicite et, si vitam puriter egi,
20   eripite hanc pestem perniciemque mihi,

1 **desinas ineptire** 'cease to play the fool' (jussive subjunctive).
4 **cum ventitabas** 'when you used to go'.
5 **quantum amabitur nulla** 'as much as no girl shall be loved', i.e. 'more than any girl ...'. **nobis** 'by me' (dative of the agent).
6 **ibi ... cum** 'then, when ...'.
9 **volt = vult**. **impotens** 'lacking in self-control', 'weakling'.
10 **nec ... sectare** 'and don't keep pursuing' (**sector**, **sectari** is a frequentative form of **sequor**).
11 **obdura** 'harden (your heart)', 'endure'.
14 **nulla** 'not at all', 'never'.
15 **vae te** 'alas, for you'.
18 **cui labella mordebis?** 'whose lips will you bite?'
19 **destinatus** 'resolute(ly)'.

---

1 How is the poem constructed, i.e. into what blocks of sense is it divided? The clue is given by the persons of the verbs; who is addressed in each section?
2 What is the tone of each section?
3 At the end of the poem does it seem to you that Catullus has succeeded in hardening his heart?

---

2 **pium**: **pius** is a complex word; it means conscientious, loyal, fulfilling one's duties to gods, country and fellow-men.
3 **foedere nullo = foedere ullo** 'in any pact'.
4 **divum**, *gen. pl.* 'of the gods'; **numine** 'divine power', 'divinity'; the gods were thought to punish perjurers.
9 **credita** 'entrusted to'.
10 **quare** 'and so'. **iam ... excrucies** 'why should you go on torturing yourself?'
11 **quin tu animo offirmas?** 'why are you not firm in mind?' **quin =** 'why not?' **istinc** 'from there', i.e. 'from where you are, from your unhappy love'.
14 **verum** 'but'. **qua lubet efficias** 'you must achieve somehow or other'; the subjunctive is jussive, equivalent to an imperative.
16 **pote** 'possible' (here used as the neuter of **potis**, but in *l.* 24 **potis** itself is neuter, being treated as indeclinable).
17 **si vestrum est misereri** 'if it is in your nature (part of you) to feel pity'.
20 **pestem perniciemque** 'plague and destruction' = 'destructive plague'.

quae mihi subrepens imos ut torpor in artus
    expulit ex omni pectore laetitias.
non iam illud quaero, contra me ut diligat illa,
    aut, quod non potis est, esse pudica velit.
25 ipse valere opto et taetrum hunc deponere morbum.
    o di, reddite mi hoc pro pietate mea.

(76; metre: elegiac couplets)

*The man who stole Clodia from Catullus was probably Marcus
Caelius Rufus, the young friend with whom Cicero had
corresponded when he was in Cilicia (see pp. 40–43 above). He
was a close friend of Catullus but had betrayed him.*

Rufe, mihi frustra ac nequiquam credite amice,
    (frustra? immo magno cum pretio atque malo),
sicine subrepsti mi atque intestina perurens
    ei misero eripuisti omnia nostra bona?
5 eripuisti, heu heu, nostrae crudele venenum
    vitae, heu heu, nostrae pestis amicitiae.

(77; metre: elegiac couplets)

*But Caelius was tougher than Catullus and, when he learnt
Clodia's true nature, he threw her over. Wild with rage she
decided to take her revenge by getting her brother Clodius to
bring a law case against him. This case was a cause célèbre;
Cicero undertook the defence and Caelius also spoke on his own
behalf. In his defence Cicero took the line that the case had no
substance but had been brought to satisfy the whims of a wicked
and immoral woman; he devoted much of his speech to destroying
her character and undermining her evidence. The prosecution,
and indeed the whole court, must have been aghast when Cicero
launched into this attack, in which he openly called one of the
leading ladies of Roman society a shameless whore.*

si quae non nupta mulier domum suam patefecerit omnium
cupiditati palamque sese in meretricia vita conlocarit, si hoc in
urbe, in hortis, si in Baiarum illa celebritate faciat, si denique ita
se gerat non incessu solum sed ornatu et comitatu, non flagrantia
5 oculorum, non libertate sermonum, sed etiam complexu,
osculatione, actis, navigatione, conviviis, ut non solum meretrix
sed etiam proterva meretris videatur: cum hac si qui adulescens

21 **subrepens imos ... in artus** 'creeping down into my innermost being (limbs)'. **ut torpor** 'like a paralysis'.

23 **contra** adverb, 'in return'.

25 **taetrum** 'foul'.

26 **pro** 'in return for'.

---

1 The poem falls into three blocks of sense. What are these and what is the tone of each? Where do you feel the emotion is strongest?

2 How has Catullus shown *pietas* and how has Clodia failed to do so?

3 Explain in your own words the complex emotions Catullus is feeling.

---

1 **mihi ... credite** 'trusted by me'. **frustra ac nequiquam** 'for nothing and in vain'.

2 **immo magno cum pretio** 'no, at great cost ...'; **immo** corrects what has been just said.

3 **sicine subrepsti mi** 'is that how you have crept up on me?' **sicine** an emphatic form of **sic**; **subrepsti = subrepisti**.

4 **ei misero (mihi)**. **ei** is an exclamatory particle, expressing grief, usually found with **misero mihi**.

5–6 **crudele venenum ... pestis** take as vocatives; Caelius is the cruel poison of Catullus' life and the ruin of his love.

---

1 **non nupta** Clodia's husband was dead. **patefecerit** 'opened up'.

2 **cupiditati** 'to the lust'. **palam ... conlocarit** 'openly set herself up in the life of a whore'.

3 **in hortis** 'in her gardens'. She owned gardens on the banks of the Tiber where she used to watch the young men swimming. **in Baiarum illa celebritate** 'in all those crowds at Baiae'; Baiae was a fashionable seaside resort on the Bay of Naples.

4 **non incessu solum** 'not just by her gait/the way she walked'.

4–5 **flagrantia oculorum** 'by the flashing of her eyes'.

6 **osculatione** 'by her way of kissing'. **actis** 'her beach parties'. **navigatione** 'her yachting parties'.

7 **proterva** 'shameless'.

forte fuerit, utrum hic tibi, L. Herenni, adulter an amator videatur?
obliviscor iam iniurias tuas, Clodia, depono memoriam doloris mei;
10 quae abs te crudeliter in meos absente me facta sunt neglego; ne
sint haec in te dicta quae dixi. sed ex ipsa te requiro ... si quae
mulier sit eius modi qualem ego paulo ante descripsi, tui dissimilis,
vita institutoque meretricio, cum hac aliquid adulescentem
hominem habuisse rationis num tibi perturpe aut perflagitiosum
15 esse videatur.

(Cicero: *pro Caelio* 49–50)

*Cicero was a model of respectability but in this case was in the
awkward position of having to defend the character of a young man
who had certainly sown more than his share of wild oats. He does
this with great skill and wit and his attack on Clodia's character is
devastating. The acquittal of Caelius was equivalent to a
condemnation of Clodia; she disappeared from the scene without
further trace.*

8 **adulter an amator** to be an adulterer was disgraceful, to be a
lover quite respectable.

9 **iniurias tuas** 'the wrongs you did me'; while Cicero was in exile,
Clodia had hounded his family.

10–11 **ne sint haec in te dicta quae dixi** 'let's suppose what I have said
was not said against you'.

12 **tui dissimilis** 'different from you'.

13 **vita institutoque meretricio** 'by her set way of life a whore';
ablatives of description.

13–14 **aliquid ... habuisse rationis** 'had some dealings'.

14 **perturpe aut perflagitiosum** 'absolutely disgraceful and
scandalous'.

Cupid on a dolphin

3 The sequel

When Catullus had recovered to some extent, he sent two friends to take a message to Clodia, which marks the final rupture.

sagittifer Parthus

Furi et Aureli, comites Catulli,
sive in extremos penetrabit Indos,
litus ut longe resonante Eoa
    tunditur unda,
5   sive in Hyrcanos Arabesve molles,
seu Sagas sagittiferosve Parthos,
sive quae septemgeminus colorat
    aequora Nilus,
sive trans altas gradietur Alpes,
10 Caesaris visens monimenta magni,
Gallicum Rhenum horribile aequor ulti-
    mosque Britannos,
omnia haec, quaecumque feret voluntas
caelitum, temptare simul parati,
15 pauca nuntiate meae puellae
    non bona dicta.
cum suis vivat valeatque moechis,
quos simul complexa tenet trecentos,
nullum amans vere, sed identidem omnium
20   ilia rumpens;
nec meum respectet, ut ante, amorem,
qui illius culpa cecidit velut prati
ultimi flos, praetereunte postquam
    tactus aratro est.

(11; metre: sapphic stanzas)

He decided to go abroad to try to forget Clodia and joined the staff of the governor of Bithynia. He had to stay there for a full year. He made many friends there but disliked his governor as well as the place and the climate. At last the year was over and he says goodbye to his friends, glad to leave the sultry plains of Bithynia and looking forward to a sight-seeing tour on his way home.

iam ver egelidos refert tepores,
iam caeli furor aequinoctialis
iucundis Zephyri silescit auris.
linquantur Phrygii, Catulle, campi

1–2 **comites Catulli, sive ... penetrabit** 'the companions of Catullus' = 'who will accompany Catullus, whether he penetrates to ...'. The travelogue lists the remotest and wildest places of the world, the Indians to the extreme east, the Hyrcani on the southern shore of the Caspian sea, the Arabians to the south, the Sagae, nomads on the northern border of Persia, the Parthians, whose great empire reached to India, the Rhine, which Caesar reached in the summer of 55 BC, and Britain, at the furthest edge of the world.

3–4 **longe resonante Eoa/tunditur unda** 'is pounded by the far echoing eastern wave(s).' **Eoa** is pronounced as three long syllables.

5 **molles** the Arabs were often characterized as soft or effeminate.

6 **sagittiferos** 'arrow-carrying'; the Parthian army included mounted archers.

7–8 **septemgeminus colorat/aequora Nilus** the seven streams of the Nile delta carried silt out to sea and darkened the waters.

10 **visens** 'going to visit'.

3–14 **voluntas/caelitum** 'the will of the heavenly ones', i.e. the gods.

17 **vivat valeatque** 'let her live and good luck to her'.   **moechis** 'adulterers', 'lovers'.

20 **ilia rumpens** 'bursting the balls'; Clodia is insatiable.

21 **nec ... respectet** 'and let her not look for'.

22–3 **prati/ultimi** 'the edge of the meadow'.

---

1 How is the poem constructed? What is the tone of each part?

2 **non bona dicta** (*l.* 16): why do these words give the reader a shock?

3 The first twelve lines list the remote and dangerous places Furius and Aurelius would visit with Catullus. But there is one more mission even more dangerous. What is it?

4 There are some striking sound effects in *ll.* 3–4 and again in *ll.* 17–20. Can you spot them? How in each case do the sounds reinforce the sense?

5 What would you say was Catullus' state of mind when he wrote this poem? How did he feel towards Clodia and their past love?

---

1 **egelidos ... tepores** 'not chill warmths' i.e. 'warm days which are no longer chilly'.

2 **aequinoctialis** the spring equinox was a time of gales.

3 **Zephyri** 'of Zephyr' (the warm west wind of spring).

4 **Phrygii ... campi** 'the plains of Phrygia' (the western part of Bithynia).

5   Nicaeaeque ager uber aestuosae.
      ad claras Asiae volemus urbes.
      iam mens praetrepidans avet vagari,
      iam laeti studio pedes vigescunt.
      o dulces comitum valete coetus,
10   longe quos simul a domo profectos
      diversae varie viae reportant.

(46; metre: hendecasyllables)

1 What was the weather like when Catullus wrote this poem? Why should he spend three lines of a short poem on the weather?

2 What does he intend to do and how does he feel about it? Which word particularly emphasizes his feelings?

3 What does he say about his friends' journey from home and about their return journey? Is there a change of tone in these last three lines? Are they an anti-climax?

4 The poem is divided into two halves, joined by a linking line. Explain this structure. The opening lines of the second half contain sound echoes of the first two lines; can you spot them? Why should Catullus have made these sound echoes?

The theatre at Ephesus

He made his tour in a yacht, calling in at famous places en route. One place he visited was the Troad, but he made this stop not simply to see the famous site of Troy, but to pay his last respects to his brother, who had died there.

Troy

     multas per gentes et multa per aequora vectus
       advenio has miseras, frater, ad inferias,
     ut te postremo donarem munere mortis
       et mutam nequiquam alloquerer cinerem.
5   quandoquidem fortuna mihi tete abstulit ipsum,
       heu miser indigne frater adempte mihi,
     nunc tamen interea haec, prisco quae more parentum
       tradita sunt tristi munere ad inferias,

5 **Nicaeae** Nicaea was the capital of Bithynia. **uber** 'fertile'.
aestuosae 'sweltering'. Nicaea was unhealthy and unbearably hot
in summer.

7 **praetrepidans** 'trembling in anticipation'. **avet** 'longs', 'is eager'.

9 **comitum ... coetus** 'company of friends', i.e. his friends on the
staff of the governor.

0–11 Catullus and his friends had set out from Rome together to serve in
Bithynia; now they are all going home by different routes.

11 **diversae varie viae** 'opposite roads differently'. (Most of them no
doubt would be sailing west to Italy, but Catullus was going south
to Asia.)

A boating scene from Pompeii

2 **inferias** 'offerings to the dead'.

3 **munere mortis** 'the gift due to death'; **donarem** is here
constructed with the accusative of the person (**te**) and the ablative
of the gift, 'to present you with ...'.

4 **nequiquam** 'in vain', because his brother's ashes are dumb and
cannot reply.

5 **quandoquidem** 'since'. **tete** an emphatic form of **te**.

6 **indigne** 'cruelly'.

7 **prisco ... more parentum** 'by the ancient custom of our
ancestors'; the traditional gifts offered at the grave were wine, milk
and honey.

8 **tradita ... inferias** (which) are given as a sad duty to be a funeral
offering'; **munus** means either a gift or a duty, obligation; both
meanings are here intended.

accipe fraterno multum manantia fletu,
10   atque in perpetuum, frater, ave atque vale.

(101; metre: elegiac couplets)

Consider the diction (i.e. the sort of words used and their associations) of this poem. Does the diction successfully convey the feelings of the poem?

He celebrated his homecoming with a poem of pure happiness at being back at last.

paene insularum, Sirmio, insularumque
ocelle, quascumque in liquentibus stagnis
marique vasto fert uterque Neptunus,
quam te libenter quamque laetus inviso,
5   vix mi ipse credens Thuniam atque Bithunos
liquisse campos et videre te in tuto.
o quid solutis est beatius curis,
cum mens onus reponit, ac peregrino
labore fessi venimus larem ad nostrum,
10   desideratoque acquiescimus lecto?
hoc est quod unum est pro laboribus tantis.
salve, o venusta Sirmio, atque ero gaude
gaudente, vosque, o Lydiae lacus undae,
ridete quidquid est domi cachinnorum.

(31; metre: limping iambics)

1   Express the meaning of the first three lines in simple terms.
2   Summarize the meaning of *ll.* 7–10.
3   Explain the structure of the poem.
4   A Victorian critic describes the poem as 'a most unartificial and joyous outpouring of feeling'. Is this a fair description? Is the poem entirely 'unartificial'?

9   **manantia** '(gifts) wet'.

1–2   Catullus greets Sirmio as the jewel (**ocelle** 'little eye', an endearing
      diminutive) of (all) nearly-islands (i.e. peninsulas) and islands.
      Sirmio is a rocky peninsula on the south shore of Lake Benacus
      (now Lago di Garda), about twenty miles from Verona.

2   **quascumque** 'whichever', 'all which ...'. **in liquentibus stagnis**
      'in clear pools'.

3   **uterque Neptunus** Catullus speaks as if there were two Neptunes,
      one the god of fresh water, the other the god of the salt sea.

5–6   **Thuniam atque Bithunos/campos** the Thyni and the Bithyni were
      the two tribes which made up the native people of Bithynia.
      Catullus makes a jingle of these names; the feeling conveyed is that
      he is glad to be shot of the whole place.

6   **te** i.e. Sirmio.

7   **solutis ... curis** 'than cares cast off' = 'than casting off one's cares'.

8   **peregrino** 'foreign'.

11   **pro laboribus tantis** 'in return for such toils', i.e. 'which make
      such toils worthwhile'.

12–13 **ero ... gaudente** 'as your master rejoices'.

13   **vosque** 'and you'; he turns from the peninsula of Sirmio to the
      waters of the lake; he calls the waves Lydian because the original
      settlers there were Etruscans who were said to have come from
      Lydia (modern Turkey).

14   **ridete ... cachinnorum** 'laugh whatever of laughter there is at
      home', i.e. 'laugh with all the laughter you have in you'. The splash
      of the waves on the shore is like laughter greeting Catullus'
      homecoming.

When he had reached home and the yacht was laid up on Lake Benacus, near the family villa, he wrote a poem about it. He imagines that he is showing the yacht to some friends who are dining with him and makes the yacht tell its own story:

route of
Catullus's yacht

phaselus ille, quem videtis, hospites,
ait fuisse navium celerrimus,
neque ullius natantis impetum trabis
nequisse praeterire, sive palmulis
5   opus foret volare sive linteo.
et hoc negat minacis Hadriatici
negare litus insulasve Cycladas
Rhodumque nobilem horridamque Thraciam
Propontida trucemve Ponticum sinum,
10   ubi iste post phaselus antea fuit
comata silva; nam Cytorio in iugo
loquente saepe sibilum edidit coma.
Amastri Pontica et Cytore buxifer,
tibi haec fuisse et esse cognitissima
15   ait phaselus: ultima ex origine
tuo stetisse dicit in cacumine,
tuo imbuisse palmulas in aequore,
et inde tot per impotentia freta
erum tulisse, laeva sive dextera
20   vocaret aura, sive utrumque Iuppiter
simul secundus incidisset in pedem;
neque ulla vota litoralibus deis
sibi esse facta, cum veniret a mari
novissimo hunc ad usque limpidum lacum.
25   sed haec prius fuere: nunc recondita
senet quiete seque dedicat tibi,
gemelle Castor et gemelle Castoris.

(4; metre: iambic trimeters)

How is the yacht characterized in this poem?

2   **ait fuisse ... celerrimus** 'says it was the fastest'.

3–4   **neque ullius ... nequisse** 'and that the speed of no (other) boat could overtake it'; **nequeo** = 'I cannot'; Catullus doubles the negatives for emphasis.

4–5   **sive palmulis ... sive linteo** 'whether with oars ... or with sails (canvas)'.

6–7   **hoc negat ... negare** 'it denies that the shore of the Adriatic denies this', i.e. 'it says that the shore confirms this'. Catullus now traces the journey he had made in the yacht backwards from the Adriatic to the Cyclades islands, to Rhodes, to the Propontis, to the Black Sea (Pontus) and finally to the forests in the mountains of Bithynia where the yacht had been originally a tree (see map). **minacis** 'threatening'; the Adriatic was a dangerous sea for sailors.

8–9   **horridam Thraciam Propontida** 'the horrid Thracian Propontis', another dangerous sea (**Propontida** is Greek accusative).

9   **trucemve Ponticum sinum** 'or the savage Pontic gulf' = 'the savage Black Sea'.

10   **iste post phaselus** 'that (which was) afterwards a yacht'.

11   **comata** 'leafy'. **Cytorio in iugo** 'on the hills of Cytorus'; Cytorus and Amastris were ports on the Black Sea behind which rose mountains.

12   **loquente ... coma** 'as its leaves chattered'.

13   **Amastri ... Cytore** vocatives; Catullus addresses the hills as one entity (**tibi**). **buxifer** 'bearing box trees' (the area was famous for its box wood, used in shipbuilding).

16   **cacumine** 'peak'.

17   **imbuisse palmulas** 'dipped its little oars'; but **imbuo** has the secondary meaning of 'initiate' and both meanings are here intended.

18   **impotentia freta** 'wild seas'.

19–20   **laeva sive dextera ... aura** 'whether the wind called on the left or on the right', i.e. from port or starboard.

20–21   **sive utrumque ... in pedem** 'or whether a following wind fell on each foot together', i.e. 'or whether the boat was running before the wind'. Jupiter, the sky god, can mean 'weather' or, as here, 'wind'. **in pedem** the sails were square and so had a 'foot' at each lower corner.

22   **vota** sailors in trouble made vows to the gods of the shore, promising offerings if they were saved. Catullus' yacht never had to do this.

23–4   **a mari/novissimo** 'from its last sea', i.e. the Adriatic, from which it sailed up the River Po to Lake Benacus.

25–6   **recondita ... quiete** 'in sequestered/remote quiet'.

26   **senet** 'grows old'.

27   **gemelle Castor et gemelle Castoris** 'twin Castor and Castor's twin', i.e. Castor and Pollux, the heavenly twins, who guarded seafarers.

Serapis

He soon returned to Rome and revisited old friends. One day he met Varus in the Forum, who took him to visit his latest girlfriend. She proved attractive enough, but the visit was not a success.

Varus me meus ad suos amores
visum duxerat e foro otiosum,
scortillum (ut mihi tum repente visum est)
non sane illepidum neque invenustum;
5   huc ut venimus, incidere nobis
sermones varii, in quibus quid esset
iam Bithynia, quo modo se haberet,
et quonam mihi profuisset aere.
respondi id quod erat, nihil neque ipsis
10   nec praetoribus esse nec cohorti,
cur quisquam caput unctius referret –
praesertim quibus esset irrumator
praetor, nec faceret pili cohortem.
'at certe tamen,' inquiunt 'quod illic
15   natum dicitur esse, comparasti
ad lecticam homines.' ego (ut puellae
unum me facerem beatiorem)
'non' inquam 'mihi tam fuit maligne,
ut, provincia quod mala incidisset,
20   non possem octo homines parare rectos.'
at mi nullus erat nec hic neque illic,
fractum qui veteris pedem grabati
in collo sibi collocare posset.
hic illa, ut decuit cinaediorem,
25   'quaeso,' inquit 'mihi, mi Catulle, paulum
istos commoda: nam volo ad Serapim
deferri.' 'mane,' inquii puellae,
'istud quod modo dixeram me habere,
fugit me ratio: meus sodalis –
30   Cinna est Gaius – is sibi paravit.

1	**amores** 'his beloved', 'his girlfriend'.
2	**visum** 'to visit her' (supine expressing purpose).
3	**scortillum** 'a little tart'.
4	**non sane ... invenustum** 'certainly not without charm and attraction', i.e. 'extremely charming and attractive'.
6–7	**quid esset/iam Bithynia** 'what Bithynia was like now'.
7	**quo modo se haberet** 'how it was getting on'.
8	**quonam ... aere** 'by what money it had benefited me', i.e. 'how much money I had made out of it'. Romans serving on the staff of a provincial governor expected to come back with their pockets well lined.
9–10	**nihil neque ipsis ... cohorti** 'there was nothing for (the natives) themselves nor for the governors nor for his staff'. **praetoribus** the governors of most provinces were ex-praetors and their title was *propraetor*. **cohorti** the governor's staff were called his *cohors*.
11	**cur quisquam ... referret** '(no reason) why anyone should bring back his head better oiled', i.e. no one could make enough money even to buy a better hair oil.
12	**irrumator** 'a bugger' (a term of indiscriminate abuse).
13	**faceret pili** 'cared a straw for'.
14	**quod illic/natum dicitur esse** 'what is said to be born there', i.e. the native product. Bithynia was evidently well known for producing litter-bearers; eight strong men were required for carrying a litter, which was the usual mode of transport for wealthy women in Rome (wheeled vehicles were not allowed in the streets in daylight hours).
15	**comparasti = comparavisti** 'you have got'.
16–17	**ut puellae ... beatiorem** 'to make myself out to the girl to be the one luckier man'.
18	**non ... maligne** 'I didn't do so badly'.
19	**incidisset** 'had fallen to my lot'.
20	**homines ... rectos** 'straight-backed men'.
22	**veteris pedem grabati** 'the foot of an old camp-bed'.
24	**hic** 'at this point'. **ut decuit cinaediorem** 'as suited (= as you would expect from) a shameless whore'.
26	**commoda** 'lend'. **Serapim** 'to the temple of Serapis'; the worship of Serapis had been introduced from Egypt in 105 BC and was extremely popular, although the authorities tried repeatedly to suppress it.
28–30	Catullus in his confusion becomes rather incoherent.
29	**fugit me ratio** 'reason escaped me' = 'I made a mistake'. **sodalis** 'friend'.
30	**Cinna est Gaius** 'it's Cinna, that is Gaius Cinna'. The Cinna referred to must be C. Helvius Cinna, a minor poet, who may have served with Catullus in Bithynia. He is the poet who after the murder of Julius Caesar was torn to pieces by the mob, who mistook him for another Cinna who was one of the conspirators (see Shakespeare's *Julius Caesar*).

verum, utrum illius an mei, quid ad me?
utor tam bene quam mihi pararim.
sed tu insulsa male et molesta vivis,
per quam non licet esse neglegentem.'

(10; metre: hendecasyllables)

It must have been soon after this that Catullus died at the age of thirty. We do not know the cause of his death.

We have seen that Catullus published his poems in his own lifetime. For two hundred years after his death his poetry was well known and is often quoted by ancient authors. After this references to his poetry become rare. His works were not considered suitable for schools and were not part of the school syllabus. And so few copies of his poetry were circulating and he seems to have been forgotten. A thousand years later, at the time of the Renaissance, when interest in classical literature revived, his works were unknown until one precious manuscript was found by chance early in the fourteenth century; this was shortly afterwards lost, but copies had been made of which three survive. In two of these copies the 'resurrection' of Catullus is recorded as follows.

versus domini Benevenutio de Campexanis de Vicencia de resurrectione Catulli poetae Veronensis:

ad patriam venio longis a finibus exul;
    causa mei reditus compatriota fuit ...
quo licet ingenio vestrum celebrare Catullum,
    cuius sub modio clausa papirus erat.

Verses of Lord Benevenuto Campesani of Vicenza about the resurrection of the poet Catullus of Verona:

I, Catullus, come back to my country, an exile from far off lands; the reason for my return was a compatriot. Through his genius you can celebrate your Catullus, whose papyrus (manuscript) was shut at the bottom of a box.

Supposing this manuscript had not been discovered, how great a loss would we have suffered?

31   **quid ad me**? 'What does it matter to me?'

32   **tam bene quam mihi pararim** (= **paraverim**, perfect subjunctive) 'as well as if I had got them for myself.'

33   **sed tu ... vivis** 'but you are a very silly and tiresome girl'; **vivis** almost = **es**; **insulsa male** literally, 'badly stupid'.

34   **per quam ... neglegentem** 'through whom it is not allowed to be careless', i.e. 'who won't let a man make a mistake'.

1   What is Catullus' intention in this poem? Is it serious or humorous? If humorous, who is he laughing at?

2   Examine the diction of the poem, i.e. what sort of words and idioms is he using and what emotional connotations do they have? Compare the diction of this poem with that he wrote at his brother's tomb (poem 101, p. 130 above).

3   Compare the tone and diction of this poem with Horace's Satire on the Bore (Part III, pp. 72–4).

VIRGIL

The greatest poet of the extraordinary flowering of Golden Age literature was Publius Vergilius Maro, known in English as Virgil. He was born in Mantua in North Italy in 70 BC, and grew up amid the terrible civil wars which rent the Roman world. His early poetry celebrated the beauty of the Italian countryside but set it against the background of civil strife. This had caused a quarter of the land of Italy to change hands in the proscriptions and confiscations, and had taken the farmers from the soil and pressed them into arms. Like most of his contemporaries, Virgil was profoundly grateful when Augustus reestablished peace after the Battle of Actium in 31 BC.

In his last and finest poem, the *Aeneid*, Virgil expressed what he felt about Augustan Rome, but he chose a legend from the distant past in order to do this. The story concerns the flight of the Trojan Aeneas from the ruins of his sacked city and his journey to Italy where he establishes a foothold for the Roman nation. Virgil fully recognized the greatness and importance of Aeneas' Roman mission. It was eventually to lead to the new golden era of peace and stability created by Augustus. But he was equally aware of the suffering caused not only to their enemies but also to the Romans themselves by their imperial destiny. We give here Virgil's story of Dido, the Carthaginian queen who is tragically destroyed by her

Virgil

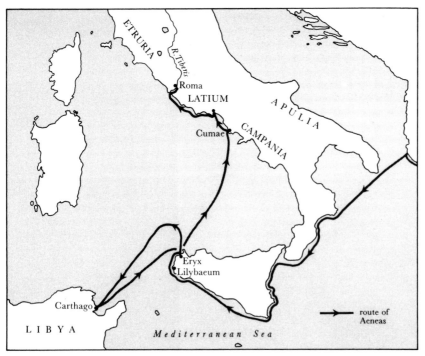

Rome and Carthage

love affair with Aeneas. Virgil asks us to consider whether even the greatness of Rome is sufficient to justify such torment.

Some of the finest passages of the *Aeneid* proudly proclaim the glory of the city which civilized the Western world. But there is a more private voice to be heard. No poet has seen deeper into the mysteries of the human heart or conveyed more movingly the pain involved in human experience.

The *Aeneid* was incomplete when Virgil died in 19 BC and the poet asked that it should be destroyed. Augustus overruled this request. Thus we owe it to the emperor that we can read the only poem in Latin able to stand comparison with Homer's great epics, the *Iliad* and the *Odyssey*.

The bay of Carthage

1 Aeneas arrives at Carthage

The Greeks had laid siege to Troy for ten years before they finally captured it by trickery. On the dreadful night when the city was sacked, the ghost of Hector, who had been Troy's greatest warrior, appeared to his cousin Aeneas in a dream and told him to flee from the burning ruins. He must take with him the sacred emblems and the guardian gods of Troy and found a home for them in a new city across the sea.

Aeneas obeys and wanders with his followers for seven years. In all this time, he fails to reach the place where Fate and the gods wish him to build his city. Only when he does so will he fulfil his mission by founding a new Troy from which Rome will spring.

Virgil begins his story about Aeneas as his fleet is at last approaching the destined land of Italy.

Juno, queen of the gods, loves Carthage, but hates the Trojans.

Juno

    urbs antiqua fuit (Tyrii tenuere coloni)
    Karthago, Italiam contra Tiberinaque longe
    ostia, dives opum studiisque asperrima belli,
    quam Iuno fertur terris magis omnibus unam
5   posthabita coluisse Samo: hic illius arma,
    hic currus fuit; hoc regnum dea gentibus esse,
    si qua fata sinant, iam tum tenditque fovetque.
    progeniem sed enim Troiano a sanguine duci
    audierat Tyrias olim quae verteret arces;
10 hinc populum late regem belloque superbum
    venturum excidio Libyae; sic volvere Parcas.
    his accensa super iactatos aequore toto
    Troas, reliquias Danaum atque immitis Achilli,
    arcebat longe Latio, multosque per annos
15 errabant acti fatis maria omnia circum.
    tantae molis erat Romanam condere gentem.

(Aeneid 1.12–22, 29–33)

Juno persuades Aeolus, the god of the winds, to stir up a terrible storm. The Trojan fleet, which has set sail from Sicily and has now almost reached its destination of Italy, is driven off course and suffers much damage and loss. Neptune calms the storm and Aeneas and most of his men reach the coast of Libya safely. They are utterly demoralized but Aeneas puts a brave face on things.

Jupiter now sends his messenger Mercury down to Libya to make sure that the Carthaginians give Aeneas a friendly welcome. Venus, disguising herself as a huntress, meets her son Aeneas as he explores the country he has come to. She tells him the history of Dido, queen of Carthage.

1 **Tyrii tenuere (= tenuerunt) coloni**
'colonists from Tyre held it', i.e. lived
there. The Carthaginians are repeatedly
called Tyrians because they come from
Tyre, the Phoenician city on the coast
of Syria.

2–3 **Italiam … ostia = contra Italiam**
Tiberinaque ostia longe 'facing Italy
and the mouth of the Tiber (i.e. Italy
where the Tiber runs into the sea) at a
distance' – see map. **dives opum** 'rich
in resources'.

4–5 **quam Iuno fertur … unam …**
coluisse 'which Juno is said to have
loved more than any other land'.

5 **posthabita Samo** 'with (even) Samos
coming second'. On Samos, an Aegean
island, there was a famous temple to
Juno.

5–6 **hic illius arma,/hic currus fuit** i.e. in
the temple was a statue of Juno armed and in a chariot.

6–7 **hoc … fovetque = iam tum dea tendit fovetque** ('intends and
nurtures') **hoc esse regnum** ('this to be a kingdom' = 'to be the ruler')
gentibus. si qua 'if in any way'.

8 **sed enim** 'but in fact' (take at start of line). **progeniem … Troiano a**
sanguine duci 'offspring was being drawn from Trojan blood' = 'a
race was even now springing from Trojan blood'.

9 **Tyrias … arces = quae olim verteret Tyrias arces** 'which would
one day overturn the Tyrians' citadels'. The reference is to the Punic
Wars.

10–11 Indirect statement continues after **audierat. late regem** 'wide-ruling'.

11 **venturum (esse). excidio** 'for a destruction
to …' (predicative dative) = 'to destroy'. **sic**
volvere Parcas 'thus the Fates ordained'.
venturum (esse) and **volvere** are infinitives
in indirect statement, part of what Juno had
heard.

12 **his accensa super** 'inflamed (= enraged) over
these things'.

13 **Troas** 'the Trojans' (accusative plural).
reliquias Danaum atque immitis Achilli
'the remnants left by the Greeks and savage
Achilles'. **Danai** = 'the Greeks'. **Achilli**
genitive.

14 **Latio** Latium is the area south of the Tiber;
see map.

15 **maria … circum = circum omnia maria**.

16 **tantae molis erat** 'it was a matter involving
(literally, of) such effort …'.

Tyre

The storm

'Punica regna vides, Tyrios et Agenoris urbem;
sed fines Libyci, genus intractabile bello.
imperium Dido Tyria regit urbe profecta,
20   germanum fugiens. longa est iniuria, longae
ambages; sed summa sequar fastigia rerum.
huic coniunx Sychaeus erat, ditissimus agri
Phoenicum, et magno miserae dilectus amore,
cui pater intactam dederat primisque iugarat
25   ominibus. sed regna Tyri germanus habebat
Pygmalion, scelere ante alios immanior omnis.
quos inter medius venit furor. ille Sychaeum
impius ante aras atque auri caecus amore
clam ferro incautum superat, securus amorum
30   germanae; factumque diu celavit et aegram
multa malus simulans vana spe lusit amantem.
ipsa sed in somnis inhumati venit imago
coniugis ora modis attollens pallida miris;
crudelis aras traiectaque pectora ferro
35   nudavit, caecumque domus scelus omne retexit.
tum celerare fugam patriaque excedere suadet
auxiliumque viae veteres tellure recludit
thesauros, ignotum argenti pondus et auri.
his commota fugam Dido sociosque parabat.
40   conveniunt quibus aut odium crudele tyranni
aut metus acer erat; navis, quae forte paratae,
corripiunt onerantque auro. portantur avari
Pygmalionis opes pelago; dux femina facti.
devenere locos ubi nunc ingentia cernes
45   moenia surgentemque novae Karthaginis arcem.'

(*Aeneid* 1.338–66)

*The disguised Venus now tells Aeneas that all the
men and ships he had thought lost have in fact
escaped the storm. She sends him on his way.*

corripuere viam interea, qua semita monstrat.
iamque ascendebant collem, qui plurimus urbi
imminet adversasque aspectat desuper arces.
miratur molem Aeneas, magalia quondam,
50   miratur portas strepitumque et strata viarum.
instant ardentes Tyrii: pars ducere muros
molirique arcem et manibus subvolvere saxa,

miratur molem Aeneas

17 **Punica** 'Carthaginian'. **Agenoris urbem** 'Carthage' (Agenor was an ancestor of Dido).

18 **fines (sunt) Libyci** 'the surrounding country is Libyan', i.e. belonging to native Africans. The colonizing Carthaginians are hedged in by enemies. **intractabile bello** 'fierce in war'.

20 **germanum** '(her) brother'. **longa** '(a) long (story of)'.

20–21 **longae ambages** 'a long involved story'.

22 **summa sequar fastigia rerum** 'I shall follow (= trace) the main outlines of the story'.

22–3 **ditissimus agri/Phoenicum** 'the wealthiest of the Phoenicians (i.e. Tyrians) in land'.

23 **magno miserae dilectus amore** 'loved by great love of the unhappy girl' = 'greatly loved by the unhappy girl'.

24 **intactam** 'untouched' = 'as a virgin'.

24–5 **primis iugarat (= iugaverat) ominibus** 'had joined in her first wedding ceremony' (i.e. she had not been married before).

25 **regna Tyri** 'the kingdom of Tyre' (**regna** is poetic plural for singular). **germanus** '(her) brother'.

26 **omnis = omnes** (**-is** is a common variant for **-es** in the acc. plur. of the 3rd decl.).

27 **quos inter = inter quos**, referring to Pygmalion and Sychaeus.

29–30 **securus amorum/germanae** 'caring nothing for his sister's love'.

30 **aegram** 'sick' = 'distraught'.

31 **malus** 'wickedly', 'in his wickedness'. **vana spe lusit amantem** 'he deluded the loving (wife) with vain hope'.

32–3 **ipsa ... inhumati ... imago/coniugis** 'the ghost (itself) of her unburied husband'.

33 **ora modis attollens pallida miris** 'lifting his face to her, pale in wondrous ways' = 'strangely pale'. **ora** poetic plural for singular.

34 **traiecta** 'transfixed'.

35 **nudavit** 'he stripped bare' = 'he revealed'.

36 **celerare** 'speed up' = 'embark hastily upon'. **suadet** 'he urges (her to …)'.

37–8 **auxilium viae veteres tellure recludit/thesauros** 'he revealed to her ancient treasures (hidden) in the ground (as a) help for the journey'.

40 **conveniunt (ei) quibus. tyranni** 'of the tyrant', i.e. of Pygmalion.

41 **paratae (erant)**.

42 **portantur** 'are carried off'.

43 **pelago** 'over the sea'. **dux ... facti = dux facti (fuit) femina.**

44 **devenere = devenerunt** 'they came down (from the sea)' = 'they landed at'. **locos = in locos.**

46 **corripuere (= corripuerunt) viam** 'they (i.e. Aeneas and his companion) hastened on their way'.

47 **plurimus** 'with its huge mass'.

48 **aspectat** 'looks towards'. **adversas** = 'facing them'.

49 **molem** i.e. 'the massive structures'. **magalia quondam** 'once huts'.

50 **strata** 'the paving'.

51 **instant** 'press on (with the work)'. **ardentes** 'burning', i.e. enthusiastically.

51–3 **pars ... pars** 'some ... others'. **ducere** (= 'build'), **moliri** (= 'toil at'), **subvolvere** (= 'roll up'), **optare**, **concludere** (= 'enclosed') are all historic infinitives.

pars optare locum tecto et concludere sulco;
iura magistratusque legunt sanctumque senatum.
55 hic portus alii effodiunt; hic alta theatri
fundamenta locant alii, immanisque columnas
rupibus excidunt, scaenis decora alta futuris.
qualis apes aestate nova per florea rura
exercet sub sole labor, cum gentis adultos
60 educunt fetus, aut cum liquentia mella
stipant et dulci distendunt nectare cellas,
aut onera accipiunt venientum, aut agmine facto
ignavum fucos pecus a praesepibus arcent:
fervet opus redolentque thymo fragrantia mella.
65 'o fortunati, quorum iam moenia surgunt!'
Aeneas ait et fastigia suspicit urbis.

apis

(*Aeneid* 1.418–38)

*Aeneas proceeds into the city. He is greatly moved by the fact that
in this remote place the walls of the temple of Juno have been
decorated with scenes from the Trojan War. As he gazes at these,
Dido appears.*

haec dum Dardanio Aeneae miranda videntur,
dum stupet obtutuque haeret defixus in uno,
regina ad templum, forma pulcherrima Dido,
70 incessit magna iuvenum stipante caterva.
qualis in Eurotae ripis aut per iuga Cynthi
exercet Diana choros, quam mille secutae
hinc atque hinc glomerantur Oreades; illa pharetram
fert umero gradiensque deas supereminet omnis
75 (Latonae tacitum pertemptant gaudia pectus);
talis erat Dido, talem se laeta ferebat
per medios instans operi regnisque futuris.
tum foribus divae, media testudine templi,
saepta armis solioque alte subnixa resedit.
80 iura dabat legesque viris, operumque laborem
partibus aequabat iustis aut sorte trahebat.

Dido and Aeneas at the banquet

(*Aeneid* 1.494–508)

*Dido welcomes Aeneas warmly and he swears undying gratitude.
Venus, wishing to make doubly sure that Dido remains friendly to
Aeneas, substitutes her son Cupid for Aeneas' son Ascanius,
sometimes called Iulus.*

*At a great dinner party, Dido cradles the false Ascanius in her
lap, unaware that he is in fact the god of love. Little by little, she
begins to forget Sychaeus as her love for Aeneas grows. After
dinner, Aeneas tells the story of the fall of Troy and his subsequent
adventures. Dido hangs on his lips.*

53 **tecto** 'for a building'. **sulco** 'with a trench'. This was the way the Romans marked out the site for city walls.

54 **legunt** 'choose', 'elect'. They establish laws and elect magistrates and a government.

55–6 **alta theatri/fundamenta locant** 'they lay the deep foundations of a theatre'.

57 **scaenis decora alta futuris** 'lofty adornments for the stage which is going to be (built)'.

58–9 **qualis apes … exercet … labor** 'like the work which keeps bees busy'. **qualis** (= 'what sort of') commonly introduces a simile: **qualis labor** 'what sort of work' = 'like the work which …'.

59–60 **gentis adultos … fetus** 'the young offspring of their race'.

60–61 **liquentia mella/stipant** 'they cram in the liquid honey'.

61 **dulci distendunt nectare cellas** 'they fill to bursting the honeycomb cells with sweet nectar'.

62 **venientum** = **venientium** i.e. 'of the bees coming back from the meadows'.

63 **ignavum … arcent** 'they keep off the drones (**fucos**), an idle tribe, from their hives'.

64 **fervet** literally, 'boils'. **redolent thymo fragrantia mella** 'the sweet-smelling honey is scented with thyme'.

66 **fastigia suspicit** 'looks up at the tops of the buildings'. As he looks at the building operations, Aeneas has been walking down the hill.

67 **Dardanio Aeneae** 'to Trojan Aeneas'. Dardanus was the founder of the Trojan race.

68 **obtutu haeret defixus in uno** 'he sticks, held fast in a single gaze' = 'stands there, rooted to the spot in total concentration'.

70 **stipante** 'pressing (round her)'.

71 **Eurotae** 'of the Eurotas' (the river on which Sparta stood). **iuga Cynthi** 'the ridges of Cynthus' (the hill on Delos).

72 **exercet Diana choros** 'Diana sets (her followers) singing and dancing'.

73 **hinc atque hinc** 'on this side and on that'. **glomerantur** 'gather together'. **Oreades**, *f. pl.* 'mountain nymphs'.

74 **gradiens** 'as she goes'. **deas** i.e. the mountain nymphs. **supereminet** 'overtops'.

75 **pertemptant gaudia** 'joy thrills …'. **Latonae** the mother of Diana.

76 **talis** picks up **qualis**, the word which began the simile in *l.* 71.

77 **instans** (+ dative) 'pressing on with'.

78 **foribus divae** 'at the doors of the goddess'. **media testudine** 'beneath the centre of the vault'.

79 **saepta** 'hedged about'. **solio alte subnixa** 'taking her place high up on her throne'.

81 **partibus aequabat iustis** 'she was making equal in fair parts' = 'she was dividing up justly and equally'. **sorte trahebat** 'was assigning by lot'.

Cupid strings his bow

2 The love of Dido and Aeneas

Dido is wounded by her love.

at regina gravi iamdudum saucia cura
vulnus alit venis et caeco carpitur igni.
multa viri virtus animo multusque recursat
gentis honos: haerent infixi pectore vultus
5   verbaque, nec placidam membris dat cura quietem.

(*Aeneid* 4.1–5)

cerva

*Encouraged by her sister Anna, Dido gives free rein to her passion
for Aeneas. She tries vainly to win the gods' favour by sacrifices.*

heu, vatum ignarae mentes! quid vota furentem,
quid delubra iuvant? est mollis flamma medullas
interea et tacitum vivit sub pectore vulnus.
uritur infelix Dido totaque vagatur
10   urbe furens, qualis coniecta cerva sagitta,
quam procul incautam nemora inter Cresia fixit
pastor agens telis liquitque volatile ferrum
nescius: illa fuga silvas saltusque peragrat
Dictaeos; haeret lateri letalis harundo.
15   nunc media Aenean secum per moenia ducit
Sidoniasque ostentat opes urbemque paratam,
incipit effari mediaque in voce resistit;
nunc eadem labente die convivia quaerit
Iliacosque iterum demens audire labores
20   exposcit pendetque iterum narrantis ab ore.
post ubi digressi, lumenque obscura vicissim
luna premit suadentque cadentia sidera somnos,
sola domo maeret vacua stratisque relictis
incubat. illum absens absentem auditque videtque,
25   aut gremio Ascanium genitoris imagine capta
detinet, infandum si fallere possit amorem.
non coeptae adsurgunt turres, non arma iuventus
exercet portusve aut propugnacula bello
tuta parant: pendent opera interrupta minaeque
30   murorum ingentes aequataque machina caelo.

(*Aeneid* 4.65–89)

pastor nescius

*Juno plots with Venus to strengthen the union between Dido and
Aeneas. Her aim is to keep Aeneas in Carthage and thus prevent
him from fulfilling his destiny in Italy. Venus is glad to see the bonds
of hospitality strengthened.*

1   **cura** is often used of the care of love.

2   **alit venis** 'feeds with her life-blood'. **carpitur** 'is wasted', 'pines away'.

3   **multa viri virtus** 'many (a thought of) the courage of the man'. **recursat** 'comes swiftly back'.

3–4   **multus gentis honos** 'many (a thought of) the great distinction of his race' (**honos = honor**).

4   **haerent infixi vultus** 'his features (**vultus**) remain firmly fixed in …'.

6   **vatum** 'of the soothsayers' (who are advising her how to win the gods' favour). **quid vota (iuvant)**. **furentem** 'her in her frenzy'.

7   **ēst** 'eats', not to be confused with **est** 'he is'. **mollis … medullas** 'the soft marrow of her bones'.

8   **tacitum** she cannot speak of her love to Aeneas.

10   **coniecta … sagitta** 'when the arrow has been fired'.

11   **nemora inter Cresia** 'amid the woods of Crete'.

12   **agens** 'pursuing (her)'.

13–14   **silvas saltusque … Dictaeos** 'the wooded defiles (literally, the woods and defiles) of Crete'. Dicte is a mountain on Crete.

14   **harundo** 'shaft (literally, reed)'.

15   **Aenean** accusative.

16   **Sidonias** 'of Tyre'. Virgil refers to Tyre and Sidon as if they were the same place. **ostentat** 'shows off'.

17   **effari** 'to speak out', i.e. 'to declare her love'. **resistit** 'stops'.

18   **eadem … convivia** i.e. repetitions of the first banquet at which Aeneas had told his tale.

19   **Iliacos** 'Trojan'. **demens** 'in her madness'.

21   **digressi (sunt)** 'they have parted'. **vicissim** 'in turn'.

23–4   **stratis relictis/incubat** 'she lies on the couch he has left (i.e. had reclined on at the banquet)'.

25   **gremio** 'in her lap'. **genitoris** 'of his father'.

26   **detinet** 'she clings on to'. **si** 'if' = 'in the hope that'. **infandum … amorem** 'a love she could not speak of'. She tries to hoodwink love and herself.

27   **coeptae** 'which had been begun'.

28–9   **propugnacula bello/tuta** 'the ramparts bringing safety in war'.

29   **parant** subject *they*, the young men. **pendent** 'are suspended' = 'are idle'. **interrupta** 'broken off'.

29–30   **minae murorum ingentes** 'the vast threats of the walls' = 'the vast threatening walls'.

30   **aequata machina caelo** 'the crane towering to the sky'.

Dido and Aeneas go hunting.

Ascanius spumantem dari optat aprum

Oceanum interea surgens Aurora reliquit.
it portis iubare exorto delecta iuventus,
retia rara, plagae, lato venabula ferro,
Massylique ruunt equites et odora canum vis.
35 reginam thalamo cunctantem ad limina primi
Poenorum exspectant, ostroque insignis et auro
stat sonipes ac frena ferox spumantia mandit.
tandem progreditur magna stipante caterva;
cui pharetra ex auro, crines nodantur in aurum,
40 aurea pupuream subnectit fibula vestem.
nec non et Phrygii comites et laetus Iulus
incedunt. ipse ante alios pulcherrimus omnis
infert se socium Aeneas atque agmina iungit.
qualis ubi hibernam Lyciam Xanthique fluenta
45 deserit ac Delum maternam invisit Apollo
instauratque choros, mixtique altaria circum
Cretesque Dryopesque fremunt pictique Agathyrsi:
ipse iugis Cynthi graditur mollique fluentem
fronde premit crinem fingens atque implicat auro,
50 tela sonant umeris: haud illo segnior ibat
Aeneas, tantum egregio decus enitet ore.
postquam altos ventum in montis atque invia lustra,
ecce ferae saxi deiectae vertice caprae
decurrere iugis; alia de parte patentis
55 transmittunt cursu campos atque agmina cervi
pulverulenta fuga glomerant montisque relinquunt.
at puer Ascanius mediis in vallibus acri
gaudet equo iamque hos cursu, iam praeterit illos,
spumantemque dari pecora inter inertia votis
60 optat aprum, aut fulvum descendere monte leonem.

The hunt

31 **Oceanum** the stream of Ocean which surrounded the world. **Aurora** the goddess of dawn.

32 **iubare exorto** 'when the sun's beams arose'.

33 **retia rara** 'wide-meshed nets'. **plagae** 'trap-nets'. **lato venabula ferro** 'broad-bladed hunting-spears'. The horsemen pour along with their gear of nets, spears, etc.

34 **Massyli** 'African'. The Massyli were a North African tribe. **odora canum vis** 'the keen-scented strength of dogs' = 'keen-scented, strong dogs'.

35 **thalamo** 'in her bedroom'.

36 **ostro insignis** 'standing out in purple'.

37 **sonipes** '(her) steed'. **frena ferox spumantia mandit** 'proudly champs the foaming bit'.

39 **cui pharetra (est)** 'to whom there is a quiver' = 'she has a quiver'. **crines nodantur in aurum** 'her hair is knotted onto a golden clasp'.

40 **aurea ... vestem** 'a golden brooch fastens her purple dress'.

41 **Phrygii** 'Trojan'.

43 **infert se socium** 'brings himself as a companion' = 'goes to join her'.

44 **hibernam Lyciam** 'Lycia, his winter home'. **Xanthi fluenta** 'the streams of Xanthus' (in Lycia, where Apollo dwelt at Patara in the winter).

45 **Delum maternam** 'his mother's Delos' = 'Delos, where his mother gave him birth'.

46 **instaurat choros** 'starts up the dance afresh'. **mixti altaria circum** 'mingled around the altars'.

47 **picti** 'tattooed'. The Dryopes were from northern Greece, the Agathyrsi from Scythia; Cretans, Dryopes and Agathyrsi all gather at Delos for Apollo's festival.

48 **ipse** Apollo himself, the master.

48–9 **molli fluentem ... auro** 'shaping his flowing hair, he garlands (literally, presses) it with soft foliage and entwines it with gold', i.e. 'he puts on his hair (**crinem**) a crown of leaves entwined with gold wire'.

50 **haud ... segnior** 'no more sluggish than ...' = 'even more briskly than...'.

51 **enitet** 'shines forth'.

52 **ventum (est). invia lustra** 'the trackless lairs (of the beasts)'.

53 **ecce** 'look!'. **deiectae vertice** 'dislodged from the top of ...'. The beaters have driven the goats down.

54 **decurrere = decurrerunt**.

55 **transmittunt** 'they cross'. **cervi** 'stags' (subject of **transmittunt** and **glomerant**).

56 **pulverulenta** 'dusty'. **glomerant** 'mass' (transitive).

57 Aeneas' son is known both as Ascanius and Iulus.

58 **hos ... illos** referring to his fellow hunters.

59–60 **spumantem ... aprum** 'a foaming wild boar'. **pecora inter inertia** 'amid (these) harmless creatures'. He prays to be given a serious challenge.

interea magno misceri murmure caelum
incipit. insequitur commixta grandine nimbus,
et Tyrii comites passim et Troiana iuventus
Dardaniusque nepos Veneris diversa per agros
65 tecta metu petiere; ruunt de montibus amnes.
speluncam Dido dux et Troianus eandem
deveniunt. prima et Tellus et pronuba Iuno
dant signum; fulsere ignes et conscius aether
conubiis, summoque ulularunt vertice Nymphae.
70 ille dies primus leti primusque malorum
causa fuit; neque enim specie famave movetur
nec iam furtivum Dido meditatur amorem:
coniugium vocat, hoc praetexit nomine culpam.

(*Aeneid* 4.129–36, 138–72)

speluncam eandem deveniunt

*The malevolent goddess Rumour brings the news of the love affair
to an African king, the Gaetulian Iarbas. He has himself been
rejected as a suitor by Dido and is especially indignant that she
preferred to himself a man he thinks of as an effeminate oriental.
He prays to his father Jupiter to take action.*

*Jupiter is angry to discover that Aeneas is neglecting the will of
Destiny and he sends Mercury down to him with a stinging rebuke.
Mercury flies to Carthage.*

61 **misceri** 'to be disturbed'.

62 **commixta grandine** 'with hail mixed in' = 'mixed with hail'.

63 **passim** 'in every direction'.

64 **Dardanius nepos Veneris** 'the Trojan grandson of Venus', i.e. Ascanius.

64–5 **diversa ... tecta** 'various shelters'.

65 **petiere = petierunt.**

66 **speluncam ... eandem** supply **ad. Dido ... Troianus = Dido et dux Troianus.**

67 **prima Tellus** 'primeval Earth'. **pronuba** 'goddess of marriage'.

68 **fulsere = fulserunt** 'blazed'.

68–9 **conscius aether/conubiis** 'the upper air, the witness to the marriage'.

69 **summo ulularunt (= ululaverunt) vertice Nymphae** 'the Nymphs cried out on the mountain top'. Virgil conjures up the language and ritual of a Roman wedding. Earth and Juno give the signal for the ceremony to begin. The flashes of lightning are the marriage torches, the upper air is the witness, and the Nymphs sing the marriage song.

71 **specie** 'by appearance' = 'by how things appear'.

72 **nec iam furtivum ... meditatur amorem** 'and no longer practises a secret love' = 'and she no longer conceals her love'.

73 **coniugium vocat** 'she calls it (i.e. her liaison with Aeneas) a marriage'. **praetexit ... culpam** 'she masks her sin'.

A Roman wedding

Mercury

ut primum alatis tetigit magalia plantis,
75   Aenean fundantem arces ac tecta novantem
conspicit. atque illi stellatus iaspide fulva
ensis erat Tyrioque ardebat murice laena
demissa ex umeris, dives quae munera Dido
fecerat, et tenui telas discreverat auro.
80   continuo invadit: 'tu nunc Karthaginis altae
fundamenta locas pulchramque uxorius urbem
exstruis? heu, regni rerumque oblite tuarum!
ipse deum tibi me claro demittit Olympo
regnator, caelum ac terras qui numine torquet:
85   ipse haec ferre iubet celeris mandata per auras:
quid struis? aut qua spe Libycis teris otia terris?
si te nulla movent tantarum gloria rerum,
Ascanium surgentem et spes heredis Iuli
respice, cui regnum Italiae Romanaque tellus
90   debetur.' tali Cyllenius ore locutus
mortalis visus medio sermone reliquit
et procul in tenuem ex oculis evanuit auram.
      at vero Aeneas aspectu obmutuit amens,
arrectaeque horrore comae et vox faucibus haesit.
95   ardet abire fuga dulcisque relinquere terras,
attonitus tanto monitu imperioque deorum.
heu, quid agat? quo nunc reginam ambire furentem
audeat adfatu? quae prima exordia sumat?
atque animum nunc huc celerem nunc dividit illuc
100   in partisque rapit varias perque omnia versat.

(Aeneid 4.259–86)

*Aeneas makes preparations to go, but still cannot find the right way
to break the news to Dido. She senses what is happening, and her
instinct is confirmed by Rumour. In a frenzy, she summons Aeneas
and speaks these words to him:*

      'dissimulare etiam sperasti, perfide, tantum
posse nefas tacitusque mea decedere terra?
nec te noster amor nec te data dextera quondam
nec moritura tenet crudeli funere Dido?
105   quin etiam hiberno moliris sidere classem
et mediis properas Aquilonibus ire per altum,
crudelis? quid, si non arva aliena domosque
ignotas peteres, et Troia antiqua maneret,
Troia per undosum peteretur classibus aequor?

74   **alatis ... plantis** 'with his winged feet'.

75   **fundantem** 'laying foundations for'. **tecta novantem** 'renewing buildings' = 'building new dwellings'.

76–7   **stellatus iaspide fulva/ensis** 'a sword starred with tawny jasper'.

77   **Tyrio ardebat murice laena** '(his) cloak was glowing with Tyrian dye'.

78–9   **dives ... fecerat = munera quae dives Dido fecerat**.

79   **tenui telas discreverat auro** 'had interwoven the fabric with fine (strands of) gold'.

80   **invadit** Mercury 'went for' him.

81   **fundamenta locas** 'are you laying the foundations?' **uxorius** 'enslaved to a wife'.

82   **heu ... oblite** 'alas, you who have forgotten ...' = 'alas that you have forgotten ...'.

83   **deum = deorum**.

84   **caelum ... qui ... torquet = qui caelum ... torquet. numine torquet** 'controls with his divine power'.

85   **iubet (me)**.

86   **struis** 'are you aiming at?' **teris otia** 'are you wasting your time?'

88   **heredis** 'of (your) heir'.

89   **respice** 'consider'.

90   **debetur** 'is owed', i.e. rule over Italy and the soil of Rome are being held in trust for Ascanius. Aeneas must pay his debt. **tali ... ore** 'with such a mouth' = 'with such words'. **Cyllenius** Mercury, born on Mount Cyllene in Arcadia.

91   **mortalis visus** 'the sight of men'.

92   **evanuit** 'he vanished'.

93   **aspectu obmutuit amens** 'was beside himself (**amens**) and dumbfounded at what he had seen'.

94   **arrectae (sunt) horrore comae** 'his hair stood on end with dread'. **faucibus haesit** 'stuck in his throat'.

95   **ardet** 'he is on fire', 'he longs'.

96   **attonitus** 'thunderstruck', 'dazed'.

97   **quid agat?** 'what was he to do?'

97–8   **quo ... ambire ... audeat adfatu** 'with what words (**quo adfatu**) could he have the courage to approach ...'.

98   **prima exordia** 'beginning (of a speech)'.

99   **celerem** 'rapidly' (adjective used adverbially).

100   **in partis ... varias** 'to all sorts of considerations'.

101   **sperasti = speravisti. perfide** 'traitor'.

102   **nefas** 'a sinful thing'.

103   **data ... quondam = dextera (manus) quondam data** 'your right hand once given me'. Bride and groom joined hands at a Roman marriage ceremony.

105   **quin etiam** 'what is more, are you even ...?' **hiberno ... sidere** 'in the wintry season'. **moliris ... classem** 'are you preparing your fleet?'

106   **mediis ... Aquilonibus** 'amid the north winds (of winter)'.

107   **quid, si** 'what if ...' = 'tell me, suppose that ...'. **arva aliena** 'foreign fields'.

109   **per undosum ... aequor** 'over the swollen sea'. Dido implies that Aeneas would not even return home (if home still existed) at this season. Can he really be thinking of sailing into the unknown in winter?

110 mene fugis? per ego has lacrimas dextramque tuam te
(quando aliud mihi iam miserae nihil ipsa reliqui),
per conubia nostra, per inceptos hymenaeos,
si bene quid de te merui, fuit aut tibi quicquam
dulce meum, miserere domus labentis, et istam,
115 oro, si quis adhuc precibus locus, exue mentem.

Because of you, the Libyan tribes and the Nomad chieftains
Hate me, the Tyrians are hostile: because of you I have lost
My old reputation for faithfulness – the one thing that could
    have made me
Immortal. Oh, I am dying! To what, my guest, are you leaving
    me?
120 'Guest' – that is all I may call you now, who have called you
    husband.
Why do I linger here? Shall I wait till my brother, Pygmalion,
Destroys this place, or Iarbas leads me away captive?

                                        (C. Day Lewis)

saltem si qua mihi de te suscepta fuisset
ante fugam suboles, si quis mihi parvulus aula
125 luderet Aeneas, qui te tamen ore referret,
non equidem omnino capta ac deserta viderer.'

                                (*Aeneid* 4.305–30)

The ruins of Troy

110–15 **per ego … te … oro** = **per has lacrimas … ego te … oro** (*l.* 115).
111 **quando** 'since'.
112 **conubia** 'union'. **inceptos hymenaeos** 'the marriage we have begun'.
113–14 **fuit … meum** 'or if there was anything about me that was sweet to you'.
114 **miserere** 'pity' (imperative of **misereor** + genitive). **domus labentis** 'slipping house' = 'doomed house'.
114–15 **istam … exue mentem** 'put off that mind' = 'give up that idea'.

123–4 **si qua … suboles** 'if a child (**suboles**) from you had been taken up by me (i.e. in my arms) before your flight'.
124 **parvulus** 'darling little'. **aula** 'in my hall'.
125 **te … ore referret** could bring you back with his face' = 'could remind me of you by his features'. **tamen** i.e. 'though you yourself have deserted me'.
126 **equidem** 'I indeed'. **capta ac deserta** 'cheated and abandoned'.

The story of Dido and Aeneas is told in a mosaic from Low Ham in Somerset

3 The death of Dido

Aeneas replies to Dido.

dixerat. ille Iovis monitis immota tenebat
lumina et obnixus curam sub corde premebat.
tandem pauca refert: 'ego te, quae plurima fando
enumerare vales, numquam, regina, negabo
5   promeritam, nec me meminisse pigebit Elissae
dum memor ipse mei, dum spiritus hos regit artus.
pro re pauca loquar. neque ego hanc abscondere furto
speravi (ne finge) fugam, nec coniugis umquam
praetendi taedas aut haec in foedera veni.
10 me si fata meis paterentur ducere vitam
auspiciis et sponte mea componere curas,
urbem Troianam primum dulcisque meorum
reliquias colerem, Priami tecta alta manerent,
et recidiva manu posuissem Pergama victis.
15 sed nunc Italiam magnam Gryneus Apollo,
Italiam Lyciae iussere capessere sortes;
hic amor, haec patria est. si te Karthaginis arces
Phoenissam Libycaeque aspectus detinet urbis,
quae tandem Ausonia Teucros considere terra
20 invidia est? et nos fas extera quaerere regna.
me patris Anchisae, quotiens umentibus umbris
nox operit terras, quotiens astra ignea surgunt,
admonet in somnis et turbida terret imago;
me puer Ascanius capitisque iniuria cari,
25 quem regno Hesperiae fraudo et fatalibus arvis.
nunc etiam interpres divum Iove missus ab ipso
(testor utrumque caput) celeris mandata per auras
detulit: ipse deum manifesto in lumine vidi
intrantem muros vocemque his auribus hausi.
30 desine meque tuis incendere teque querelis;
Italiam non sponte sequor.'

(*Aeneid* 4.331–61)

'pius' Aeneas takes his father and
son from the burning city of Troy

1 **monitis** 'because of the advice'.

2 **obnixus** 'with great effort'. **sub corde** 'deep in his heart.
premebat 'he stifled'.

3 **refert** 'he replies'.

3–5 **ego te ... promeritam = ego numquam negabo te promeritam
(esse) plurima quae fando enumerare vales** 'I shall never deny
that you have deserved (from me) as many things as you can
possibly list in speaking'.

5 **me meminisse pigebit** 'shall I be sorry to remember'. **Elissae**
Elissa is Dido's Tyrian name.

6 **dum (sum) memor**.

7 **pro re** 'for the situation' = 'pleading my case'. **abscondere furto** 'to
conceal with deceit'.

8 **ne finge** 'don't suppose (that)'.

8–9 **coniugis ... praetendi taedas** 'did I hold out a bridegroom's
torches'.

9 **haec ... foedera** 'this bond', i.e. marriage. A torchlight procession
escorted the bride and groom home after their wedding.

10–11 **meis ... auspiciis** 'by my own authority' = 'on my own terms'.

11 **sponte mea componere curas** 'to settle my cares to my liking'.

13 **colerem** 'I should be looking after'. **tecta**, *n.pl.* 'the palace'.

14 **recidiva ... Pergama** 'rebuilt Troy' (**Pergama**, *n.pl.* 'Troy'). **victis**
'for the conquered'.

15 **Gryneus Apollo** 'Grynian Apollo'. At Grynium in Lydia there was a
wood sacred to Apollo where Aeneas had consulted Apollo's oracle.

16 **Lyciae iussere (= iusserunt) capessere sortes** 'the oracle of Lycia
has ordered me to make for ...'. Lycia was Apollo's winter home.

17–18 **te ... Phoenissam** 'you, a Tyrian'.

18 **Libycae aspectus detinet urbis** 'the sight of the Libyan city (i.e.
Carthage) holds you (here)'.

19–20 **quae ... invidia est? = quae tandem invidia est Teucros
considere Ausonia terra** 'why, I ask you (**tandem**), do you resent
the Trojans' settling in Italian (**Ausonia**) territory?' (**quae ... invidia
est** literally, 'what is your grudge?').

20 **et** 'too', 'also'. **fas (est)** 'it is right'. **extera** 'foreign'.

21 **patris Anchisae ... imago** (*l.* 23) (**imago** 'the ghost of). **umentibus
umbris** 'with moist shadows'.

23 **turbida** 'troubled'.

24 **Ascanius** '(the thought of) Ascanius'. Supply **admonet**. **capitis
iniuria cari** 'the wrong of (= done to) his beloved head (= person)'.

25 **Hesperiae** 'of the Western Land' = 'of Italy'. **fraudo** (+ ablative)
'cheat of'. **fatalibus arvis** i.e. 'the land fated to be his'.

26 **interpres** 'the messenger'.

27 **testor utrumque caput** 'I call both of our heads (= both of us) to
witness'.

29 **hausi** 'I drank in', 'heard'.

31 **sponte** 'of my own accord'.

Dido replies furiously, with bitter complaints about his lack of humanity and his ingratitude. She refuses to believe that the gods have intervened and scornfully sends him on his way, hoping that he will die at sea with her name on his lips. Her ghost will pursue him to the underworld. She then runs from his sight.

        at pius Aeneas, quamquam lenire dolentem
        solando cupit et dictis avertere curas,
        multa gemens magnoque animum labefactus amore,
35   iussa tamen divum exsequitur classemque revisit.
        tum vero Teucri incumbunt et litore celsas
        deducunt toto navis. natat uncta carina,
        frondentisque ferunt remos et robora silvis
        infabricata fugae studio.
40   migrantis cernas totaque ex urbe ruentis.
        ac velut ingentem formicae farris acervum
        cum populant hiemis memores tectoque reponunt,
        it nigrum campis agmen praedamque per herbas
        convectant calle angusto; pars grandia trudunt
45   obnixae frumenta umeris, pars agmina cogunt
        castigantque moras, opere omnis semita fervet.
        quis tibi tum, Dido, cernenti talia sensus,
        quosve dabas gemitus, cum litora fervere late
        prospiceres arce ex summa, totumque videres
50   misceri ante oculos tantis clamoribus aequor!
        improbe Amor, quid non mortalia pectora cogis!
        ire iterum in lacrimas, iterum temptare precando
        cogitur et supplex animos summittere amori,
        ne quid inexpertum frustra moritura relinquat.

(Aeneid 4.393–415)

formica

Dido sends her sister Anna down to the harbour to plead with Aeneas to stay just long enough to enable her to come to terms with his departure. Aeneas, however, stands firm in his resolve to leave.

    Dido is now utterly determined to die. She pretends that a priestess has told her that she can find release from her love if she builds a great funeral pyre and puts on it her marriage bed and the arms and clothes which Aeneas has left behind. These, she claims, she must burn.

    Mercury now appears in a dream to Aeneas and tells him to leave at once. When she sees the Trojan ships sailing away, Dido calls down a terrible curse upon Aeneas. She says:

55   'Sol, qui terrarum flammis opera omnia lustras,
        tuque harum interpres curarum et conscia Iuno,
        nocturnisque Hecate triviis ululata per urbes
        et Dirae ultrices et di morientis Elissae,
        accipite haec, meritumque malis advertite numen

32 **lenire** 'to soothe'. **(eam) dolentem.**

33 **solando** 'by consoling her'.

34 **multa gemens** 'sighing much'. **animum labefactus** 'shaken to the heart'.

35 **iussa … divum exsequitur** 'he carries out the commands of the gods'.

36 **Teucri incumbunt** 'the Trojans get down to work'.

37 **natat uncta carina** 'the well-tarred vessel is afloat' (**carina** is a poetic singular for plural).

38–9 **frondentis** 'with leaves on'. **infabricata** 'unfinished'. They have time neither to strip all the leaves from the branches which they use as oars nor to finish shaping the timber.

40 **migrantis cernas** 'you could have seen (them) on the move'.

41–2 **velut … cum** 'just as when'. **ingentem … farris acervum** 'a huge heap of grain'. **formicae** 'ants'. **populant** 'pillage' = 'take as plunder'. What imagery is used throughout this simile, i.e. what are the ants implicitly compared to?

43 **campis** 'over the plain'.

44 **calle** 'on a path'. **pars … pars … = alii … alii … . grandia** 'vast'.

45 **obnixae** 'with great effort'. **cogunt** 'marshal'.

46 **castigant moras** 'they punish delays' = 'discipline the stragglers'. **fervet** 'boils' = 'is in a ferment of activity'.

47 **quis … sensus = quis tum sensus (fuit) tibi, Dido, cernenti talia.**

49 **prospiceres** 'you looked out at …'.

49–50 **totum … misceri … aequor** 'the whole sea mixed up' = 'the whole sea a mass of confusion'.

51 **quid** 'to what (extremes)'.

53 **supplex animos summittere amori** 'to submit her (proud) spirit to her love as a suppliant (i.e. to Aeneas)'.

54 **frustra moritura** i.e. 'and so die in vain'. If Aeneas would come back to her, she need not die.

55 **terrarum** translate with **opera omnia**. **lustras** 'light up'.

56 **interpres … et conscia** 'mediator and witness'.

57 **nocturnis Hecate triviis ululata** 'Hecate whose name is shrieked at the crossroads at night'. Hecate is a goddess of the underworld, associated with black magic. **per urbes** 'through the cities' = 'in every city'.

58 **Dirae ultrices** 'avenging Furies'. **Elissae** i.e. of Dido.

59 **meritum malis advertite numen** 'turn to my wrongs the divine power I deserve' = 'turn your power upon my wrongs, the power they are entitled to'.

60 et nostras audite preces. si tangere portus
infandum caput et terris adnare necesse est,
et sic fata Iovis poscunt, hic terminus haeret,
at bello audacis populi vexatus et armis,
finibus extorris, complexu avulsus Iuli,
65 auxilium imploret videatque indigna suorum
funera; nec, cum se sub leges pacis iniquae
tradiderit, regno aut optata luce fruatur,
sed cadat ante diem mediaque inhumatus harena.
haec precor, hanc vocem extremam cum sanguine fundo.
70 tum vos, o Tyrii, stirpem et genus omne futurum
exercete odiis, cinerique haec mittite nostro
munera. nullus amor populis nec foedera sunto.
exoriare aliquis nostris ex ossibus ultor
qui face Dardanios ferroque sequare colonos,
75 nunc, olim, quocumque dabunt se tempore vires.
litora litoribus contraria, fluctibus undas
imprecor, arma armis: pugnent ipsique nepotesque.'

(Aeneid 4.607–29)

Dido now sends for her sister.

at trepida et coeptis immanibus effera Dido
sanguineam volvens aciem, maculisque trementis
80 interfusa genas et pallida morte futura,
interiora domus inrumpit limina et altos
conscendit furibunda gradus ensemque recludit
Dardanium, non hos quaesitum munus in usus.
hic, postquam Iliacas vestis notumque cubile
85 conspexit, paulum lacrimis et mente morata
incubuitque toro dixitque novissima verba:
'dulces exuviae, dum fata deusque sinebat,
accipite hanc animam meque his exsolvite curis.
vixi et quem dederat cursum fortuna peregi,

Dido on her pyre

60–61	**si … necesse est = si necesse est infandum caput tangere portus**.
61	**infandum caput** '(for that) unspeakable being'. Dido will not name Aeneas. **terris adnare** 'to sail to land'.
62	**hic terminus haeret** 'this bound stands firmly fixed', i.e. there is no possibility of passing the boundary stone set by fate.
63–8	All of these curses were fulfilled. Aeneas was harried by the Italian tribe, the Rutuli. He never saw Troy again. He left Iulus in order to seek help from Evander. He saw many of his men die. The peace he made with the Italians was far from favourable to the Trojans. He ruled his people for only three years, and he either drowned in a river or was killed in a battle and his body not recovered.
63	**at** 'even so'. **bello … et armis** 'by armed conflict with' (hendiadys, i.e. the two nouns are used to express a single idea).
64	**finibus extorris** 'exiled from his home', i.e. Troy. **avulsus** 'torn from'.
65	**imploret** 'may he beg'.
66	**sub leges pacis iniquae** 'under the conditions of an unjust peace'.
67	**luce** i.e. 'the light of life'.
68	**ante diem** 'before his day'. **harena** 'on the sand'. She visualizes him lying shipwrecked on a beach, with no hope of being buried and thus finding rest in the underworld.
70	**genus** i.e. of the Trojans.
71	**exercete** 'harass'.
72	**sunto** 'let there be'.
73	**exoriare (= exoriaris) … ultor** 'may you arise, some avenger, from my bones'.
74	**face … ferroque** 'with firebrand and the sword'. **qui … Dardanios … sequare (= sequaris) colonos** 'who may harry the Trojan settlers'.
75	**olim** 'at some time'. **quocumque … vires = quocumque tempore vires se dabunt** 'at whatever time strength offers (itself)'.
76–7	**contraria … imprecor** 'I pray for … in conflict with …'.
77	**ipsi nepotesque** 'themselves and their sons' sons'.
78	**coeptis immanibus effera** 'wild in her dreadful design'.
79	**sanguineam … aciem** 'her bloodshot eyes'.
79–80	**maculis trementis/interfusa genas** 'her quivering cheeks blotched with stains (of red)'.
80	**pallida** 'pale at'.
81	**interiora … limina** 'inner door' (poetic plural). The pyre is in a courtyard of the palace.
82	**furibunda** 'in a frenzy'. **gradus** 'the steps' (to the top of the pyre). **ensem recludit** 'unsheathes a sword'.
83	i.e. Dido had asked Aeneas for the Trojan sword but had not intended to use it for this purpose.
84	**notum cubile** 'the familiar bed'.
85	**lacrimis et mente** 'in tearful thought' (hendiadys).
86	**novissima** 'last'.
87	**exuviae** 'things he sloughed off' = 'things which once were his'. **dulces … dum** 'dear, as long as'.
89	**quem … peregi = peregi** (= 'I have completed') **cursum quem fortuna dederat**.

90   et nunc magna mei sub terras ibit imago.
        urbem praeclaram statui, mea moenia vidi,
        ulta virum poenas inimico a fratre recepi,
        felix, heu nimium felix, si litora tantum
        numquam Dardaniae tetigissent nostra carinae.'
95   dixit, et os impressa toro 'moriemur inultae,
        sed moriamur' ait. 'sic, sic iuvat ire sub umbras.
        hauriat hunc oculis ignem crudelis ab alto
        Dardanus, et nostrae secum ferat omina mortis.'
           dixerat, atque illam media inter talia ferro
100   conlapsam aspiciunt comites, ensemque cruore
        spumantem sparsasque manus. it clamor ad alta
        atria: concussam bacchatur Fama per urbem.
        lamentis gemituque et femineo ululatu
        tecta fremunt, resonat magnis plangoribus aether,
105   non aliter quam si immissis ruat hostibus omnis
        Karthago aut antiqua Tyros, flammaeque furentes
        culmina perque hominum volvantur perque deorum.

                        (*Aeneid* 4.642–71)

Anna's lament.

        audiit exanimis trepidoque exterrita cursu
        unguibus ora soror foedans et pectora pugnis
110   per medios ruit, ac morientem nomine clamat:
        'hoc illud, germana, fuit? me fraude petebas?
        hoc rogus iste mihi, hoc ignes araeque parabant?
        quid primum deserta querar? comitemne sororem
        sprevisti moriens? eadem me ad fata vocasses:
115   idem ambas ferro dolor atque eadem hora tulisset.
        his etiam struxi manibus patriosque vocavi
        voce deos, sic te ut posita, crudelis, abessem?
        exstinxti te meque, soror, populumque patresque
        Sidonios urbemque tuam. date vulnera lymphis
120   abluam et, extremus si quis super halitus errat,
        ore legam.' sic fata gradus evaserat altos,

90 **sub** (+ accusative) includes the idea of motion towards. **mei ... imago** 'the ghost of me' = 'my ghost'.

91 **statui** 'I set up', 'founded'.

92 **poenas recepi** 'I exacted punishment'.

93 **heu nimium felix, si ... tantum** 'alas, too happy, if only ...'.

94 **Dardaniae ... carinae** 'the Trojan keels (= ships)'. King Dardanus was the founder of the Trojan race.

95 **os impressa toro** 'pressing her face in the bed'. **moriemur ...** Dido uses the royal 'we'.

96 **iuvat** 'it pleases me' = 'I choose'.

97 **hauriat** 'let him drink in (the sight of)'. **ab alto** 'from the high sea'.

98 **Dardanus** 'the Trojan' (= Aeneas).

100 **conlapsam** '(her) having fallen on'. **comites** her friends watch from the ground, powerless to help.

–101 **ensem cruore/spumantem** 'the sword foaming with blood'.

101 **sparsas manus** '(her) hands spattered (with blood)'.

102 **concussam ... urbem** 'the stricken city'. **bacchatur Fama** 'Rumour runs wildly'.

103 **lamentis ... ululatu** 'with lamentations and groaning and the wailing of women'.

104 **plangoribus** 'with sounds of mourning'. **aether** 'the high heaven'. **non aliter quam si** 'not otherwise than if' = 'just as if'. **immissis ruat**

105 **hostibus** 'were falling, after the enemy had been sent in' = 'had broken in'.

106 **Tyros** (nominative feminine) 'Tyre'.

107 **culmina ... deorum** = **perque culmina hominum perque (culmina) deorum**.

108 **exanimis** 'out of her mind'. **trepido ... cursu** 'in her panic-stricken running'. Anna makes straight for the scene.

109 **ora ... foedans** 'marring her face with her finger-nails'; **ora** is a poetic plural. **pugnis** 'with her fists' (from **pugnus**).

110 **morientem (Didonem)**.

111 **hoc illud ... fuit?** 'was this (what all) that (pretence of yours meant)?' **fraude** 'in deceit'. **petebas** i.e. my help.

112 **hoc ... hoc** the objects of **parabant** (= 'had in store').

113 **querar** deliberative subjunctive. **comitem** i.e. 'as your companion'.

114 **eadem ... ad fata** 'to the same fate (as yourself)'. **vocasses** (= **vocavisses**) 'you should have called'.

115 **ferro ... tulisset** 'should have taken (us both) off with the sword'.

116 **struxi** 'did I build (the pyre)'.

117 **sic ... abessem = ut abessem te sic posita** ('from you, placed thus (in death)'), **crudelis**.

118 **exstinxti** (= **exstinxisti**) 'you have destroyed'.

9–20 **date (ut) ... abluam** 'grant that I may wash' = 'let me wash. **lymphis** 'with water'.

120 **extremus ... halitus = si quis extremus halitus** 'if any last breath'. **super** 'left over', i.e. 'still'.

121 **legam** 'let me catch it'. **fata** 'having spoken'. **evaserat** 'she had climbed'.

semianimemque sinu germanam amplexa fovebat
cum gemitu atque atros siccabat veste cruores.
illa, gravis oculos conata attollere, rursus
125   deficit; infixum stridit sub pectore vulnus.
ter sese attollens cubitoque adnixa levavit,
ter revoluta toro est oculisque errantibus alto
quaesivit caelo lucem ingemuitque reperta.
tum Iuno omnipotens longum miserata dolorem
130   difficilisque obitus Irim demisit Olympo
quae luctantem animam nexosque resolveret artus.
nam quia nec fato merita nec morte peribat,
sed misera ante diem subitoque accensa furore,
nondum illi flavum Proserpina vertice crinem
135   abstulerat Stygioque caput damnaverat Orco.
ergo Iris croceis per caelum roscida pennis
mille trahens varios adverso sole colores
devolat et supra caput astitit. 'hunc ego Diti
sacrum iussa fero teque isto corpore solvo.'
140   sic ait et dextra crinem secat: omnis et una
dilapsus calor atque in ventos vita recessit.

Iris

(*Aeneid* 4.672–705)

122 **semianimem … fovebat** 'embracing her still-living (literally, half alive) sister in her arms, she caressed her'.

123 **atros siccabat … cruores** 'she tried to staunch the dark blood'.

124 **illa** i.e. Dido.

125 **deficit** 'she failed'. **infixum** 'driven in', 'deep'. **stridit** 'hissed'.

126 **cubito adnixa levavit** 'supporting herself on her elbow, she lifted herself up'.

127 **revoluta toro est** 'she fell back on the bed'.

128 **(luce) reperta**.

129 **miserata** 'pitying'.

130 **difficilis obitus** 'her difficult death'. Iris, Juno's messenger, is the goddess of the rainbow.

131 **nexos … artus** 'close-locked limbs'.

132 **merita nec morte** = nec merita morte.

133 **ante diem** 'before her time'. **accensa** 'on fire with'.

134-5 **illi flavum … vertice crinem/abstulerat** 'had taken away from her the golden locks on her head' = 'had taken a golden lock from her hair'. The goddess Proserpina would cut off a lock of hair from someone who died normally, as if from an animal to be sacrificed.

135 **Stygio caput damnaverat Orco** 'had condemned her life to Stygian Orcus'. **Orcus** another name for Dis or Pluto, the king of the underworld.

136 **croceis … roscida pennis** 'dewy on her saffron wings' = 'with dew on her saffron wings'.

137 **adverso sole** 'as the sun shone on her'.

138 **supra** 'above'. **hunc** i.e. the lock of hair.

139 **iussa** '(as I have been) ordered'.

40-41 **omnis … calor** = et una omnis calor dilapsus **(est)** 'and together (with the lock) all heat slipped from her'.

LIVY

In the middle of the first century BC, Cicero complained that there was no good history of Rome. Livy, the English name for Titus Livius (59 BC–AD 17), supplied this need with the monumental work to which he devoted most of his life. The 142 books of his *History of Rome* covered the time from the foundation of the city to 9 BC. Most of this great history has been lost.

Livy was on good terms with the emperor Augustus, but his work is certainly not Augustan propaganda. He wrote out of a passionate love for traditional Roman values, illustrating the qualities that had brought the nation to greatness, and describing what he saw as its moral decline. In his account of the Second Punic War, he writes with a grim admiration of Hannibal, the great Carthaginian general who almost extinguished these values together with the city itself. His comments on the value of history are interesting: 'What makes the study of history a particularly helpful medicine is that it sets before you a clear record of the infinite variety of human experience. This enables you to find models for yourself and your country to imitate, as well as courses of action which were disgraceful from start to finish and should be avoided.' History is good for you because it educates you.

Hannibal

In the last chapter, you read the terrible curses which Dido called down upon Aeneas and his descendants. She ended her speech with these dreadful words:

exoriare aliquis nostris ex ossibus ultor
qui face Dardanios ferroque sequare colonos,
nunc, olim, quocumque dabunt se tempore vires.
litora litoribus contraria, fluctibus undas
imprecor, arma armis: pugnent ipsique nepotesque.

In our chapters from Livy's *History*, we see how this part of her curse was fulfilled. The description of Hannibal's crossing of the Alps is one of the highlights of Livy's work. This historian is always exciting and he has the gift of making his readers live through the events he describes. He conveys with startling immediacy the despair of the Carthaginians on the frozen heights of the Alps, and then, as Hannibal moves forward onto a ridge and addresses his troops, the historian vividly illustrates the qualities which go to make a great general. Livy responds with wide-eyed admiration to the epic nature of Hannibal's journey and conveys the dreadful threat posed by an enemy which was to test the courage and determination of the Romans to the full.

Carthage

1 Hannibal prepares to invade Italy

Livy introduces the greatest war in history.

in parte operis mei licet mihi praefari bellum maxime omnium
memorabile quae unquam gesta sint me scripturum, quod
Hannibale duce Carthaginienses cum populo Romano gessere.
nam neque validiores opibus ullae inter se civitates gentesque
5   contulerunt arma neque his ipsis tantum unquam virium aut
roboris fuit; et haud ignotas belli artes inter sese sed expertas
primo Punico conferebant bello, et adeo varia fortuna belli fuit ut
propius periculum fuerint qui vicerunt. odiis etiam prope
maioribus certarunt quam viribus, Romanis indignantibus quod
10 victoribus victi ultro inferrent arma, Poenis quod superbe avareque
crederent imperitatum victis esse.

(21.1.1–3)

*The young Hannibal swears an oath of undying hatred against the
Romans.*

fama est etiam Hannibalem annorum ferme novem, pueriliter
blandientem patri Hamilcari ut duceretur in Hispaniam, cum
exercitum eo traiecturus sacrificaret, altaribus admotum, tactis
15 sacris, iure iurando adactum se cum primum posset hostem fore
populo Romano.
       mors Hamilcaris peropportuna et pueritia Hannibalis
distulerunt bellum. medius Hasdrubal inter patrem ac filium octo
ferme annos imperium obtinuit.

(21.1.4, 2.3)

*Livy describes how Hannibal was greeted in Spain when he joined
Hasdrubal there. The character of Hannibal.*

20 missus Hannibal in Hispaniam primo statim adventu omnem
exercitum in se convertit; Hamilcarem iuvenem redditum sibi
veteres milites credere; eundem vigorem in vultu vimque in oculis
intueri. dein brevi effecit ut pater in se minimum momentum ad
favorem conciliandum esset.
25   nunquam ingenium idem ad res diversissimas, parendum atque
imperandum, habilius fuit. itaque haud facile discerneres utrum
imperatori an exercitui carior esset; neque Hasdrubal alium
quemquam praeficere malle ubi quid fortiter ac strenue agendum
esset, neque milites alio duce plus confidere aut audere. plurimum
30 audaciae ad pericula capessenda, plurimum consilii inter ipsa

1   **in parte** i.e. 'in this part'. **praefari** 'to state first'.

1–2   **bellum maxime … memorabile** 'the most remarkable war'.

2   **me scripturum (esse)** indirect statement after **praefari** (**scribo** 'write about', 'tell the story of').

3   **gessere = gesserunt.**

4   **validiores opibus** 'stronger in resources'.

5–6   **neque his ipsis tantum unquam virium aut roboris fuit** 'and not (even) was there ever so much strength and vigour to themselves' = 'and the Romans and Carthaginians themselves were at the peak of their power'.

6–7   **haud ignotas belli artes … conferebant** 'they brought together not unknown skills of warfare' = 'they were by no means strangers to each other's methods of fighting'. **expertas** 'practised'. **primo Punico … bello** the First Punic War lasted from 265 to 241 BC. The Romans had won the war and gained, in Sicily, the beginnings of an overseas empire.

8   **propius periculum** 'rather close to defeat'. **qui vicerunt = ei qui vicerunt**, i.e. the Romans. **prope** 'almost'.

9   **certarunt = certaverunt. indignantibus** from **indignor** (1) 'I am indignant that'.

10   **ultro** 'unprovoked'. **Poenis** 'Carthaginians'.

10–11   **superbe avareque … imperitatum victis esse** 'that when they had been conquered they had been treated (literally, ordered about) with lordly arrogance and greed'. **imperitatum … esse** impersonal use of passive.

12–13   **Hannibalem … pueriliter blandientem** (+ dat.) 'Hannibal, childishly coaxing'.

13   **Hamilcari** the leading Carthaginian general. **Hispania** 'Spain'.

14   **eo** i.e. to Spain. **traiecturus** 'on the point of crossing' (from Carthage to Spain). **altaribus** 'the altar' (plural for singular). **admotum** agrees with **Hannibalem** (*l.* 12).

15   **sacris** 'the sacred objects'. **iure iurando adactum (esse)** 'was made to swear an oath'. **se** 'that he' (Hannibal). **cum primum** 'as soon as'.

17   **peropportuna** 'very timely'.

18   **distulerunt** 'postponed'. **Hasdrubal** Hamilcar's son-in-law.

19   **obtinuit** 'held'.

21   **in se convertit** 'turned upon himself' = 'attracted the attention of'. **redditum (esse).**

22   **credere** 'they (the old soldiers) believed' (historic infinitive). **vigorem** 'liveliness'.

23   **intueri** 'they saw' (historic infinitive). **brevi** understand **tempore. in se** 'in his case'. **minimum momentum** 'of very little importance'.

26   **habilius** 'more adaptable'. **haud facile discerneres** 'one (literally, you) could not easily have distinguished'.

28   **malle** 'preferred' (historic infinitive).

28–9   **ubi quid … esset** 'whenever anything was …'.

29   **confidere, audere** historic infinitives.

30   **capessenda** from **capesso** 'I grasp', 'grapple with'.

pericula erat. nullo labore aut corpus fatigari aut animus vinci
poterat. caloris ac frigoris patientia par; cibi potionisque desiderio
naturali, non voluptate modus finitus; vigiliarum somnique nec die
nec nocte discriminata tempora. multi saepe militari sagulo
35   opertum humi iacentem inter custodias stationesque militum
conspexerunt. equitum peditumque idem longe primus erat;
princeps in proelium ibat, ultimus conserto proelio excedebat.

   has tantas viri virtutes ingentia vitia aequabant, inhumana
crudelitas, perfidia plus quam Punica, nihil veri, nihil sancti,
40   nullus deum metus, nulla religio. cum hac indole virtutum atque
vitiorum triennio sub Hasdrubale imperatore meruit, nulla re quae
agenda videndaque magno futuro duci esset praetermissa.

(21.4)

*In 221 BC Hasdrubal was murdered and Hannibal was chosen as
his successor. According to Livy, it was already Hannibal's
ambition to conquer Italy. In 219 BC he laid siege to Saguntum, a
Spanish city which was allied to Rome, and captured it. War
between Rome and Carthage was now inevitable.*

Hannibal gives his Spanish troops leave to go home for the winter.

Saguntum

Hannibal Sagunto capto Carthaginem Novam in hiberna
concesserat, ibique auditis quae Romae quaeque Carthagine acta
45   decretaque forent, seque non ducem solum sed etiam causam esse
belli, partitis divenditisque reliquiis praedae, nihil ultra differendum
ratus, Hispani generis milites convocat.

   'credo ego vos,' inquit, 'socii, et ipsos cernere pacatis omnibus
Hispaniae populis aut finiendam nobis militiam exercitusque
50   dimittendos esse aut in alias terras transferendum bellum. itaque
cum longinqua ab domo instet militia incertumque sit quando
domos vestras visuri sitis, si quis vestrum suos invisere vult,
commeatum do. primo vere edico adsitis, ut dis bene iuvantibus
bellum ingentis gloriae praedaeque futurum incipiamus.' omnibus

31 **erat** supply **ei**: 'there was to him' = 'he had'.

32 **patientia** 'endurance': supply **erat**.

32–3 **cibi potionisque … modus finitus** 'his appetite for food and drink was limited …'. **desiderio naturali** 'by natural desire'.

33 **vigiliarum** and **somni** are dependent on **tempora** (**vigiliae**, *f.pl.* 'waking').

34 **discriminata (sunt)** 'were marked off'. **militari sagulo** 'with a military cloak'.

35 **opertum** '(him) covered'. **inter custodias stationesque** 'amid the guard-posts and the sentry-stations' (i.e. not in the **praetorium**).

36 **idem** 'the same man', i.e. 'in the same way, he (Hannibal) …'.

37 **conserto proelio** 'when battle was joined'.

39 **Punica** 'Carthaginian'. (*Punica fides* was a proverbial expression for 'treachery'). **nihil veri** 'nothing of truth'. **nihil sancti** 'nothing of sanctity', i.e. he showed no sense of truth and no sense of sanctity.

40 **cum hac indole** 'with this character'.

41 **triennio** 'for three years'.

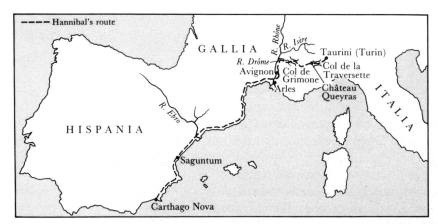

Hannibal's route to Italy

43 **Carthaginem Novam** New Carthage, now Cartagena, was a town on the south-east coast of Spain, founded by the Carthaginians.

44–5 **auditis quae … forent** = **eis** ('those things') **auditis quae … acta decretaque forent**; translate **forent** as **essent**.

45 **seque … ducem … esse** 'and (hearing) that he was the leader …'.

46 **partitis divenditisque reliquiis** 'having divided out the rest or sold it piecemeal'.

46–7 **nihil ultra differendum (esse) ratus** 'thinking that he should postpone matters no further'.

48 **et ipsos** 'yourselves (also)', i.e. as I do.

48–9 **pacatis … populis** 'the tribes having been won over'. **omnibus Hispaniae populis** Hannibal had in fact conquered only the hostile Spanish tribes who lived south of the Ebro.

49 **militiam** 'campaign'.

53 **commeatum** 'military leave', 'furlough'. **edico adsitis** supply **ut**: 'I order you to be here'.

54 **bellum ingentis gloriae praedaeque futurum** 'a war which will be one of (i.e. bringing) great glory and great booty'.

55 fere visendi domos oblata ultro potestas grata erat. per totum tempus
hiemis quies inter labores aut iam exhaustos aut mox exhauriendos
renovavit corpora animosque ad omnia de integro patienda; vere
primo ad edictum convenere.

(21.21.1–8)

*In May 218 BC, Hannibal crossed the Ebro. In July and August he
crossed the Pyrenees and was then confronted with the wide river
Rhône.*

*Hannibal sends a detachment of his men to cross over the river
upstream and attack the enemy on the far bank from behind.*

iamque omnibus satis comparatis ad traiciendum terrebant ex
60 adverso hostes omnem ripam equites virique obtinentes. quos ut
averteret, Hannonem vigilia prima noctis cum parte copiarum,
maxime Hispanis, adverso flumine ire iter unius diei iubet et, ubi
primum possit quam occultissime traiecto amni, circumducere
agmen ut adoriatur ab tergo hostes. ad id dati duces Galli edocent
65 inde milia quinque et viginti ferme supra parvae insulae
circumfusum amnem minus alto alveo transitum ostendere.
   ibi raptim caesa materia ratesque fabricatae in quibus equi virique
et alia onera traicerentur. Hispani sine ulla mole flumen tranavere. et
alius exercitus ratibus iunctis traiectus, castris prope flumen positis,
70 nocturno itinere atque operis labore fessus quiete unius diei reficitur,
intento duce ad consilium opportune exsequendum. postero die
profecti, ex loco edito fumo significant transisse et haud procul
abesse; quod ubi accepit Hannibal, dat signum ad traiciendum.
   navium agmen, ad excipiendum adversi impetum fluminis, parte
75 superiore transmittens tranquillitatem infra traicientibus lintribus
praebebat. Galli occursant in ripa cum variis ululatibus cantuque
moris sui, quatientes scuta super capita vibrantesque dextris tela,
quamquam ex adverso terrebat tanta vis navium cum ingenti sono
fluminis et clamore vario nautarum militumque, et qui nitebantur
80 perrumpere impetum fluminis et qui ex altera ripa traicientes suos
hortabantur.
   iam satis paventes adverso tumultu terribilior ab tergo adortus
clamor, castris ab Hannone captis. mox et ipse aderat ancepsque
terror circumstabat, et e navibus tanta vi armatorum in terram
85 evadente et ab tergo improvisa premente acie. Galli postquam
utroque vim facere conati pellebantur, qua patere visum maxime iter
perrumpunt trepidique in vicos passim suos diffugiunt. Hannibal,
ceteris copiis per otium traiectis, spernens iam Gallicos tumultus
castra locat.

(21.27.1–8, 28.1–4)

55 **fere** 'almost'. **visendi … potestas** 'opportunity of seeing'. **ultro** 'unasked'.

56 **aut iam exhaustos aut mox exhauriendos** 'which they had already endured and which they soon had to endure'.

57 **de integro** 'afresh'.

58 **ad edictum** 'in accordance with his command'. **convenere = convenerunt**.

9–60 **ex adverso** 'on the other side'.

60 **viri = pedites**.

61 **averteret** 'he might draw them off'. **Hannonem** the nominative of this name is **Hanno**.

62 **adverso flumine** 'with the river against them' = 'upstream'.

63 **traiecto amni** 'after crossing the river'.

64 **ad id dati** 'appointed for this purpose'.

64–6 **edocent … amnem … transitum ostendere** 'told them that … the river … afforded a crossing'. **supra** 'above' = 'upstream'. **minus alto alveo** 'because of its shallower channel'.

67 **caesa (est)**. **materia** 'timber'.

68 **sine ulla mole** 'without any trouble, difficulty'. **tranavere** 'swam across'.

69 **alius exercitus** 'the rest of the army'. **ratibus iunctis** 'on the rafts which they had made'.

70 **nocturno itinere** 'by the night march'. **operis** 'of the construction work', i.e. the raft-building. **reficitur** 'was restored, rested'.

71 **intento duce ad** 'the general (being) intent on …, eager to …'. **exsequendum** from **exsequor** 'I carry out'.

72 **ex loco edito** 'from a high place'. **fumo** 'by a smoke signal'.

72–3 **transisse … abesse** understand **se** as the subject of these infinitives.

74–5 **navium agmen … parte superiore transmittens** 'sending across the column of ships upstream'. **ad excipiendum adversi impetum fluminis** 'in order to take the force of the current' (literally, the onslaught of the river against them).

75 **tranquillitatem** 'calm water'. **infra** 'below' = 'downstream'. **lintribus** 'for the small boats'. Hannibal is the subject of **praebebat**.

76 **ululatibus** 'with war-whoops'. **cantu** 'with singing'.

77 **moris sui** 'of their custom' = 'in their customary manner'. **vibrantes** 'shaking'. **dextris** 'in their right hands'.

78 **ex adverso** 'opposite them'.

80 **traicientes** agrees with **suos**.

82 **iam satis paventes adverso tumultu** 'as they (the Gauls) were already extremely frightened by the noise to their front'.

2–3 **paventes … clamor = (eos) paventes adortus (est)** ('assailed') **clamor**. The shouting which arose 'hit' them.

3–4 **anceps terror** 'a twofold terror'.

4–5 **vi … evadente** 'a force coming out (of the river)'.

85 **improvisa … acie** 'an unexpected line' = 'troops …' = 'troops unexpectedly …'.

86 **utroque vim facere** 'to fight in both directions'. **pellebantur** 'they were being driven back'. **qua patere visum (est) maxime iter** 'where the way seemed most to lie open' = 'by the route which seemed to offer the best escape'.

88 **per otium** 'undisturbed'.

2 Hannibal reaches the Alps

Hannibal's men are confronted by the fearsome sight of the Alps.

Hannibal ab Druentia, campestri maxime itinere, ad Alpes cum
bona pace incolentium ea loca Gallorum pervenit. tum ex
propinquo visa montium altitudo nivesque caelo prope immixtae,
tecta informia imposita rupibus, pecora iumentaque torrida frigore,
5 homines intonsi et inculti, animalia inanimaque omnia rigentia gelu
terrorem renovarunt.

(21.32.6–7)

The Alps

*The mountain people threaten Hannibal's advance; he sends his
spies among them.*

erigentibus in primos agmen clivos apparuerunt imminentes
tumulos insidentes montani, qui, si valles occultiores insedissent,
coorti ad pugnam repente, ingentem fugam stragemque dedissent.
10   Hannibal consistere signa iussit; Gallisque ad visenda loca
praemissis, postquam comperit transitum ea non esse, castra quam
extentissima potest valle locat. tum per eosdem Gallos, haud sane
multum lingua moribusque abhorrentes, cum se immiscuissent
conloquiis montanorum, edoctus interdiu tantum obsideri saltum,
15 nocte in sua quemque dilabi tecta, luce prima subiit tumulos, ut ex
aperto atque interdiu vim per angustias facturus.

(21.32.8–10)

1   **Druentia** the river Durance. **maxime** 'for the most part'.

2   **ea loca**, *n.pl.* 'those places' (the object of **incolentium**).

3   **visa** agrees with **altitudo**, the first noun in the list, but it should be taken with all the subjects of **renovarunt**: 'the sight of (all these things) renewed their terror'. **nives … prope immixtae** 'the snow (literally, the snows) almost merging with …'.

4   **tecta informia** 'shapeless huts'. **torrida** 'frost-bitten'.

5   **intonsi et inculti** 'shaggy and shabby'. **inanima** 'inanimate objects'. **rigentia gelu** 'stiff with cold'.

6   **renovarunt = renovaverunt**.

7   **erigentibus in primos agmen clivos** 'to them leading their column up into the first slopes' = 'as their column began to climb the first slopes'.

7–8 **imminentes tumulos insidentes** 'occupying the overhanging hill-tops'.

8   **montani** 'mountain dwellers' (the subject of the sentence).

9   **coorti** 'springing out'.

10   **consistere signa iussit** 'he ordered the standards to halt' = 'he ordered a (general) halt'. **Gallis** these were the Gauls serving in Hannibal's army.

11   **transitum ea (via) non esse** 'that there was no crossing that way' = 'that it was impossible to cross there'.

1–12 **quam extentissima potest valle** 'in the broadest valley he could find'.

2–13 **haud sane multum … abhorrentes** 'not very different' (i.e. from the Gauls of the neighbourhood).

3–14 **cum se immiscuissent conloquiis montanorum** 'when they had mixed themselves in the conversations of the mountain people' = 'when they had infiltrated the mountain people and picked up their conversations'.

15   **dilabi** 'melted away'. **ut** (+ future participle) 'as though in order to'.

5–16 **ex aperto** 'openly'.

16   **vim per angustias facturus** 'to force his way through the narrow pass'.

Fighting with barbarians

Hannibal's stratagem.

die deinde simulando aliud quam quod parabatur consumpto, cum
eodem quo constiterant loco castra communissent, ubi primum
degressos tumulis montanos laxatasque sensit custodias, pluribus
20 ignibus quam pro numero manentium in speciem factis
impedimentisque cum equite relictis et maxima parte peditum, ipse
cum expeditis raptim angustias evadit iisque ipsis tumulis quos
hostes tenuerant consedit.
　　prima deinde luce castra mota et agmen reliquum incedere
25 coepit. iam montani signo dato ex castellis ad stationem solitam
conveniebant, cum repente conspiciunt alios arce occupata sua
super caput imminentes, alios via transire hostes. utraque simul
obiecta res oculis animisque immobiles parumper eos defixit;
deinde, ut trepidationem in angustiis suoque ipsum tumultu misceri
30 agmen videre, quidquid adiecissent ipsi terroris satis ad perniciem
fore rati, diversis rupibus decurrunt.

(21.32.11–33.4)

A narrow escape.

tum vero simul ab hostibus, simul ab iniquitate locorum Poeni
oppugnabantur, plusque inter ipsos, sibi quoque tendente ut
periculo prius evaderet, quam cum hostibus certaminis erat. et equi
35 maxime infestum agmen faciebant, qui et clamoribus dissonis, quos
nemora etiam repercussaeque valles augebant, territi trepidabant,
et icti forte aut vulnerati adeo consternabantur, ut stragem
ingentem simul hominum ac sarcinarum omnis generis facerent;
multosque turba, cum praecipites utrimque angustiae essent, in
40 immensum altitudinis deiecit; et iumenta cum oneribus
devolvebantur.
　　quae quamquam foeda visu erant, stetit parumper tamen
Hannibal ac suos continuit, ne tumultum ac trepidationem augeret;
deinde, postquam interrumpi agmen vidit, decurrit ex superiore
45 loco et, cum impetu ipso fudisset hostem, suis quoque tumultum
auxit. sed is tumultus momento temporis, postquam liberata itinera
fuga montanorum erant, sedatur, nec per otium modo sed prope
silentio mox omnes traducti.
　　castellum inde, quod caput eius regionis erat, viculosque
50 circumiectos capit et capto cibo ac pecoribus per triduum exercitum
aluit; et, quia nec montanis primo perculsis nec loco magno opere
impediebantur, aliquantum eo triduo viae confecit.

(21.33.5–11)

17 **simulando** 'in pretending (to do)'. **aliud quam quod parabatur**
'something other than what was being prepared'.

19 **laxatas … custodias** 'they had relaxed their vigilance'.

9–20 **pluribus ignibus quam pro numero manentium** 'more fires
than in proportion to (= were needed by) the number of those who
stayed', i.e. he lit more fires than necessary.

20 **in speciem** 'as a pretence'.

22 **cum expeditis** 'with the light-armed soldiers'. **raptim angustias
evadit** 'speedily emerged at the top of the pass'.

24 **mota (sunt)**. **incedere** 'to advance'.

25 **ex castellis** 'from (their) fortified villages'.

26–7 **alios … alios … hostes** i.e. they saw some of their enemy in one
place, others in another.

28 **obiecta** 'presented to'. **immobiles … eos defixit** 'fixed them
motionless to the spot'.

29 **trepidationem** 'panic', i.e. of Hannibal's men.

9–30 **suoque ipsum tumultu misceri agmen** 'and that the column was
being thrown into disorder by its own confusion'.

30 **quidquid adiecissent ipsi terroris satis ad perniciem fore rati**
'thinking that whatever terror (**quidquid terroris**) they
themselves could add would be sufficient to destroy them'.

31 **diversis** 'on both sides'.

32 **ab iniquitate locorum** the ground was uneven, with many defiles
and no room to deploy.

33–4 **plus … certaminis erat** 'there was more of a struggle'. **sibi
quoque tendente** 'as each man strove for himself'. **prius** 'first'.

36 **repercussae** 'echoing' (agreeing with both **nemora** and **valles**).
trepidabant 'began to panic'.

37 **consternabantur** from **consterno** (1) 'I alarm'.

39 **turba** 'the confusion'.

9–40 **in immensum altitudinis** 'to an enormous depth'.

42 **foeda visu** 'dreadful to behold'.

44 **interrumpi** 'was being broken apart'.

45 **cum** 'although'.

46 **liberata** 'cleared'.

47 **sedatur** 'was calmed'. **per otium** 'without harassment'.

48 **traducti (sunt)**.

9–50 **viculos circumiectos** 'the outlying villages'.

51 **aluit** from **alo, alere, alui** 'I feed'. **montanis primo perculsis**
'by the mountain people, utterly demoralized at the outset'. **loco**
'by the (nature of the) country'. **magno opere = magnopere**.

52 **aliquantum … viae** 'some distance'. **eo triduo** 'in those three
days'.

*The treachery of the Gauls leads the Carthaginians into another
extremely dangerous situation.*

perventum inde ad frequentem cultoribus alium populum. ibi non
bello aperto sed suis artibus, fraude et insidiis, est prope
55 circumventus. magno natu principes castellorum oratores ad
Poenum veniunt, alienis malis doctos memorantes amicitiam malle
quam vim experiri Poenorum; itaque oboedienter imperata
facturos; commeatum itinerisque duces et ad fidem promissorum
obsides acciperet.
60   Hannibal nec temere credendum nec aspernandos ratus, ne
repudiati aperte hostes fierent, benigne cum respondisset, obsidibus
quos dabant acceptis et commeatu quem in viam ipsi detulerant
usus, composito agmine duces eorum sequitur. primum agmen
elephanti et equites erant; ipse post cum robore peditum
65 circumspectans sollicitus omnia incedebat.
        ubi in angustiorem viam et ex parte altera subiectam iugo
ventum est, undique ex insidiis barbari a fronte ab tergo coorti,
comminus eminus petunt, saxa ingentia in agmen devolvunt.
maxima ab tergo vis hominum urgebat. tunc quoque ad extremum
70 periculi ac prope perniciem ventum est; nam dum cunctatur
Hannibal demittere agmen in angustias, occursantes per obliqua
montani interrupto medio agmine viam insedere, noxque una
Hannibali sine equitibus atque impedimentis acta est.
        postero die, iam segnius incursantibus barbaris, iunctae copiae
75 saltusque haud sine clade, maiore tamen iumentorum quam
hominum pernicie, superatus. inde montani pauciores iam et
latrocinii magis quam belli more concursabant modo in primum,
modo in novissimum agmen, utcumque aut locus opportunitatem
daret aut progressi morative aliquam occasionem fecissent.
80 elephanti sicut per artas vias magna mora agebantur, ita tutum ab
hostibus quacumque incederent, quia insuetis adeundi propius
metus erat, agmen praebebant.

(21.34–35.3)

elephantus

53 **perventum (est)** impersonal use of the passive, 'they came'. **ad frequentem cultoribus … populum** 'to a people (= a settlement) crowded with inhabitants' = 'to a well-populated settlement'.

54 **suis artibus** 'by his (i.e. Hannibal's) own devices'. This is a reference to the treacherous reputation of the Carthaginians. **prope** 'nearly'.

55 **circumventus** 'outmanœuvred'. **magno natu principes** 'the elder headmen'. **oratores** 'as speakers' = 'as a deputation'.

56 **Poenum** 'the Carthaginian', i.e. Hannibal. **alienis malis** 'by other men's evils'. **memorantes** 'saying' (take before **alienis malis**). **malle** understand **se** before **malle**.

57 **oboedienter** 'obediently'.

58 **facturos (esse). ad fidem promissorum** 'as a pledge that they would fulfil their promises'.

59 **acciperet** 'let him accept'.

60 **nec temere credendum nec aspernandos ratus** 'thinking that they should neither be blindly trusted nor treated with contempt'.

63 **composito agmine** 'with his column formed' = 'he formed his column and …'.

66 **ex parte altera subiectam iugo** 'overhung on one side by a ridge'; **subiectam** (= 'overhung') agrees with **viam**.

68 **comminus eminus** 'at close quarters and at long range'.

69 **vis hominum** 'force (= number) of men'. **tunc quoque** 'on this occasion too'.

71–2 **occursantes per obliqua montani** 'the mountain people, making an attack on the flank'.

72 **interrupto** from **interrumpo** 'I break through'.

73 **Hannibali** 'by Hannibal' (dative of the agent).

74 **segnius** 'less vigorously'. **iunctae (sunt)** i.e. the cavalry and baggage train rejoined the rest of the force.

76 **superatus (est)** 'was topped', i.e. they reached the top of the pass.

77 **latrocinii** 'of brigandage' (dependent, like **belli**, on **more**). **concursabant** 'were skirmishing'.

77–8 **modo … modo** 'sometimes … sometimes'.

78 **novissimum** 'rear'. **utcumque** 'in whatever way'. **opportunitatem** 'a chance'.

79 **-ve** 'or'. It is attached to the second of the two alternatives (compare **-que**), e.g. **bonus malusve** = 'good or bad'.

80 **sicut … ita** 'just as … so' = 'even though … still'. **artas** 'narrow'.

80–82 **tutum … agmen praebebant** ('made'). **quacumque incederent** 'wherever they went'. **insuetis** '(to their enemies who were) unaccustomed (to the elephants)'.

3 Hannibal crosses the Alps

The Carthaginians reach the top of the Alps.

nono die in iugum Alpium perventum est per invia pleraque et
errores, quos aut ducentium fraus aut temere initae valles a
coniectantibus iter faciebant. biduum in iugo stativa habita
fessisque labore ac pugnando quies data militibus; iumenta aliquot,
5 quae prolapsa in rupibus erant, sequendo vestigia agminis in castra
pervenere.

    fessis taedio tot malorum nivis etiam casus ingentem terrorem
adiecit. per omnia nive oppleta cum signis prima luce motis
segniter agmen incederet pigritiaque et desperatio in omnium vultu
10 emineret, praegressus signa Hannibal in promuntorio quodam, unde
longe ac late prospectus erat, consistere iussis militibus Italiam
ostentat subiectosque Alpinis montibus Circumpadanos campos,
moeniaque eos tum transcendere non Italiae modo sed etiam urbis
Romanae; cetera plana, proclivia fore; uno aut summum altero
15 proelio arcem et caput Italiae in manu ac potestate habituros.

(21.35.4–9)

The hazardous descent.

procedere inde agmen coepit iam nihil ne hostibus quidem praeter
parva furta per occasionem temptantibus. ceterum iter multo quam
in adscensu fuerat difficilius fuit; omnis enim ferme via praeceps,
angusta, lubrica erat, ut neque sustinere se ab lapsu possent aliique
20 super alios et iumenta in homines occiderent.

    ventum deinde ad multo angustiorem rupem atque ita rectis
saxis ut aegre expeditus miles temptabundus manibusque retinens
virgulta ac stirpes circa eminentes demittere sese posset. natura
locus iam ante praeceps recenti lapsu terrae in pedum mille
25 admodum altitudinem abruptus erat. ibi cum velut ad finem viae
equites constitissent, miranti Hannibali quae res moraretur agmen
nuntiatur rupem inviam esse. degressus deinde ipse ad locum
visendum. haud dubia res visa quin per invia circa nec trita antea,
quamvis longo ambitu, circumduceret agmen.

(21.35.10–36.4)

But this route proved totally impassable. Above the old, untouched
snow there was a new layer of moderate depth and at first they
found it easy to gain a foothold as they advanced, since it was soft
and not too deep. However, as it melted under the feet of so many
men and animals, they had to make their way over the bare ice
underneath and the liquid slush of the melting snow.

    There was a grim struggle here, since the slippery path did not

1	**nono die** i.e. from the foot of the Alps.
1–2	**per invia pleraque et errores** 'travelling mostly through pathless tracts and by wrong routes'.
2–3	**temere initae valles a coniectantibus iter** 'valleys blindly entered by (the Carthaginians) guessing the way'.
3	**stativa** 'a camp'.
7	**taedio** (+ genitive) 'by discouragement at'. **nivis ... casus** it was now late September.
8	**oppleta** 'covered'.
9	**segniter** 'sluggishly'. **pigritia** 'weariness'.
10	**emineret** 'were obvious' (the verb is singular in Latin because the weariness and the despair form one idea). **praegressus signa** 'going ahead of the standards'. **in promuntorio** 'on a ledge'.
12	**ostentat** 'he shows'. **Circumpadanos** 'around the river Po'.
13	**eos ... transcendere** accusative + infinitive: supply 'he said that' to introduce this: **moenia** is the object of **transcendere**.
14	**proclivia** 'downhill and easy'. **summum altero** 'at most by a second', i.e. 'at most two'.

A warrior on horseback

16–17	**nihil ne hostibus quidem ... temptantibus** 'with the enemy no longer making any assaults ...'. **furta** 'stealthy attacks'. **per occasionem** 'as opportunity offered'.
17	**ceterum** 'but'.
19	**lubrica** 'slippery'. **neque ... que** 'they could not stop themselves from slipping (**ab lapsu**) but ...'.
20	**occiderent** 'fell'.
21	**ventum (est)**. **rupem** 'precipitous cliff'.
21–2	**ita rectis saxis** 'with such sheer rocks' (ablative of description).
22	**aegre** 'with difficulty'. **expeditus** unencumbered'. **temptabundus** 'feeling his way'.
23	**virgulta ac stirpes circa eminentes** 'the bushes and roots which projected all around'.
24–5	**in pedum mille admodum altitudinem** 'to a depth of nearly 1,000 feet'.
25	**velut** 'as though'.
28–9	**haud dubia res visa quin ... circumduceret** 'there seemed no doubt that he must lead round ...'. **per invia circa nec trita antea** 'through the trackless and previously untrodden areas round about'. **quamvis longo ambitu** 'however long the detour might prove'.

*afford a foothold and the downward slope made their feet slide even
more quickly, so that, whether they used their knees or their hands
to try to get up, even these supports would slip from under them
and they would fall down again. And there were no stems or roots
thereabouts for them to get a hold on with their hands and feet to
help them struggle up. There was only the smooth ice and the
slushy snow, on which they constantly rolled about. The baggage
animals sometimes even cut into the bottommost crust of snow as
they went along; they slipped forward and, as they struck out
strongly with their hooves, they broke right through so that a large
number of them stuck fast in the hard and deep-frozen snow as if
caught in a trap.*

The Carthaginians make a road across the precipice.

30   tandem nequiquam iumentis atque hominibus fatigatis, castra in
iugo posita, aegerrime ad id ipsum loco purgato: tantum nivis
fodiendum atque egerendum fuit. inde ad rupem muniendam per
quam unam via esse poterat milites ducti, cum caedendum esset
saxum, arboribus circa immanibus deiectis struem ingentem
35   lignorum faciunt eamque, cum et vis venti apta faciendo igni coorta
esset, succendunt ardentiaque saxa infuso aceto putrefaciunt. ita
torridam incendio rupem ferro pandunt molliuntque anfractibus
modicis clivos ut non iumenta solum sed elephanti etiam deduci
possent.

(21.37.1–3)

They reach the lowlands.

40   quadriduum circa rupem consumptum, iumentis prope fame
absumptis; nuda enim fere cacumina sunt et, si quid est pabuli,
obruunt nives. inferiora vallis apricosque quosdam colles habent
rivosque prope silvas et iam humano cultu digniora loca. ibi
iumenta in pabulum missa et quies muniendo fessis hominibus data.
45   triduo inde ad planum descensum et iam locis mollioribus et
accolarum ingeniis.
    hoc maxime modo in Italiam perventum est ...

(21.37.4–38.1)

31 **posita (sunt). aegerrime** 'with the greatest difficulty'. **ad id
    ipsum** 'for this purpose'. **purgato** from **purgo** (1) 'I clear'.

32 **fodiendum** from **fodio** 'I hack out'. **egerendum** from **egero** 'I
    dig out'. **muniendam** from **munio** 'I make passable'.

33 **unam** 'alone'.

34–5 **struem … lignorum** 'pile of logs'.

36 **ardentia** 'glowing'. **infuso aceto** 'pouring on vinegar'.
    putrefaciunt 'they cause to crumble'.

37 **torridam** 'heated'. **pandunt** 'they make passable', 'make a road
    across'.

37–8 **molliunt anfractibus modicis clivos** 'they make the slopes
    easier with short zig-zag tracks'.

Monte Viso, which towers over the col
by which Hannibal crossed the Alps

40 **quadriduum … consumptum** 'four days were spent'.

40–41 **prope absumptis** 'nearly killed'.

41 **pabuli** from **pabulum** 'fodder'.

42 **obruunt** 'cover'. **nives** is the subject. **inferiora** 'the lower
    slopes' (subject of **habent**). **apricos quosdem colles** 'certain
    sunny hills' = 'a number of sunny hills'.

42–3 **-que … -que** 'both … and'.

44 **muniendo** 'by their road-building'.

45 **planum** 'the plain'. **mollioribus** goes with both **locis** and
    ingeniis (ablative absolute): 'they now went through places
    where both the terrain and the characters of the natives were
    milder'.

46 **accolarum** 'of the inhabitants'.

47 **maxime** 'by and large'.

*Hannibal won a series of great victories over the Romans. The most
devastating was the battle fought in 216 BC at Cannae, when
perhaps 70,000 Romans were killed. However, though he stayed in
Italy for sixteen years, he never succeeded in breaking the might of
Rome. Eventually a Roman army led by Scipio took the war over to
Africa and Hannibal was forced to return there. He was
conclusively defeated by Scipio at the Battle of Zama in 202 BC.*

*Hannibal now set about rebuilding the prosperity of Carthage.
But he had many enemies both among his fellow-citizens and at
Rome, and seven years later he was exiled. We take up his story in
182 BC. King Prusias of Bithynia has guaranteed him a safe refuge
but receives a distinguished Roman visitor.*

ad Prusiam regem legatus T. Quinctius Flamininus venit. ibi quia
ipse Prusias, ut gratificaretur praesenti Flaminino Romanisque, per
50   se necandi aut tradendi eius in potestatem consilium cepit, a primo
colloquio Flaminini milites extemplo ad domum Hannibalis
custodiendam missi sunt.

    semper talem exitum vitae suae Hannibal prospexerat animo, et
Romanorum inexpiabile odium in se cernens et fidei regum nihil
55   sane confisus; Prusiae vero levitatem etiam expertus erat; Flaminini
quoque adventum velut fatalem sibi horruerat. ad omnia undique
infesta, ut iter semper aliquod praeparatum fugae haberet, septem
exitus e domo fecerat, et ex iis quosdam occultos, ne custodia
saepirentur.

60   sed totius circuitum domus ita custodiis complexi sunt, ut nemo
inde elabi posset. Hannibal, postquam est nuntiatum milites regios
in vestibulo esse, postico, quod devium maxime erat, fugere
conatus, ut id quoque occursu militum obsaeptum sensit et omnia
circa clausa custodiis dispositis esse, venenum, quod multo ante
65   praeparatum ad tales habebat casus, poposcit. 'liberemus,' inquit,
'diuturna cura populum Romanum, quando mortem senis
exspectare longum censent. nec magnam nec memorabilem ex
inermi proditoque Flamininus victoriam feret.'

    exsecratus deinde in caput regnumque Prusiae et hospitales deos
70   violatae ab eo fidei testes invocans, poculum exhausit. hic vitae
exitus fuit Hannibalis.

(39.51)

49 **gratificaretur** (+ dative) 'he might do a favour to'. **praesenti** 'who was on the spot'.

49–50 **per se** 'on his own initiative'.

50 **necandi** and **tradendi** are dependent on **consilium**. **tradendi eius** 'of handing him over'. **potestatem** i.e. of the Romans.

50–51 **a primo colloquio** (+ gen.) 'as a result of his first conversation with …'.

54 **inexpiable** 'implacable'. **in se** 'against himself'.

54–5 **nihil sane** 'by no means'.

55 **vero** 'indeed'. **levitatem** 'untrustworthiness'.

56 **velut fatalem** 'as if (it would prove) fatal'. **horruerat** 'he had felt fear at'.

56–7 **ad omnia undique infesta** 'in the face of all the dangers which surrounded him'. **iter** 'route'.

57 **praeparatum fugae** 'prepared for flight' = 'available for escape'.

58–9 **ne custodia saepirentur** 'so that they could not be blocked off by guards'.

60 **circuitum** 'the perimeter'. **custodiis complexi sunt** 'they (i.e. the king's men) surrounded with guards'.

62 **in vestibulo** 'in the entrance-court'. **postico** from **posticum** 'back-door'. **devium** 'secret'.

63 **occursu militum obsaeptum (esse)** 'was blocked off by the soldiers stationed there'.

64 **circa** 'round about'. **custodiis dispositis** 'by the guards positioned there'.

65 **praeparatum** 'ready'. The story goes that he carried the poison with him concealed in a signet ring.

66–7 **quando mortem senis exspectare longum censent** 'since they consider it (a) long (business) to wait for the death of an old man', i.e. they are too impatient to wait for me to die in the course of nature.

69 **exsecratus … in** (+ accusative) 'having cursed'. **caput** 'the life'. **hospitales deos** 'the gods of hospitality'.

70 **violatae** 'violated', 'abused' (agreeing with **fidei**). **testes invocans** 'calling upon as witnesses of …'. **poculum** 'the draught', 'drink'.

Prusias of Bithynia

Flamininus

*The satirical writer Juvenal, who wrote in the first half of the
second century AD, used the story of Hannibal to demonstrate
what he saw as the ultimate futility of military ambition. After you
have read this passage, you might consider what your attitude is
to the achievements of Hannibal or any other great military
leader.*

      expende Hannibalem: quot libras in duce summo
      invenies? hic est, quem non capit Africa Mauro
      percussa oceano Niloque admota tepenti.
      additur imperiis Hispania, Pyrenaeum
5   transilit. opposuit natura Alpemque nivemque:
      diducit scopulos et montem rumpit aceto.
      iam tenet Italiam, tamen ultra pergere tendit.
      'actum,' inquit, 'nil est, nisi Poeno milite portas
      frangimus et media vexillum pono Subura.'
10   o qualis facies et quali digna tabella,
      cum Gaetula ducem portaret belua luscum.
      exitus ergo quis est? o gloria, vincitur idem
      nempe et in exsilium praeceps fugit atque ibi magnus
      mirandusque cliens sedet ad praetoria regis
15   donec Bithyno libeat vigilare tyranno.
      finem animae quae res humanas miscuit olim,
      non gladii, non saxa dabunt nec tela, sed ille
      Cannarum vindex et tanti sanguinis ultor
      anulus. i demens et saevas curre per Alpes
20   ut pueris placeas et declamatio fias.

A balance from Pompei

(Juvenal: *Satires* 10.147–67)

Gaetula belua

1 **expende** 'weigh in the scale'. **quot libras**, *acc. pl.* 'how many pounds' (of weight), i.e. how much do the ashes of the dead Hannibal weigh?

2 **non capit** 'cannot contain'.

2–3 **Mauro/percussa oceano** 'pounded by the Moorish Ocean' (i.e. the Atlantic).

3 **Nilo admota tepenti** 'stretching as far as the warm Nile'.

4 **Pyrenaeum** 'the Pyrenees'.

5 **opposuit** 'put in his way'. **Alpemque nivemque** 'the Alpine snows' (hendiadys: literally, 'the Alp and the snow').

6 **diducit scopulos**' he splits the rocks'.

7 **tendit** 'he strives'.

8 **Poeno milite** singular for plural, i.e. 'with the Carthaginian soldiers'. **portas** 'the gates' (of Rome).

9 **vexillum** 'standard'. **Subura** a district of Rome. This is humorous since it was the red-light district.

10 **facies** 'sight'. **quali digna tabella** 'how worthy of a picture!' = 'how fit for caricature!'.

11 **Gaetula ... belua** 'an African monster', i.e. an elephant. **luscum** 'one-eyed' (agreeing with **ducem**). In 217 BC Hannibal crossed the Apennines on his one surviving elephant and lost an eye through disease.

12 **vincitur** Hannibal suffered his one and only defeat at Zama in 202 BC. **idem** 'that same man'.

13 **nempe** 'to be sure': the word conveys scorn.

14 **cliens** 'client', 'hanger-on'. **praetoria** 'palace'.

15 **libeat** (+ dative) 'it might please'. **vigilare** 'to wake up' (and admit his visitor). **tyranno** the Greek word for 'king'.

16 **animae** 'life', 'spirit': dative, indirect object of **dabunt**. **miscuit** 'turned upside-down'.

18 **Cannarum vindex** 'avenger of Cannae' (216 BC, Hannibal's greatest victory over the Romans). **ultor** (+ genitive) 'exacting revenge for'.

19 **anulus** 'a ring' (in which he carried his poison). **demens** 'madman'.

20 **declamatio** 'a subject for debates in school'.

OVID

The last of the great Augustan poets was Publius Ovidius Naso (43 BC–AD 17). The range of his poetry is wider than any of his predecessors': in the following extracts you will be sampling his autobiographical writings, his love poetry and his huge work on mythological subjects, the *Metamorphoses*.

Ovid's love poems do not aim at the passionate intensity of Catullus or the profound melancholy of Virgil. For him, being in love is fun, and even when things go wrong, it is not a matter for serious grief. A cheerful sensualist in his poetry, he offended the Emperor, who was trying to clean up the morals of Rome. He was exiled to a remote spot on the Black Sea – where he eventually died – and in these bleak surroundings his writing took on a grimmer character. But his unhappiness gave him a new subject for his verse. The elegant couplets in which he had penned his love poetry became in his poems from exile the medium for lament.

The reasons for Ovid's banishment remain mysterious. The poet himself refers to a poem (*carmen*) and a mistake (*error*). We are unlikely ever to find out exactly what the mistake was. He may have innocently overheard part of a conspiracy against the Emperor and done nothing about it.

On the subject of the poem, however, we are on surer ground. Augustus was eager to improve the lax moral standards of the Rome of his day. Yet in AD 2 he had to banish his only daughter Julia for flagrant adultery and six years later Julia's daughter had to be banished too, also for immorality. The Emperor would have felt little affection for the poet who had so often encouraged the sexual permissiveness which he himself had been at such pains to suppress.

Sulmo

All of Ovid's love poetry must have seemed a provocation to him, but the *Ars Amatoria* – from which you will be reading an excerpt – would have struck him as especially offensive. When he banished Ovid, Augustus had this poem banned from Rome's three public libraries.

Ovid's love poetry may seem to us too lighthearted to deserve serious disapproval, and it may seem strange that Ovid, unlike any of the other major Augustan poets, was a respectable married man. But in seeming to encourage adultery, which Augustus had made a criminal offence, and in sending up traditional Roman stories (like that of Romulus and the Sabine women), Ovid was asking for trouble. Even now his poetry has a *risqué* element, a whiff of sexual excitement, as the poet pursues love to the exclusion of everything else.

The statue of Ovid at Sulmo

1 Ovid tells the story of his life

Ovid was born on 20 March 43 BC in Sulmo (modern Sulmona) in the Apennines about ninety miles east of Rome. He had one brother, born exactly a year before. Their family was an old-established and fairly wealthy equestrian one and Ovid had the right background to pursue a successful senatorial career. But he found himself irresistibly drawn to poetry. He was to be the last of the Augustan love poets.

Ovid introduces himself and his brother.

> ille ego qui fuerim, tenerorum lusor amorum,
> quem legis, ut noris, accipe, posteritas.
> Sulmo mihi patria est, gelidis uberrimus undis,
> milia qui novies distat ab urbe decem.
> 5 editus hic ego sum, nec non, ut tempora noris,
> cum cecidit fato consul uterque pari.
> nec stirps prima fui; genito sum fratre creatus,
> qui tribus ante quater mensibus ortus erat.
> Lucifer amborum natalibus affuit idem:
> 10 una celebrata est per duo liba dies.

(*Tristia* 4.10.1–12, abridged)

The eduction of the poet and his brother.

> protinus excolimur teneri curaque parentis
> imus ad insignes urbis ab arte viros.
> frater ad eloquium viridi tendebat ab aevo
> fortia verbosi natus ad arma fori;
> 15 at mihi iam puero caelestia sacra placebant,
> inque suum furtim Musa trahebat opus.
> saepe pater dixit, 'studium quid inutile temptas?
> Maeonides nullas ipse reliquit opes.'
> motus eram dictis, totoque Helicone relicto
> 20 scribere temptabam verba soluta modis.
> sponte sua carmen numeros veniebat ad aptos,
> et quod temptabam scribere versus erat.

(*Tristia* 4.10.15–26)

1–2 **ille ... posteritas** = **accipe** ('listen'), **posteritas** ('future generations'), **ut noris** (= **noveris**) **qui** (= **quis**) **ille ego fuerim, lusor tenerorum amorum quem legis. ille ego** 'that famous I', i.e. 'I, the famous poet Ovid' (**ille** frequently means 'the famous'). **lusor** 'playful poet'.

4 **novies decem** 'nine times ten' = 'ninety'. **distat** 'is away'. **urbe** i.e. Rome.

5 **editus** 'born'. **nec non** 'and also'.

6 **fato ... pari** 'by the same fate'. The two consuls Hirtius and Pansa were killed fighting Antony in the year of Ovid's birth (43 BC).

7 **stirps prima** 'the first born'. **genito ... fratre** 'my brother already born' = 'after the birth of my brother'.

8 **tribus ... quater** 'four times three', i.e. twelve.

9 **Lucifer ... idem** 'the same dawn'. **natalibus** 'at the birthday': Ovid and his brother had the same birthday. **affuit** = **adfuit**.

10 **una ... dies** 'one day' (**dies**, referring to a specific day, can be feminine). **liba**, *n. pl.* 'cakes', offered to the deity who protected the birthday child.

11 **protinus excolimur teneri** 'we started our education right away, while still young'.

12 **ad insignes ... viros** = **ad viros urbis ab arte insignes** ('famous because of their skill'). Like Horace, Ovid went to Rome to be educated.

13 **ad eloquium** 'towards public speaking'. **viridi ... ab aevo** 'from his youngest years', literally, 'from his green age'.

The nine Muses

14 **ad arma** 'for the warfare. **verbosi ... fori** 'of the wordy law court'. The lawcourts were in the Forum.

15 **caelestia sacra** 'the holy rites of poetry' (inspiration comes from heaven (**caelum**)).

16 **trahebat** understand **me**.

18 **Maeonides** i.e. Homer, from Maeonia (= Lydia).

19 **Helicone** (ablative) Mount Helicon in Boeotia was the home of the Muses. Ovid means that he totally abandoned poetry.

20 **verba soluta modis** 'words freed from metre', i.e. prose.

21 **numeros ... ad aptos** 'into the appropriate metre'.

They both prepare for a career in public life.

> interea tacito passu labentibus annis
>> liberior fratri sumpta mihique toga est,
25 > induiturque umeris cum lato purpura clavo,
>> et studium nobis, quod fuit ante, manet.
> iamque decem vitae frater geminaverat annos,
>> cum perit, et coepi parte carere mei.
> cepimus et tenerae primos aetatis honores,
30 >> eque viris quondam pars tribus una fui.

(*Tristia* 4.10.27–34)

But Ovid abandons this ambition in favour of poetry.

> curia restabat: clavi mensura coacta est;
>> maius erat nostris viribus illud onus.
> nec patiens corpus, nec mens fuit apta labori,
>> sollicitaeque fugax ambitionis eram,
35 > et petere Aoniae suadebant tuta sorores
>> otia, iudicio semper amata meo.

(*Tristia* 4.10.35–40)

His admiration for older poets of his time.

> temporis illius colui fovique poetas
>> quotque aderant vates, rebar adesse deos.
> saepe suos solitus recitare Propertius ignes,
40 >> iure sodalicii, quo mihi iunctus erat.
> et tenuit nostras numerosus Horatius aures,
>> dum ferit Ausonia carmina culta lyra.
> Vergilium vidi tantum: nec avara Tibullo
>> tempus amicitiae fata dedere meae.

(*Tristia* 4.10.41–52, abridged)

A young man in a toga

He publishes his first poems which are inspired by Corinna.

45 > utque ego maiores, sic me coluere minores,
>> notaque non tarde facta Thalia mea est.
> carmina cum primum populo iuvenalia legi,
>> barba resecta mihi bisve semelve fuit.

24 **liberior … toga** 'the toga which gave more freedom', i.e. the adult's toga, the *toga virilis*, which was worn (**sumpta … est**) by boys from about the age of sixteen. **fratri … mihique** 'by my brother and me' (dative of the agent).

25 **cum lato purpura clavo** 'the purple (toga) with the broad stripe' = 'the toga with the broad purple stripe'. The *latus clavus* was worn by senators, sons of senators and *equites illustres*, i.e. sons of knights whom Augustus wished to encourage to embark on a senatorial career.

26 Ovid's brother remained an enthusiast for the law, Ovid for poetry.

27 **geminaverat** 'had doubled', i.e. he had reached the age of twenty.

29 **cepimus et = et cepimus** 'and I took'. **tenerae primos aetatis honores** 'the first offices open to (someone of my) tender age'.

30 Ovid served as one of a Board of Three, dealing with prisons or the mint.

31 **restabat** 'awaited (me)'. At the age of thirty, he could start on the *cursus honorum* by becoming a quaestor. **clavi mensura coacta est** 'the width of my purple stripe was narrowed'. He withdrew from public life, becoming an *eques* of the second class and thus having a narrower stripe on his toga.

32 **maius** 'too great for …'.

33 **nec patiens (laboris) corpus (erat).**

34 **sollicitae fugax ambitionis** 'a runaway from political life with all its anxieties': literally, **ambitio** means 'going round', canvassing for a political cause.

35 **Aoniae sorores** the sisters from Mount Helicon in Boeotia (= Aonia), i.e. 'the Muses'.

35–6 **petere … otia = Aoniae sorores suadebant (mihi) petere tuta otia.**

38 **quot aderant vates** 'as many poets as were present' = 'any poets who were present'.

39 **solitus (est). suos … ignes** 'his fiery poetry' = 'his love poetry'.

40 **iure sodalicii** 'by the ties of comradeship'.

41 **numerosus** 'with his many metres'.

42 **ferit Ausonia carmina culta lyra** 'accompanied his sophisticated poetry on his Ausonian (= Italian) lyre'. **ferit** 'struck', i.e. struck the strings with his plectrum.

43 **tantum** 'only', i.e. Ovid never spoke to him.

44 **dedere = dederunt.** Fate gave Tibullus no time for friendship with Ovid (**meae amicitiae**). Tibullus died when Ovid was about twenty-four.

Horace

45 **maiores … minores** 'older (poets) … younger (poets)'.

46 **Thalia mea** 'my Muse'. Thalia was the Muse of comedy and light verse.

47 **legi** 'I read aloud'. Poetry was usually first made known by a public recitation.

48 **resecta (erat)** 'had been cut'. **bisve semelve** 'once or twice', i.e. when he was eighteen or so.

moverat ingenium totam cantata per urbem
50   nomine non vero dicta Corinna mihi.
molle Cupidineis nec inexpugnabile telis
   cor mihi, quodque levis causa moveret, erat.
cum tamen hic essem minimoque accenderer igni,
   nomine sub nostro fabula nulla fuit.

(*Tristia* 4.10.55–68, abridged)

Sleeping Cupid

Ovid falls foul of the Emperor.

55   iam mihi canities pulsis melioribus annis
      venerat, antiquas miscueratque comas,
   cum maris Euxini positos ad laeva Tomitas
      quaerere me laesi principis ira iubet.

(*Tristia* 4.10.93–8, abridged)

Ovid's last night in Rome.

cum subit illius tristissima noctis imago,
60   quae mihi supremum tempus in urbe fuit,
cum repeto noctem, qua tot mihi cara reliqui,
      labitur ex oculis nunc quoque gutta meis.
iam prope lux aderat, qua me discedere Caesar
      finibus extremae iusserat Ausoniae.
65   nec spatium nec mens fuerat satis apta parandi:
      torpuerant longa pectora nostra mora.
non mihi servorum, comites non cura legendi,
      non aptae profugo vestis opisve fuit.
non aliter stupui, quam qui Iovis ignibus ictus
70   vivit et est vitae nescius ipse suae.

(*Tristia* 1.3.1–12)

49 **moverat ingenium** 'had stirred my genius': **Corinna** (*l.* 50) is the
subject of **moverat.**

50 **dicta … mihi** 'called by me'. It was customary for poets to give their
mistress a 'poetical' name (**nomine non vero**); cf. Catullus' Lesbia.
Corinna, Ovid's first love (if she was a real person), is the subject of
many of his early love poems.

51 **Cupidineis nec inexpugnabile telis** 'and not proof against the darts of
Cupid': take **nec** before **Cupidineis.**

52 **quod** (+ subjunctive) generic, i.e. 'the sort of heart which…'.

53 **hic** 'like this'. **accenderer** 'could be set on fire'.

54 **fabula** 'scandal'. **sub** 'attached to'.

55 **pulsis melioribus annis** 'when my better (= more youthful) years were
gone'.

55 **miscuerat** 'had flecked', 'had sprinkled'.

57–8 **cum … Tomitas … iubet = cum ira principis me iubet quaerere** (=
'to make for') **Tomitas** (*acc. pl.*). **maris … Tomitas** 'the people of
Tomis who live (literally, are placed) on the left of the Euxine Sea (i.e.
the Black Sea)'. **laesi principis** of the offended emperor'. Augustus
banished Ovid in AD 8 when the poet was fifty-one. The reasons for this
banishment are discussed above, pp. 190–91.

60 **quae** the antecedent is **noctis.**

62 **gutta** 'a teardrop'.

63 **prope** 'nearly'. **lux** 'the dawn', i.e. 'the day'.

64 **finibus extremae … Ausoniae** 'from the boundaries of furthest Italy' =
'from the furthest boundaries of Italy'.

65 **spatium** 'time'. **nec spatium nec mens … parandi** 'neither time nor
spirit for getting ready'. **satis apta** 'sufficiently suitable things' = 'the
sort of things which were needed'.

66 **torpuerant** 'had become numb'.

67 **non … legendi = non (fuit cura) mihi servorum (legendorum), non
(mihi fuit) cura legendi comites.**

68 **profugo** 'for an exile'. **vestis opisve** genitives; understand **cura** 'I took
no thought for…'. **opis** 'what could be of help to me'.

69 **non aliter … quam** 'not otherwise than' = 'just like'. **stupui** 'I was
dumbfounded'. **Iovis ignibus ictus** 'struck by the thunderbolt (literally
by the fires) of Jupiter'.

70 **et** (here) = 'though'. **nescius** (+ genitive) 'unconscious of'.

He bids farewell to his friends and his wife.

> ut tamen hanc animi nubem dolor ipse removit,
>   et tandem sensus convaluere mei,
> adloquor extremum maestos abiturus amicos,
>   qui modo de multis unus et alter erant.
> 75 uxor amans flentem flens acrius ipsa tenebat,
>   imbre per indignas usque cadente genas.
> nata procul Libycis aberat diversa sub oris,
>   nec poterat fati certior esse mei.
> quocumque aspiceres, luctus gemitusque sonabant,
> 80   formaque non taciti funeris intus erat.

(Tristia 1.3.13–22)

His wife wishes to follow him into exile.

> tum vero coniunx umeris abeuntis inhaerens
>   miscuit haec lacrimis tristia verba meis:
> 'non potes avelli. simul hinc, simul ibimus,' inquit;
>   'te sequar et coniunx exulis exul ero.
> 85 te iubet e patria discedere Caesaris ira,
>   me pietas. pietas haec mihi Caesar erit.'
> talia temptabat, sicut temptaverat ante,
>   vixque dedit victas utilitate manus.

(Tristia 1.3.79–89, abridged)

Caesar Augustus

73 **extremum** 'for the last time'.

74 **modo de multis** 'out of the many (I had had) recently'. **unus et alter** 'one or two'.

75 **acrius** his wife is in even greater anguish than he is.

76 **imbre** (ablative) 'a shower (of tears)'. **per indignas ... genas** 'down her cheeks which did not deserve (such disfigurement)'. **usque** 'continually'.

77 **nata** '(my) daughter'. **diversa** 'distant'. **sub** 'on', 'near'.

78 **fati certior esse mei** = **certior fieri de fato meo**.

79 **quocumque aspiceres** 'wherever one (literally, you) might look'.

80 **intus** 'inside (the house)'.

81 **umeris abeuntis inhaerens** 'clinging to the shoulders of (me) going away' = 'with her arms flung tightly round me as we parted'.

83 **non potes avelli** 'you cannot be torn away' = 'I shall not allow you to be torn from me'.

86 **me (iubet) pietas**.

87 **sicut** 'just as'.

88 **dedit victas ... manus** literally, 'gave her hands, conquered by ...'. **manus do** is an expression meaning 'I surrender'. Translate 'she surrendered, won over by ...'. **utilitate** by practical considerations'. She stayed in Rome to work for Ovid's recall.

2 Ovid the lover

Ovid called himself tenerorum lusor amorum *(the poet who writes playfully of tender love). In this poem, written in imitation of Catullus' tributes to his girlfriend's sparrow, he writes wittily and touchingly of the death of Corinna's parrot.*

> psittacus, Eois imitatrix ales ab Indis,
>   occidit: exsequias ite frequenter, aves;
> ite, piae volucres, et plangite pectora pinnis
>   et rigido teneras ungue notate genas.
> 5   omnes, quae liquido libratis in aere cursus,
>   tu tamen ante alios, turtur amice, dole.
> plena fuit vobis omni concordia vita
>   et stetit ad finem longa tenaxque fides.
> quid tamen ista fides, quid rari forma coloris,
> 10   quid vox mutandis ingeniosa sonis,
> quid iuvat, ut datus es, nostrae plucuisse puellae?
>   infelix avium gloria nempe iaces.
> occidit illa loquax humanae vocis imago
>   psittacus, extremo munus ab orbe datum.
> 15   septima lux venit non exhibitura sequentem;
>   clamavit moriens lingua 'Corinna, vale.'

(*Amores* 2.6, abridged)

in toto nusquam corpore menda fuit

But Ovid's love poetry is not only tender and playful. On occasion it can be very sensuous. This poem is set at siesta time.

> aestus erat, mediamque dies exegerat horam;
>   adposui medio membra levanda toro.
> pars adaperta fuit, pars altera clausa fenestrae,
> 20   quale fere silvae lumen habere solent,
> qualia sublucent fugiente crepuscula Phoebo
>   aut ubi nox abiit nec tamen orta dies.
> illa verecundis lux est praebenda puellis,
>   qua timidus latebras speret habere pudor.
> 25   ecce, Corinna venit tunica velata recincta,
>   candida dividua colla tegente coma.
> deripui tunicam; nec multum rara nocebat,
>   pugnabat tunica sed tamen illa tegi;
> 30   cumque ita pugnaret tamquam quae vincere nollet,
>   victa est non aegre proditione sua.

1 **psittacus** 'parrot'. **Eois … Indis** 'imitating bird from India (literally, the Indi) in the East'.

2 **occidit** note scansion – not **occīdit**. **exsequias** 'to the funeral'.

3 **volucres** 'winged creatures'. **plangite … pinnis** 'beat with your wings'.

4 **rigido … ungue** 'with your stiff claws' (singular for plural). **notate genas** at Roman funerals, the mourners beat their breasts and tore their cheeks.

5 **omnes** understand **dolete**. **quae … libratis … cursus** 'who wing your way (literally, balance your journeys)'.

6 **ante alios** 'before (i.e.more than all) the others'. **turtur** 'turtle dove'.

7 **omni** agrees with **vita**.

8 **stetit ad finem** 'lasted to the end'.

9–10 **quid … quid … quid …** understand **iuvat** (*l.* 11) 'what help is …?' **ingeniosa** 'skilled in …'. Now the parrot is being addressed.

11 **quid iuvat … placuisse** 'what help is it to have pleased' = 'what good has it done you that you gave pleasure to'. **ut** 'as soon as'.

12 Ovid answers the questions he has just asked: **quid iuvat …?** All was of no avail, for the glory of the bird world lies dead. **nempe** (= 'to be sure', but perhaps better left untranslated) confirms this answer.

14 **extremo munus ab orbe** 'a present from the edge of the world'.

15 **lux** 'dawn', i.e. the seventh day after the onset of his illness. **non exhibitura sequentem** 'not about to reveal a following (dawn)', i.e. the bird died on the seventh day.

tutures

17 **aestus erat** 'there was heat' = 'it was sultry'. **exegerat** 'had passed'.

18 **adposui** 'I placed', 'laid'. **medio … toro** 'on the middle of the bed', i.e. he was alone. **levanda** 'to be rested', 'to rest'.

19 **pars (fenestrae) adaperta (= aperta) fuit**.

20 **quale … lumen** 'the sort of light which …'. **fere** 'generally'.

21 **qualia … crepuscula** 'the sort of twilight which …' (poetic plural). **sublucent** 'glimmers'. **Phoebo** Phoebus, god of the sun.

23 **verecundis … puellis** 'for shy girls'.

24 **latebras speret habere** 'may hope to have hiding places' = 'may hope to hide'.

25 **tunica velata recincta** 'dressed in a loose tunic'.

26 **colla**, *n. pl.* 'neck'. **dividua** (ablative) 'parted'.

27 **nec multum rara nocebat** '(since it was) thin (**rara**), it did not do much harm', i.e. it did not really hide anything.

28 Translate **sed tamen** at the start of the line. **pugnabat … tegi** 'she struggled to be covered'. The infinitive expresses purpose. She puts on a show of modesty.

29 **tamquam quae** (+ subjunctive) 'like a woman who …'.

30 **non aegre** 'not with difficulty' = 'easily'. **proditione sua** 'by her self-betrayal'.

ut stetit ante oculos posito velamine nostros,
 in toto nusquam corpore menda fuit:
quos umeros, quales vidi tetigique lacertos!
 forma papillarum quam fuit apta premi!
35 quam castigato planus sub pectore venter!
 quantum et quale latus! quam iuvenale femur!
singula quid referam? nil non laudabile vidi,
 et nudam pressi corpus ad usque meum.
cetera quis nescit? lassi requievimus ambo.
40 proveniant medii sic mihi saepe dies!

(Amores 1.5)

curvis venare theatris

*The above two poems are from Ovid's
collection of love poetry called the* Amores. *He
began this in about 25* BC *when he was not yet
twenty. A quarter of a century later, he wrote
the* Ars Amatoria (The Art of Love), *a manual
on the technique of seduction. The immorality
of this poem was one of the causes of Ovid's
exile. Here is an excerpt from it.*

*The theatre is an excellent place to pick up
girls.*

sed tu praecipue curvis venare theatris;
 haec loca sunt voto fertiliora tuo.
illic invenies quod ames, quod ludere possis,
 quodque semel tangas, quodque tenere velis.
45 ut redit itque frequens longum formica per agmen,
 granifero solitum cum vehit ore cibum,
aut ut apes saltusque suos et olentia nactae
 pascua per flores et thyma summa volant,
sic ruit ad celebres cultissima femina ludos;
50 copia iudicium saepe morata meum est.
spectatum veniunt, veniunt spectentur ut ipsae;
 ille locus casti damna pudoris habet.

(Ars Amatoria 1.89–100)

32 **menda** 'blemish'.

34 **papillarum** 'of her breasts'.

35 **castigato** 'disciplined' = 'well-formed'.

37 **singula quid referam?** 'why should I mention each (of her charms) individually?'

38 **(eam) nudam. corpus ad usque meum** 'tightly to my body'.

39 **cetera quis nescit = quis nescit cetera.**

40 **proveniant** 'may they turn out' (the subjunctive expresses a wish).

41 **tu** i.e. the young man whom Ovid is advising. **curvis** 'curving'. This refers to the curving tiers of the theatre. **venare** imperative of **venor** 'I hunt'.

42 **loca** the plural of **locus** can be neuter. **voto fertiliora tuo** 'more productive than your wish' = 'even more productive than you could wish'.

43 **quod ames** '(something) which you may love' = 'a girl to love'. **ludere** 'to deceive'.

44 **semel tangas** 'you may touch once (and then leave)' = 'have a brief affair with'.

45 **ut** 'as'. **redit itque** 'hurries to and fro'. **frequens … formica** 'many an ant'. **longum … per agmen** 'along the long column' = 'in a long column'.

46 **granifero … cibum = cum vehit solitum cibum granifero** ('grain-carrying') **ore.**

47–8 **apes** 'bees'. **saltus suos et olentia nactae/pascua** 'having got to (literally, having obtained) their glades and fragrant pastures' = 'haunting the meadows', etc.

48 **summa thyma**, *n. pl.* 'the top of the thyme'.

49 **cultissima femina** 'the most fashionable ladies' (singular for plural).

50 **morata … est** 'has delayed' = 'has confused'. He can't make up his mind because of the *embarras de richesses*.

51 **spectatum** 'to see'. The supine expresses purpose after a verb of motion. **veniunt … ipsae = veniunt ut ipsae spectentur.**

52 **casti damna pudoris** 'the losses of chaste modesty' = 'the destruction of chaste modesty'.

Romulus started this Roman tradition.

    primus sollicitos fecisti, Romule, ludos,
        cum iuvit viduos rapta Sabina viros.
55   in gradibus sedit populus de caespite factis,
        qualibet hirsutas fronde tegente comas.
    respiciunt oculisque notant sibi quisque puellam
        quam velit, et tacito pectore multa movent.

           (*Ars Amatoria* 1.101–10, abridged)

Romulus gives the sign to seize the women.

    in medio plausu (plausus tunc arte carebant)
60   rex populo praedae signa petita dedit.
    protinus exsiliunt, animum clamore fatentes
        virginibus cupidas iniciuntque manus;
    ut fugiunt aquilas, timidissima turba, columbae
        utque fugit visos agna novella lupos,
65   sic illae timuere viros sine lege ruentes;
        constitit in nulla qui fuit ante color.

           (*Ars Amatoria* 1.113–20)

Hysteria takes the women in many different ways.

    nam timor unus erat, facies non una timoris:
        pars laniat crines, pars sine mente sedet;
    altera maesta silet, frustra vocat altera matrem;
70   haec queritur, stupet haec; haec manet, illa fugit.
    si qua repugnarat nimium comitemque negarat,
        sublatam cupido vir tulit ipse sinu
    atque ita 'quid teneros lacrimis corrumpis ocellos?
        quod matri pater est, hoc tibi' dixit 'ero.'
75   Romule, militibus scisti dare commoda solus:
        haec mihi si dederis commoda, miles ero.

           (*Ars Amatoria* 1.121–32, abridged)

virginibus cupidas iniciunt manus

53 **sollicitos** 'disturbed', 'chaotic'. In its early years, Rome desperately needed women to keep its population going. Romulus invited the neighbouring Sabines to a show at Rome, planning to kidnap the women.

54 **iuvit ... viros** = **rapta Sabina iuvit viduos viros** 'the stolen Sabine woman pleased the wifeless men' = 'the wifeless men thought it a good idea to steal the Sabine women' (**rapta** (from **rapio**) 'snatched', 'stolen').

56 **qualibet ... fronde** (ablative) 'any old foliage'. They break off branches to act as sunshades (the rape occurred in August). **hirsutas** 'shaggy'.

57 **respiciunt** 'look back at'. In Augustan times, the women sat in the back rows of the theatres. Ovid makes this the custom in early Rome as well. **notant** 'mark out': plural because **quisque** (= 'each one') refers to all of them.

58 **multa movent** 'they move many things' = 'they feel deep emotion'.

59 **plausus ... arte carebant** 'their applause lacked discrimination' = 'they applauded without discrimination, good and bad alike'.

60 **praedae signa petita** 'the eagerly-awaited (literally, sought for) sign (i.e. sign for seizing) their prey (i.e. the women)'.

61 **animum ... fatentes** 'declaring their love'.

62 **iniciuntque** translate the **-que** at the start of the line.

64 **agna novella** 'the little lamb'. **visos ... lupos** the lambkin runs off the moment it spots the wolf.

65 **sine lege** 'without law and order' = 'wildly'.

66 i.e. they all changed colour.

67 i.e. they all felt the same panic but expressed it differently.

68 **pars ... pars ...** '(one) part (of them) ... (another) part (of them)' = 'some ... others ...'. **laniat** 'tears'.

69 **altera ... altera** 'one ... another'. **maesta** 'sad'. **silet** 'is silent'.

71 **si qua** 'if any (woman)'. **repugnarat** (= **repugnaverat**) 'had fought back' = 'fought back'. **nimium** 'too much'. **comitem negarat** (= **negaverat**) 'said no to her companion' i.e. the man who had seized her.

72 **sublatam cupido ... sinu** 'lifted in his passionate embrace'. **vir ... ipse** 'the man himself' = 'the man without more ado'.

73 **ita** i.e. 'and as he did so'. **corrumpis** 'do you spoil'.

74 **quod matri pater est** 'what your father is to your mother'.

75 **scisti** (= **scivisti**) **dare commoda** 'you knew the fringe benefits (**commoda**) to give' (**scisti dare** means literally 'you knew how to give'). **solus** i.e. above all others, more than anyone else.

In another poem from the Amores, *the poet displays his pick-up technique at the races in the Circus Maximus.*

He tries to chat up the girl sitting next to him.

'non ego nobilium sedeo studiosus equorum;
    cui tamen ipsa faves, vincat ut ille, precor.
ut loquerer tecum, veni, tecumque sederem,
80   ne tibi non notus, quem facis, esset amor.
tu cursus spectas, ego te: spectemus uterque
    quod iuvat atque oculos pascat uterque suos.
o, cuicumque faves, felix agitator equorum!
    ergo illi curae contigit esse tuae?

(*Amores* 3.2.1–8)

He dreams of what he would do if he were the charioteer backed by the girl.

85   hoc mihi contingat, sacro de carcere missis
        insistam forti mente vehendus equis,
et modo lora dabo, modo verbere terga notabo,
        nunc stringam metas interiore rota;
si mihi currenti fueris conspecta, morabor,
90   deque meis manibus lora remissa fluent.

(*Amores* 3.2.9–14)

The poet complains that the girl is trying to edge away from him, while other spectators are edging into her.

quid frustra refugis? cogit nos linea iungi;
    haec in lege loci commoda Circus habet.
tu tamen, a dextra quicumque es, parce puellae:
    contactu lateris laeditur illa tui;
95   tu quoque, qui spectas post nos, tua contrahe crura,
    si pudor est, rigido nec preme terga genu.

(*Amores* 3.2.19–24)

77 **studiosus** (+ genitive) 'keen on'. The poet says that it's not because he's keen on horses that he's here.

78 **cui … precor** = **precor tamen ut ille vincat cui ipsa faves**. The subject of **faves** is the girl the poet is sitting next to.

80 **quem facis … amor** '(my) love, which you are causing'.

81 **cursus** 'the races'.

83 **cuicumque** the antecedent is **agitator equorum** 'driver of horses', 'charioteer'.

84 **illi … contigit …** 'has he the luck …?'. **curae … esse tuae** 'to be your care' (predicative dative), i.e. 'to be cared for by you'.

Circus Maximus

85 **hoc mihi contingat** 'were this to be my luck'. **sacro de carcere missis** 'released (literally, sent) from the sacred starting gate'.

86 **insistam** (+ dative) 'I shall urge on'. The poet is so carried away that he switches to the indicative, imagining that he is actually participating in the race. **vehendus** 'riding'.

87 **lora dabo** 'I shall give the reins' = 'I shall give the horses their head'.

88 **stringam metas interiore rota** 'I shall graze the turning posts with the nearside wheel'. At the ends of the stadium were the turning posts (**metae**), three stone pillars with pointed tops. The charioteer's art lay in getting round these as closely as possible. Going around them too widely could waste valuable time. To bunch up with the other chariots would be to risk collision, and to strike rather than graze the posts would crash the chariot and lead to disaster.

89 **mihi** 'by me' (dative of the agent). **fueris conspecta** 'you shall have been caught sight of' = 'if you are caught sight of'.

90 **remissa** 'slack'.

91 **refugis** 'do you back away?'. **linea** 'the line', i.e. the groove in the stone which marked off the individual seats in the theatre.

92 **haec in lege loci commoda** 'these advantages in the rules of the place'.

93–6 **tu … tu … genu** the poet addresses other spectators.

94 **contactu** (+ genitive) 'by contact with …'.

95 **post** 'behind'.

The race begins; the girl's charioteer proves a failure.

> maxima iam vacuo praetor spectacula Circo
> > quadriiugos aequo carcere misit equos.
> cui studeas, video; vincet, cuicumque favebis:
> > quid cupias, ipsi scire videntur equi.
> me miserum, metam spatioso circuit orbe;
> > quid facis? admoto proximus axe subit.
> quid facis, infelix? perdis bona vota puellae;
> > tende, precor, valida lora sinistra manu.

100

(Amores 3.2.65–72)

*The spectators call for a re-start; the girl's charioteer wins the
prize; will the poet win his prize?*

> favimus ignavo. sed enim revocate, Quirites,
> > et date iactatis undique signa togis.
> en revocant; at, ne turbet toga mota capillos,
> > in nostros abdas te licet usque sinus.
> iamque patent iterum reserato carcere postes,
> > evolat admissis discolor agmen equis.
> nunc saltem supera spatioque insurge patenti:
> > sint mea, sint dominae fac rata vota meae.
> sunt dominae rata vota meae, mea vota supersunt;
> > ille tenet palmam, palma petenda mea est.'
> risit et argutis quiddam promisit ocellis:
> > 'hoc satis hic; alio cetera redde loco.'

105

110

115

(Amores 3.2.73–84)

A chariot race

97 **maxima … spectacula** i.e. 'the races, the big event'. **iam vacuo … Circo** 'the Circus (being) now empty'. The procession which preceded the races is over. **praetor** the praetor presided over the games. He began the races by dropping a white cloth.

98 **misit** the verb has two objects: the praetor 'started' the **maxima spectacula** and 'let out' the teams of four horses (**quadriiugos equos**) from the starting gate, which ensures a fair start (**aequo**).

99 **cui … favebis** = **video cui studeas** (subjunctive in indirect question) (**is**) **cuicumque favebis vincet**.

101 **me miserum** (accusative of indignant exclamation) 'unhappy me' = 'for God's sake, look at that!'. **spatioso** 'wide'.

102 **proximus** 'the man behind'. **axe** 'with his axle'.

105 **sed enim revocate** 'but come on, call them back'. **Quirites** 'Romans'.

106 **iactatis … togis** 'by waving your togas'. By doing this, the spectators give the sign (**signa**) that a re-start is necessary.

108 **abdas te licet** 'you can hide'. **in nostros … usque sinus** 'deep in the folds of my toga'.

109 **reserato carcere** 'with the starting-box unlocked'.

110 **admissis** 'released'. **discolor** 'of different colours'. The charioteers wore the colours of their sporting party. These colours, red, green, white and blue, won fanatical support.

111 **spatio** 'space'. **insurge** (+ dative) 'rise into' = 'make for' (the open space).

112 **sint … meae** = **fac (ut) mea dominae(que) meae vota rata** (fulfilled) **sint**.

113 **supersunt** 'are left' = 'are still to be fulfilled'.

114 **ille** i.e. the winner. **palmam** 'the palm of victory'.

115 **risit** 'she smiled'. Until this line the poem has been a monologue: the poet has been talking the whole time. **argutis … ocellis** 'with her lovely bright eyes' (the diminutive **ocellis** conveys the poet's emotion). **quiddam** 'something'.

116 **hoc satis (est) hic. cetera redde** 'pay the rest' (of your promises). The girl's smile prompts the poet to hope for his reward after they have left the Circus.

The playful, at times risqué, love poetry that we have included so far in this chapter should not lead us to overlook the fact that, a married man himself, Ovid also celebrated the blessings of marriage – and of pietas, *the bond that united families as well as gods and humans. This can be clearly seen in the following excerpt from his longest and, as many think, his finest work, the* Metamorphoses *(= Changes of Shape). This is a great cycle of myths and stories, linked together in an immensely long narrative of fifteen books, in which the only common feature is that each story ends with a change of shape. The following story of Baucis and Philemon comes near the end of the eighth book.*

The pious Lelex, a man mature both in mind and years (animo maturus et aevo) *tells a story to emphasize the power of the gods.*

The sacra

     immensa est finemque potentia caeli
  non habet, et quidquid superi voluere, peractum est,
  quoque minus dubites, tiliae contermina quercus
120 collibus est Phrygiis modico circumdata muro;
  ipse locum vidi …
  haud procul hinc stagnum est, tellus habitabilis olim,
  nunc celebres mergis fulicisque palustribus undae;
  Iuppiter huc specie mortali cumque parente
125 venit Atlantiades positis caducifer alis.
  mille domos adiere locum requiemque petentes,
  mille domos clausere serae; tamen una recepit,
  parva quidem, stipulis et canna tecta palustri,
  sed pia Baucis anus parilique aetate Philemon
130 illa sunt annis iuncti iuvenalibus, illa
  consenuere casa paupertatemque fatendo
  effecere levem nec iniqua mente ferendo;
  nec refert, dominos illic famulosve requiras:
  tota domus duo sunt, idem parentque iubentque.
135 ergo ubi caelicolae parvos tetigere penates
  summissoque humiles intrarunt vertice postes,
  membra senex posito iussit relevare sedili.

(*Metamorphoses* 8.618–39)

Baucis lit a fire with trembling hands and put on a pot. She put in a cabbage which her husband had brought from the garden; he took down a chine of smoked bacon and cut off a piece from the pork they had kept so long. Baucis set the table with fruit and nuts and honeycomb; Philemon brought in a jar of modest wine. While the meal was cooking, they entertained their guests with cheerful talk.

117   **immensa** 'huge'. **potentia caeli** is the subject.

118   **peractum est** 'is accomplished'.

119   **quo … minus** 'so that … less'. **tiliae contermina quercus** 'an oak (**quercus**) side by side with a lime-tree (**tiliae**)'.

120   **Phrygiis** 'Phrygian'.

122   **stagnum** 'marsh'. **habitabilis** 'habitable'.

123   **celebres … palustribus** 'crowded with gulls and marsh coots'.

125   **Atlantiades … caducifer** 'Mercury (the son of Jupiter and Maia and so grandson of Maia's father Atlas) who bears the caduceus (a wand with two snakes coiled round it in a figure of eight pattern)'. **positis … alis** 'his wings laid aside'.

126   **locum requiemque** 'a place to rest' (hendiadys).

127   **serae** 'bars'.

128   **stipulis et canna … palustri** 'with straw and marsh reeds'.

129   **anus** 'old woman'. **parili** 'equal'.

130   **iuncti** 'married'. **iuvenalibus** 'youthful'.

30–31   **illa … casa** 'in that cottage'.

131   **consenuere** 'they grew old'. **fatendo** 'by being frank about'.

132   **levem** literally 'light', i.e. 'easy to bear'. **iniqua** 'discontented'.

133   **nec refert … requiras** 'it was no use to ask for servants or masters there'.

135   **caelicolae** 'the heaven-dwellers'. **penates** 'the dwelling' (literally, 'household gods').

136   **summisso … vertice** 'stooping their heads'. **humiles … postes** 'the humble door'.

137   **posito … relevare sedili** '(them) to rest on a bench he had put out'.

unicus anser

interea totiens haustum cratera repleri
sponte sua per seque vident succrescere vina:
140 attoniti novitate pavent manibusque supinis
concipiunt Baucisque preces timidusque Philemon
et veniam dapibus nullisque paratibus orant.
unicus anser erat, minimae custodia villae,
quem dis hospitibus domini mactare parabant.
145 ille celer penna tardos aetate fatigat
eluditque diu, tandemque est visus ad ipsos
confugisse deos. superi vetuere necari
'di' que 'sumus, meritasque luet vicinia poenas
impia,' dixerunt; 'vobis immunibus huius
150 esse mali dabitur. modo vestra relinquite tecta
ac nostros comitate gradus, et in ardua montis
ite simul!' parent ambo, baculisque levati
nituntur longo vestigia ponere clivo.'

(Metamorphoses 8.679–94)

*When they were an arrow's flight from the top, they looked back
and saw the whole countryside submerged in water; only their own
house was left. While they watched in amazement and dismay, their
little cottage was turned into a temple. Marble columns took the
place of the wooden roof props; the straw thatch grew yellow and
became a roof of gold.*

*Then Mercury said, 'Tell us, good old man and wife, worthy of
your good husband, what do you wish?' After Philemon had
consulted Baucis a moment, he said, 'We ask to become your priests
and the guardians of your temple, and, since we have lived our lives
together in harmony, may the same hour carry us off together.'
Their prayer was granted. They were guardians of the temple while
life was allowed them.*

*When they were very old and were standing before the temple
steps telling over the story of the place, Baucis saw Philemon
sprouting leaves and old Philemon saw Baucis sprouting too. As the
tree tops grew over their two faces, while they still could, they
spoke to each other; each said, 'Farewell, dear wife/husband,** just
as the bark covered and hid their mouths.*

*To this day, a peasant of the place will point to two trees close to
each other, growing from a single trunk.*

***coniunx** the Latin word means either 'wife' or 'husband' (literally 'mate').

138–9   **totiens haustum cratera** 'the mixing-bowl (**cratera** is acc.
sing.), as often as it was drained'. **repleri** and **succrescere** ('was
welling up') are infinitives dependent on **vident**. **per se** 'of
itself'.

140   **manibus supinis** 'with palms turned upwards': the attitude of
prayer.

141   **concipiunt** 'utter'. **-que ... -que ...** 'both ... and ...'. **timidus**
describes both Baucis and Philemon.

142   **dapibus nullisque paratibus** 'for the meal and no preparations' =
'for the fact that they had had to improvise the meal'.

143   **unicus anser** 'a single goose'. **custodia** 'the guardian'.

144   **dis hospitibus** 'for the gods who were their guests'.

145   **celer penna** 'swift with (its) wing' = 'swift of wing'. **tardos
aetate** '(Baucis and Philemon) slow with age'.

147   **necari** understand 'the goose' as the subject of this infinitive.

148–9   **meritas ... impia** 'your impious neighbours (literally, the impious
neighbourhood) will pay the penalty they deserve'.

49–50   **vobis ... dabitur** literally, 'it will be granted to you to be immune
from this evil (i.e. punishment)'.

150   **modo** 'only'. **tecta** 'house' (poetic plural).

151   **comitate** 'accompany'. **ardua** 'the heights'.

152   **simul** i.e. **cum nobis**. **baculis levati** 'propped up on their sticks'.

3 Ovid in exile

*Ovid left for exile in Tomis on the Black Sea in December AD 8 and
had arrived there by the following autumn. He lived in this frontier
town inhabited by half-bred Greeks and barbarian Getae until his
death in AD 17.*

*He had a thoroughly uncomfortable voyage out, only just
weathering the winter storms.*

> di maris et caeli – quid enim nisi vota supersunt? –
>   solvere quassatae parcite membra ratis.
> me miserum, quanti montes volvuntur aquarum!
>   iam iam tacturos sidera summa putes.
> 5 quantae diducto subsidunt aequore valles!
>   iam iam tacturas Tartara nigra putes.
> quocumque aspicio, nihil est, nisi pontus et aer,
>   fluctibus hic tumidus, nubibus ille minax.
> inter utrumque fremunt immani murmure venti.
> 10   nescit, cui domino pareat, unda maris.
> rector in incerto est nec quid fugiatve petatve
>   invenit: ambiguis ars stupet ipsa malis.
> scilicet occidimus, nec spes est ulla salutis,
>   dumque loquor, vultus obruit unda meos.

(Tristia 1.2.1–34, abridged)

Statue of Ovid in a square at Tomis

*When he got there, he found himself living under
conditions of extreme discomfort; he writes
graphically of the horrors of the climate at Tomis,
where it is terrible even in the summer.*

> 15 siquis adhuc istic meminit Nasonis adempti,
>   et superest sine me nomen in urbe meum,
> suppositum stellis numquam tangentibus aequor
>   me sciat in media vivere barbaria.
> Sauromatae cingunt, fera gens, Bessique Getaeque,
> 20   quam non ingenio nomina digna meo!
> dum tamen aura tepet, medio defendimur Histro:
>   ille suis liquidus bella repellit aquis.

(Tristia 3.10.1–8)

1 **nisi** 'except for'. **supersunt** 'are left'. In English we should say 'what is left …?'.

2 **solvere … parcite** 'spare to loosen' = 'I beg you not to break'. **quassatae** 'shattered', agreeing with **ratis**. **membra** 'the limbs' = 'the frame'.

3 **me miserum** 'unhappy me' = 'God help me!' (accusative of exclamation).

4 **tacturos (esse)**. **putes** 'you would think'.

6 **Tartara** (*n. pl.*) 'Tartarus', i.e. the underworld.

10 **cui domino** i.e. which of the various winds.

11 **rector** 'the helmsman'. **quid fugiat** 'what to avoid', 'steer clear of'.

12 **ambiguis** 'baffling'. **ars … ipsa** 'his skill itself' = 'even his great skill'.

13 **scilicet** 'surely'.

14 **vultus … meos** 'my face'.

15 **istic** 'there', i.e. in Rome. **Nasonis adempti** 'the Naso (i.e. the Ovid) Rome has lost'. Ovid's full name was Publius Ovidius Naso.

16 **superest** 'is left', 'survives'.

17–18 **suppositum stellis** 'placed (dwelling) beneath the stars' (**suppositum** agrees with **me**). Ovid suggests the cold remoteness of Tomis by referring to the northern constellations such as the Great and Lesser Bear which never sink below the sea. **barbaria** 'the barbarian world'.

19 These are the names of three local tribes.

20 **quam non … nomine digna = nomina quam non digna**.

21 **medio defendimur Histro** 'we are defended (from the hostile tribes) by the river Hister in the middle', i.e. acting as a barrier. The Hister is the Danube.

22 **ille … liquidus** 'he (i.e. the river) as he flows'.

medio defendimur Histro

The rigours of winter.

at cum tristis hiems squalentia protulit ora,
    terraque marmoreo est candida facta gelu,
25 nix iacet, et iactam nec sol pluviaeve resolvunt,
    indurat Boreas perpetuamque facit.
tantaque commoti vis est Aquilonis, ut altas
    aequet humo turres tectaque rapta ferat.
pellibus et sutis arcent mala frigora bracis,
30 oraque de toto corpore sola patent.
saepe sonant moti glacie pendente capilli,
    et nitet inducto candida barba gelu.

        (*Tristia* 3.10.9–22, abridged)

All of nature is gripped by the ice.

quid loquar ut vincti concrescant frigore rivi,
    deque lacu fragiles effodiantur aquae?
35 quaque rates ierant, pedibus nunc itur, et undas
    frigore concretas ungula pulsat equi;
vidimus ingentem glacie consistere pontum,
    lubricaque immotas testa premebat aquas.
inclusaeque gelu stabunt in marmore puppes,
40 nec poterit rigidas findere remus aquas.
vidimus in glacie pisces haerere ligatos,
    sed pars ex illis tum quoque viva fuit.

        (*Tristia* 3.10.25–50, abridged)

The enemy attacks over the ice.

protinus aequato siccis Aquilonibus Histro
    invehitur celeri barbarus hostis equo;
45 hostis equo pollens longeque volante sagitta
    vicinam late depopulatur humum.
diffugiunt alii; nullisque tuentibus agros
    incustoditae diripiuntur opes.
pars agitur vinctis post tergum capta lacertis,
50 respiciens frustra rura Laremque suum:
pars cadit hamatis misere confixa sagittis:
    nam volucri ferro tinctile virus inest.
quae nequeunt secum ferre aut abducere, perdunt,
    et cremat insontes hostica flamma casas.

        (*Tristia* 3.10.53–66, abridged)

hostis equo pollens

23 **squalentia protulit ora** 'has thrust his rough face forth'. Like the river, the winter is personified.

24 **marmoreo ... gelu** 'with frost as hard as marble'.

25 **iactam (nivem)** 'the thrown down snow', i.e. 'the snow once it has fallen'. **resolvunt** 'melt'.

26 **indurat Boreas** 'the North wind hardens (it)'.

27 **commoti ... Aquilonis** 'of the North wind (when) set in motion' = 'of the North wind when it is blowing violently'.

28 **aequet** 'levels' = 'flattens'. **ferat** 'carries away'.

29 **pellibus et sutis ... bracis** 'with skins and sewn trousers' = 'with trousers of sewn skins' (hendiadys).

30 **patent** 'lie open', 'are exposed'.

31 **sonant** 'make(s) a noise', 'tinkle(s)'.

32 **inducto ... gelu** 'frost having been drawn over it' = 'with a layer of frost'.

33 **quid loquar ut ...** 'why should I tell how ...'. **vincti ... rivi = rivi, frigore vincti, concrescant**.

34 **fragiles** 'brittle'. It is not in fact water but ice which has to be broken.

35 **qua** 'where'. **itur** 'it is gone' = 'men go'.

36 **ungula** 'the hoof'.

38 **lubrica ... testa** 'a slippery shell' = 'a coating of ice'.

39 **stabunt** Ovid uses the future tense – he is describing something that will (i.e. is liable to) happen. **in marmore** 'on the marble (surface of the sea)'.

42 **pars** 'some (literally, part)' of the fish.

43 **aequato** 'levelled'. **siccis** 'dry' = 'freezing'.

44 **invehitur** 'rides to the attack'.

45 **pollens** 'powerful'. The enemy is noted for his prowess both on horseback and in archery.

48 **opes**, *f. pl.* 'resources'.

49 **pars agitur ... capta** 'some are driven off into captivity'.

50 **Larem** 'their household god' = 'their homes'.

51 **hamatis** 'barbed'.

52 **volucri** the 'winged iron' refers to arrows. **tinctile virus** 'poison smeared (on them)'.

53 **quae = ea quae**.

54 **insontes ... casas** 'their unoffending huts'. **hostica** 'the enemy's'.

Paralysed by fear, the natives neglect the land. All lies desolate and barren.

55 tunc quoque cum pax est, trepidant formidine belli,
   nec quisquam presso vomere sulcat humum.
 aut videt aut metuit locus hic, quem non videt, hostem;
   cessat iners rigido terra relicta situ.
 aspiceres nudos sine fronde, sine arbore, campos:
60   heu loca felici non adeunda viro!
 ergo tam late pateat cum maximus orbis,
   haec est in poenam terra reperta meam.

      (*Tristia* 3.10.67–78, abridged)

Inevitably under such conditions, Ovid fell ill and wrote a sad letter to his wife.

 haec mihi si casu miraris epistula quare
   alterius digitis scripta sit, aeger eram.
65 aeger in extremis ignoti partibus orbis,
   incertusque meae paene salutis eram.
 nec caelum patior, nec aquis adsuevimus istis,
   terraque nescio quo non placet ipsa modo.
 non domus apta satis, non hic cibus utilis aegro,
70   nullus, Apollinea qui levet arte malum,
 non qui soletur, non qui labentia tarde
   tempora narrando fallat, amicus adest.
 lassus in extremis iaceo populisque locisque,
   et subit adfecto nunc mihi, quicquid abest.
75 omnia cum subeant, vincis tamen omnia, coniunx,
   et plus in nostro pectore parte tenes.
 te loquor absentem, te vox mea nominat unam;
   nulla venit sine te nox mihi, nulla dies.

      (*Tristia* 3.3.1–18, abridged)

He kept himself going by writing poetry but complains that he has almost forgotten how to speak Latin.

 detineo studiis animum falloque dolores,
80   experior curis et dare verba meis.
 quid potius faciam desertis solus in oris,
   quamve malis aliam quaerere coner opem?
 sive locum specto, locus est inamabilis, et quo
   esse nihil toto tristius orbe potest;
85 sive homines, vix sunt homines hoc nomine digni,
   quamque lupi saevae plus feritatis habent.
 in paucis remanent Graiae vestigia linguae,
   haec quoque iam Getico barbara facta sono.

56 **sulcat** 'ploughs'. **presso vomere** 'with down-pressed ploughshare'.

57 **quem** the antecedent is **hostem**.

58 **cessat iners** 'lies idle'. **rigido ... situ** 'in unbroken neglect' = 'in neglect, unbroken by the plough'.

59 **aspiceres** 'you may see' = 'one may see'.

61 **ergo ... orbis** = **ergo, cum** ('although') **maximus orbis** ('the world') **tam late pateat**.

62 **est ... reperta** 'has been discovered'. **in poenam ... meam** 'for my punishment'.

63–4 **haec ... sit** = **si casu miraris quare haec mea epistula digitis alterius scripta sit**.

64 **aeger eram** 'I was ill' (when this letter was written) = 'I am ill'.

67 **caelum** 'the climate'. **adsuevimus** 'have we (plural for singular) become accustomed'.

68 **nescio quo ... modo** 'I don't know how' = 'in some way I cannot explain'.

69 **apta (aegro)**.

70 **nullus ... qui levet** 'no one who may relieve' = 'no one to relieve'. **Apollinea ... arte** Apollo's art was medicine.

71–2 **qui** the antecedent is **amicus** – there is no friend here to make the time pass more quickly.

74 **subit ... abest** = **quicquid abest nunc subit mihi** ('comes to my mind') **adfecto** ('affected' (with sickness), i.e. 'in my sickness').

75 **omnia cum subeant** = **cum** ('although') **omnia subeant** ('come to (my) mind').

76 **plus ... parte** 'more than half (a share)'; **pars** (here) = 'share'.

79 **detineo** i.e. 'I keep busy'.

80 **experior ... et dare** = **et experior dare**. **curis ... dare verba meis** 'to cheat my cares'.

81 **quid potius** 'what rather?' = 'what else?'.

83 **inamabilis** 'unlovely'. **quo** '(a place) than which'.

85 **sive homines (specto)**. **hoc nomine** i.e. the name of man.

87 **remanent** 'there remains', 'still exist'.

88 **facta (sunt)**.

unus in hoc nemo est populo, qui forte Latine
90   quaelibet e medio reddere verba queat.
ille ego Romanus vates – ignoscite, Musae! –
        Sarmatico cogor plurima more loqui.

(*Tristia* 5.7.39–56, abridged)

*No elegy (mourning poem) for Ovid survives. To commemorate his
death in this remote region, we quote a poem which he wrote at the
age of twenty-four on the death of his fellow poet Albius Tibullus,
celebrating the triumph of literature over mortality.* Ars longa, vita
brevis.

Memnona si mater, mater ploravit Achillem,
        et tangunt magnas tristia fata deas,
95 flebilis indignos, Elegeia, solve capillos:
        a nimis ex vero nunc tibi nomen erit.
ille tui vates operis, tua fama, Tibullus,
        ardet in exstructo corpus inane rogo.
cum rapiunt mala fata bonos, (ignoscite fasso)
100   sollicitor nullos esse putare deos.
vive pius: moriere pius; cole sacra: colentem
        mors gravis a templis in cava busta trahet.
carminibus confide bonis: iacet ecce Tibullus;
        vix manet e toto, parva quod urna capit.
105 si tamen e nobis aliquid nisi nomen et umbra
        restat, in Elysia valle Tibullus erit.
obvius huic venies hedera iuvenalia cinctus
        tempora cum Calvo, docte Catulle, tuo;
his comes umbra tua est, si qua est modo corporis umbra;
110   auxisti numeros, culte Tibulle, pios.
ossa quieta, precor, tuta requiescite in urna,
        et sit humus cineri non onerosa tuo.

(*Amores* 3.9, abridged)

A Roman funeral

89–90 **qui … queat** 'who by chance could utter in Latin any colloquial language at all'. **forte** (= 'by chance') emphasizes the remoteness of the possibility. **e medio verba** 'colloquial language', i.e. the natives speak the language, if at all, in stilted pidgin Latin. **quaelibet … verba** 'any words at all'.

91 **ille vates** 'the famous bard'.

93ff. i.e. if goddesses can mourn the death of their children, then you, Elegy, should mourn Tibullus. Elegeia, the spirit of elegiac poetry, is personified as a goddess whose children are the elegiac poets.

93 **Memnona** accusative case. The Ethiopian prince Memnon, son of Aurora (the dawn), was killed at Troy by Achilles. His mother wept tears of dew for him every morning. Achilles, son of Thetis, a sea goddess, was killed later by Paris.

95 **flebilis** 'tearful' (agreeing with **Elegeia**). **indignos … capillos** 'your hair which has not deserved such treatment'. Women loosed their hair in mourning.

96 **nimis ex vero** 'only too true'. Ovid refers to the derivation of the name Elegy from the Greek *e legei* '(he) cries woe').

97 **tua fama** i.e. 'the man who made you (Elegy) famous'.

98 **in exstructo … rogo** 'on a high (literally, built up) pyre'.

99 **fasso** (dative) 'my confession'.

100 **sollicitor** 'I am moved to'.

101 **moriere = morieris.**

102 **in cava busta** 'into a hollow tomb'.

103 **confide** the tone is ironical.

104 **parva … urna** after cremation, the bones and ashes of the dead were stored in an urn.

106 **Elysia** 'of Elysium'. Elysium was the dwelling-place of the good in the underworld.

107 **obvius** (+ dative) 'to meet'.

107–8 **hedera iuvenalia cinctus/tempora** 'bound as to your youthful temples with ivy' = 'your youthful temples bound with ivy'.

108 **Calvo** Calvus was a friend and fellow poet of Catullus (see p. 104 above). **docte** this means more than 'learned' – perhaps translate 'the great craftsman'.

109 **si … modo** 'if only'.

110 **numeros** 'verse', 'poetry'. **culte** 'cultivated', 'civilized'.

112 **onerosa** 'burdensome to' = 'a heavy weight on'.

parva quod urna capit

Cicero 1 The young Cicero

absolvō, absolvere, absolvī, absolūtum I absolve, acquit

accedō, accēdere, accessī, accessum I approach; I am added to

adversārius, -a, -um opposite; an opponent

arbitror (1) I think, judge

avus, -ī, *m.* grandfather

causa, -ae, *f.* cause, reason; law case

celebrō (1) I celebrate

cēnseō, cēnsēre, cēnsuī, cēnsum I think, judge, vote, decree

cogitō (1) I think, reflect

dēsistō, dēsistere, destitī, destitum I cease from

familiāris, -e friendly; a friend

fere (adverb) nearly, about

frāternus, -a, -um of a brother, brotherly

iūdex, iūdicis, *m.* judge, jurymen

opera, -ae, *f.* pains, attention

opīniō, opīniōnis, *f.* opinion, belief

opīnor (1) I believe

petītiō, petītiōnis, *f.* petition, candidature (for office)

petō, petere, petīvī, petītum I seek, make for, attack, stand for (office)

potius (comparative adverb) rather; **potissimum** (superlative adverb) most

quamvīs however much, although

repetō, repetere, repetīvī, repetītum I demand back, seek, recall

sensus, -ūs, *m.* feeling

studiōsus, -a, -um + gen. keen (on), enthusiastic

testis, testis, *c.* witness

ultrō (adverb) of one's own accord, on one's own initiative

verō indeed (gives emphasis to the preceding word)

versor (1) I come and go, I am involved in

vestīgium, -ī, *n.* trace, track

Cicero 2 Consulship, exile and return

abūtor, abūtī, abūsus + abl. I abuse

adsequor, adsequī, adsecūtus I follow on, overtake

annōna, -ae, *f.* corn, price of food

caedēs, caedis, *f.* slaughter, murder

cohortor (1) I encourage

concursus, -ūs, m. concourse, crowd

cūnctor (1) I delay

dolor, dolōris, *m.* pain, grief

gemitus, -ūs, *m.* groan

impetus, -ūs, *m.* charge, attack

imprōvīsus, -a, -um unforeseen, unexpected
  ex imprōvīsō unexpectedly

metus, -ūs, *m.* fear

miseriae, -ārum, *f. pl.* misery

ne ... quidem not even

necō (1) I kill, butcher

obviam (adverb) in the way of, to meet

ops, opis, *f.* help

ōrdō, ōrdinis, *m.* line, order, class (of citizens)

pateō, patēre, patuī I lie open, am revealed

pertineō, pertinēre, pertinuī, pertentum (ad) I reach, concern

plaudō, plaudere, plausī, plausum I applaud

probus, -a, -um good, upright

prōficiō, prōficere, prōfēcī, prōfectum I make progress

pudor, pudōris, *m.* shame, modesty

queō, quīre, quīvī I can

querēla, -ae, *f.* complaint

quoniam since

salvus, -a, -um safe, unharmed

scientia, -ae, *f.* knowledge

sēnsus, -ūs, *m.* feeling

sīn but if

singulāris, -e single, singular, unique

sollicitūdō, sollicitūdinis, *f.* worry, anxiety

sollicitus, -a, -um anxious

totiēns so often

vel or, even; **vel ... vel** either ... or

Cicero 3 Governor of Cilicia

approbō (1) I approve
castellum, -ī, *n.* fort
cōnferō, cōnferre, cōntulī, collātum I bring together, compare
confestim hastily
contentiō, contentiōnis, *f.* effort, struggle
contiō, contiōnis, *f.* public meeting, speech
dīmicō (1) I fight
dīripiō, dīripere, dīripuī, dīreptum I snatch away, plunder
ēligō, ēligere, ēlēgī, ēlectum I choose
ērumpō, ērumpere, ērūpī, ēruptum I break out
expugnō, expugnāre I take by storm
fructus, -ūs, *m.* fruit, profit
interest, interesse, interfuit it is important, it matters
levō, levāre I lighten
mandātum, -ī, *n.* instruction
nescioquis, nescioquid someone, something or other
obvius, -a, -um in the way, to meet
paulum/paullum a little, somewhat
peccō (1) I do wrong
pergō, pergere, perrēxī, perrēctum I go, march, proceed
potior, potīrī, potītus + gen. I obtain, possess
sempiternus, -a, -um everlasting, permanent
sententia, -ae, *f.* opinion
spatium, -ī, *n.* space (of place or time)
summa, -ae, *f.* total
sumptus, -ūs, *m.* expense
vastō (1) I lay waste

Cicero 4 Civil war and death

aliquotiēns several times
altum, -ī, *n.* the high sea
commodum, -ī, *n.* convenience, advantage
confirmō (1) I strengthen, encourage
constat, constāre, constitit it is agreed
dignitās, dignitātis, *f.* worth, importance, dignity
fors, fortis, *f.* chance
inīquus, -a, -um uneven, unfair, cruel
medicīna, -ae, *f.* cure, medicine
mereō (2) I deserve, earn
mereor, merērī, meritus I deserve

molestiae, -ārum, *f. pl.* annoyance
necessārius, -a, -um necessary
optō (1) I wish for, pray for
pār, paris equal
praetereō, praeterīre, praeteriī, praeteritum I pass by, overtake, pass over
praetermittō, praetermittere, praetermīsī, praetermissum I let pass, pass over, omit
ratiō, ratiōnis, *f.* reason, method, plan; *pl.* accounts
suprēmus, -a, -um last
trīclinium, -ī, *n.* dining room
vacō (1) I am empty, vacant
voluntās, voluntātis, *f.* wish, will, good will

Caesar 1 The first invasion of Britain

adorior, adorīrī, adortus I rise against, attack
aes, aeris, *n.* bronze
aestus, -ūs, *m.* heat, tide
āmitto, āmittere, āmīsī, āmissum I let fall, let slip, lose
ancora, -ae, *f.* anchor
angustus, -a, -um narrow
appropinquō (1) + dat. I approach
aquila, -ae, *f.* eagle; legionary standard
circiter about
compleō, complēre, complēvī, complētum I fill
coniurātiō, coniurātiōnis, *f.* conspiracy
constituō, constituere, constituī, constitūtum I place, decide, establish
cōnsuēscō, cōnsuēscere, cōnsuēvī, cōnsuētum I grow accustomed to
consuetūdō, consuetūdinis, *f.* custom
coorior, coorīrī, coortus I arise, break out
dēcernō, dēcernere, dēcrēvī, dēcrētum I judge, decide, decree
dēficiō, dēficere, dēfēcī, dēfectum I fail, am wanting
equitātus, -ūs, *m.* cavalry
etsī even if, although
exiguus, -a, -um small, tiny
existimō (1) I think
expediō, expedīre, expedīvī, expedītum I free, extricate
facultās, facultātis, *f.* opportunity
hortor (1) I encourage
idōneus, -a, -um (**ad**) suitable (for)

impediō, impedīre, impedīvī, impedītum I hinder, prevent

imperītus, -a, -um unskilled, inexperienced

incitō (1) I urge on

incolō, incolere, incoluī I dwell in, inhabit

inūtilis, inūtile useless

mandō (1) I entrust to; I command (+ dat.)

maritīmus, -a, -um maritime, sea

materia, -ae, *f.* material

mātūrus, -a, -um ripe, early

membrum, -ī, *n.* limb

nancīscor, nancīscī, nactus I obtain, get

natiō, natiōnis, *f.* tribe

opportūnus, -a, -um convenient, advantageous

ōra, -ae, *f.* coast

perturbō (1) I throw into confusion

plānus, -a, -um flat

praeda, -ae, *f.* booty

praestō, praestāre, praestitī, praestitum I stand out, excel; I show, fulfil

praeter + acc. except

premō, premere, pressī, pressum I press, press hard

pulvis, pulveris, *m.* dust

reficiō, reficere, refēcī, refectum I remake, repair

regiō, regiōnis, *f.* district, region

rota, -ae, *f.* wheel

sagitta, -ae, *f.* arrow

sōlis occāsus, -ūs, *m.* sunset, west

spatium, -ī, *n.* space (of time or place)

statiō, statiōnis, *f.* station, guard post, guard

subsequor, subsequī, subsecūtus I follow closely

subsidium, -ī, *n.* help, reinforcement

summittō, summittere, summīsī, summissum I send to help

suspicor (1) I suspect

tempestās, tempestātis, *f.* storm, weather

vis (acc. **vim**; abl. **vī**) *f.* force; **vires, virium,** *f. pl.* strength

Caesar 2 The second invasion of Britain

abdō, abdere, abdidī, abditum I remove, hide

adflīgō, adflīgere, adflīxī, adflīctum I afflict, damage

agger, aggeris, *m.* rampart

aptus, -a, um (**ad**) suitable (for)

commodus, -a, -um suitable, advantageous

cōnsīdō, cōnsīdere, cōnsēdī, cōnsessum I sit down, take up position

cōnspicor (1) I catch sight of, see

dē + abl. after (of time)

dētrimentum, -ī, *n.* loss

ēgregius, -a, -um outstanding, excellent

ēruptiō, ēruptiōnis, *f.* break-out, sally

externus, -a, -um outside, external

faber, fabrī, *m.* carpenter, engineer

imprūdens, imprūdentis ignorant, unawares

incommodum, -ī, *n.* reverse, setback, damage

īnstruō, īnstruere, īnstruxī, īnstructum I draw up

integer, integra, integrum whole, fresh

lacessō, lacessere, lacessīvī, lacessītum I provoke, challenge

mollis, molle soft

mōtus, -ūs, *m.* movement, disturbance

proelior (1) I join battle, fight

repentīnus, -a, -um sudden

Chapter 3 Revolt in Gaul 1: The ambush of Sabinus and Cotta

ācer, ācris, ācre keen, fierce

advolō (1) I fly to, swoop upon

auctor, auctōris, *m.* adviser, supporter

clamitō (1) I keep shouting, I proclaim

cōnsentiō, cōnsentīre, cōnsēnsī, cōnsēnsum I agree

cōnsulō, cōnsulere, cōnsuluī, cōnsultum I consult, consider; **mihi cōnsulō** I consult my own interest, provide for myself

cōnsuētūdō, cōnsuētūdinis, *f.* custom, habit

controversia, -ae, *f.* debate, argument

dēferō, dēferre, dētulī, dēlātum I carry down; I report

fremitus, -ūs, *m.* din

iniūria, -ae, *f.* wrong, injury

intereō, interīre, interiī, interitum I perish

minuō, minuere, minui I lessen

occultus, -a, -um hidden, secret

opprimō, opprimere, oppressī, oppressum I crush, oppress

ratiō, ratiōnis, *f.* reason, method, plan; **ratiōnēs, -um,** *f. pl.* (financial) accounts

saucius, -a, -um wounded
stīpendium, -ī, *n.* tax, pay, (a year of) military service
tenuis, tenue slender, weak
trepidō (1) I panic
ulcīscor, ulcīscī, ultus I avenge
vagor (1) I wander
valetūdō, valetūdinis, *f.* health
vigilia, -ae, *f.* wakefulness, vigilance, watch
voluntās, voluntātis, *f.* wish, desire, good will

Caesar 4 Revolt in Gaul 2: The siege of Cicero's camp

adipīscor, adipīscī, adeptus I obtain
asper, aspera, asperum rough, violent
certāmen, certāminis, *n.* contest, battle
cingō, cingere, cinxī, cinctum I surround
comminus (adverb) at close quarters
creber, crebra, crebrum frequent
deinceps (adverb) in succession
dēprehendō, dēprehendere, dēprehendī, dēprehēnsum I catch, seize
fidēs, fideī, *f.* faith, loyalty
fossa, -ae, *f.* ditch
intercipiō, intercipere, intercēpī, interceptum I intercept
intereō, interīre, interiī, interitum I perish
intermittō, intermittere, intermīsī, intermissum I leave off, leave a gap
lapis, lapidis, *m.* stone
obsidiō, obsidiōnis, *f.* siege
occāsiō, occāsiōnis, *f.* opportunity
palūs, palūdis, *f.* marsh
perfuga, -ae, *c.* deserter
perfugiō, perfugere, perfūgī, perfugitum I flee for refuge
praestō, praestāre, praestitī, praestitum I stand out, excel; I show (qualities)
quīcumque, quaecumque, quodcumque whoever, whatever
simulātiō, simulātiōnis, *f.* pretence
tolerō (1) I endure

Catullus 1 Catullus and his friends

aevum, -ī, *n.* age, generation
albus, -a, -um, white
anus, -ūs, *f.* old woman, old
āter, ātra, ātrum dark, black
crīmen, crīminis, *n.* charge, crime
culpa, -ae, *f.* blame, fault
mē decet, decēre, decuit it suits me, it is right for me
disertus, -a, -um eloquent
dīvus, -a, -um divine
dīvī, -ōrum, *m. pl.* the gods
identidem again and again
illinc from there
impius, -a, -um impious, wicked
iocus, -ī, *m.* joke, sport
laedō, laedere, laesī, laesum I hurt
Lar, Laris, *m.* guardian god, home
lūgeō, lūgēre, luxī, luctum I mourn
perennis, -e lasting, enduring
praesertim especially
pretium, -ī, *n.* price, cost
prōsum, prōdesse, prōfuī + dat. I benefit, profit
supplicium, -ī, *n.* punishment
vehemēns, vehementis violent

Catullus 2 Catullus in love

artus, -ūs, *m.* limb
bellus, -a, -um handsome, pretty
complexus, -ūs, *m.* embrace
convīvium, -ī, n. dinner party
digitus, -ī, *m.* finger
ingrātus, -a, -um thankless, ungrateful
iocor (1) I joke, play
levis, -e light
misereor (2) + gen. I pity
nūmen, nūminis, *n.* divine power
patefaciō, patefacere, patefēcī, patefactum I open up
recordor (1) I remember
sānctus, -a, -um holy
sector (1) I follow
sinus, -ūs, *m.* curve, fold (of a dress), lap

tenebrae, -ārum, *f. pl.* shadows, darkness
vīlis, -e cheap, worthless

Catullus 3 The sequel

cinis, cineris, *m.* ashes
collum, -ī, *n.* neck
diversus, -a, -um opposite, different
iugum, -ī, *n.* yoke (of oxen), mountain ridge
lacus, -ūs, *m.* lake
mūtus, -a, -um dumb
nequeō, nequīre, nequīvī I cannot
peregrīnus, -a, -um foreign
silēscō, silēscere I grow silent
vōtum, -ī, *n.* vow, prayer

Virgil 1 Aeneas arrives at Carthage

arceō, arcēre, arcuī I ward off, keep off
arx, arcis, *f.* citadel
avārus, -a, -um greedy, miserly
caecus, -a, -um blind
cernō, cernere, crēvī, crētum I perceive, decide
mōnstrō (1) I show
ōmen, ōminis, *n.* omen
pondus, ponderis, *n.* weight
spernō, spernere, sprēvī, sprētum I despise

Virgil 2 The love of Dido and Aeneas

āmēns, āmentis mad, frantic
arvum, -ī, *n.* field
ēnsis, ēnsis, *m.* sword
haereō, haerēre, haesī, haesum I stick
ignārus, -a, -um ignorant
leō, leōnis, *m.* lion
pāstor, pāstōris, *m.* shepherd
perfidus, -a, -um treacherous
sīdus, sīderis, *n.* contellation, star
speciēs, speciēī, *f.* appearance
ūrō, ūrere, ussī, ustum I burn (transitive)

Virgil 3 The death of Dido

admoneō (2) I advise, warn
celsus, -a, -um tall
fraus, fraudis, *f.* fraud, deceit
fundō, fundere, fūdī, fūsum I pour out, rout
fūnus, fūneris, *n.* funeral, death
fūrtum, -ī, *n.* theft, deceit
lūmen, lūminis, *n.* light, eye
natō (1) I swim, float
operiō, operīre, operuī, opertum I cover, conceal
secō, secāre, secuī, sectum I cut
spīritus, -ūs, *m.* breath
tectum, -ī, *n.* roof, house
testor (1) I call to witness

Livy 1 Hannibal prepares to invade Italy

calor, calōris, *m.* heat
certō (1) I contend, fight
convertō, convertere, convertī, conversum I turn
ēdoceō, ēdocēre, ēdocuī, ēdoctum I teach, inform
fabricō (1) I build, make
fatīgō (1) I tire out
humus, -ī, *f.* earth, ground; **humī** on the ground
incertus, -a, -um uncertain
mīlitia, -ae, *f.* military service, campaign
mōlēs, mōlis, *f.* mass, trouble, effort
naturālis, -e natural, innate
obtineō, obtinēre, obtinuī, obtentum I hold, obtain
pācō (1) I pacify
perfidia, -ae, *f.* treachery
vīcus, -ī, *m.* street, village
vitium, -ī, *n.* fault

Livy 2 Hannibal reaches the Alps

angustiae, -ārum, *f. pl.* narrows, pass
clīvus, -ī, *m.* slope
ēminus (adverb) from a distance
frequēns, frequentis crowded, in crowds
immōbilis, -e immobile, motionless
inanimus, -a, -um inanimate, lifeless
īnfestus, -a, -um dangerous, hostile; endangered

misceō, miscēre, miscuī, mixtum I mix, confuse
nemus, nemoris, *n.* wood, forest
saltus, -ūs, *m.* defile, mountain pass, glade

Livy 3 Hannibal crosses the Alps

abrumpō, abrumpere, abrūpī, abruptum I break away
exitus, -ūs, *m.* way out, end
extemplō (adverb) immediately
glaciēs, glaciēī, *f.* ice
hauriō, haurīre, hausī, haustum I drain, drink up
inermis, -e unarmed
iūmentum, -ī, *n.* beast of burden
libet (mihi) (2) it pleases me, I want
nequīquam in vain, to no purpose
nix, nivis, *f.* snow
nūdus, -a, -um naked, bare
oppōnō, oppōnere, opposuī, oppositum I put in the way of
ostentō (1) I show, point out
praeceps, praecipitis headlong, sheer
scopulus, -ī, *m.* rock
temerē rashly, blindly
velut just as, as though

Ovid 1 Ovid tells the story of his life

furtim secretly
gena, -ae, *f.* cheek
iuvenīlis, -e youthful, young
legō, legere, lēgī, lēctum I gather, choose, read
posteritās, posteritātis, *f.* posterity
restō (1) I remain, am left over
sonō, sonāre, sonuī, sonitum I make a sound, resound
sonus, -ī, *m.* sound
vātis, vātis, *m.* prophet, poet

Ovid 2 Ovid the lover

agna, -ae, *f.* lamb
celeber, celebra, celebrum much frequented, crowded, famous
columba, -ae, *f.* dove

habitābilis, -e habitable
lacertus, -ī, *m.* arm
nītor, nītī, nīxus I lean on, struggle
novitās, novitātis, *f.* newness, novelty
requiēs, requiētis, *f.* rest
rēfert, rēferre, rētulit it matters, it is important
saltem (adverb) at least
tegō, tegere, texī, tēctum I cover
vēnor (1) I hunt
verber, verberis, *n.* blow, lash

Ovid 3 Ovid in exile

fallō, fallere, fefellī, falsum I deceive
gelū, -ūs, *n.* frost, ice
īnsōns, īnsontis innocent
os, ossis, *n.* bone
piscis, piscis, *m.* fish
poena, -ae, *f.* punishment
quassō (1) I shake, shatter
rēmus, -ī, *m.* oar
supersum, superesse, superfuī I am left over, survive
tumidus, -a, -um swollen
volucer, volucris, volucre flying

Why learn to scan?

Latin poetry was written to be read aloud. Its publication was usually at a *recitātiō* at which poets read their poems to an audience. The sound of the verse, particularly the verse rhythms, was of paramount importance. And so, if you are to appreciate Latin poetry, you must be able to read it aloud rhythmically. If you have learnt to pronounce Latin correctly, you may be able to do this straight off and feel the rhythms for yourself. The purpose of learning scansion is to see how the various metres work and make sure that your reading is correct. The rules, quite different from those which apply to English verse, will sound complicated but are not difficult once a few basic principles are grasped.

Quantity

The scansion of Latin verse of the classical period is quantitative, not accentual as in English. Syllables are either light or heavy, regardless of where the accent falls on any given word.

(a) All syllables are heavy which contain a long vowel or diphthong, e.g. **laetī, sōlēs, Rōmānī**. For the purposes of scansion heavy syllables are marked with a macron ‾, light syllables with the symbol ˘. This convention sometimes results in a syllable containing a short vowel being marked with a macron; see below.

(b) If a short vowel is followed by two consonants, whether in the same or in different words, the syllable is heavy, e.g.

tāntae͟| mōlĭs ĕ|r͟āt Rō|mānām | cōndĕrĕ | gēntĕm.

In this line the syllables underlined are heavy although in each case the vowel is short.

(c) Exceptions to rule (b): if a short vowel is followed by a combination of mute (**p, t, c, b, d, g**) and liquid (**r** and less commonly **l**), the syllable may be scanned either light or heavy, e.g. **pătris, volŭcris, latĕbrae**. This is really a question of pronunciation; such syllables can be pronounced either **pāt-ris** or **pă-tris** (**tr** making one sound).

Elision

A final open vowel followed by a vowel in the next word is elided, as in the French *c'est*, but in Latin the elision is not written, e.g.

cōntĭcŭ|ēr(e) ōm|nēs īn|tēntīqu(e) | ōră tĕ|nēbānt

The final **e** of **conticuēre** elides before the following **o** of **omnia** and the final **e** of **que** elides before the following **ō** of **ōra**.

hūc sē| prōvēc|tī dē|sērt(ō) īn|lītŏrĕ|cōndūnt

The final **ō** of **dēsertō** elides before the following **i** of **in**.

More surprisingly, a final syllable ending **-m** elides before a following vowel, e.g.

pārs stŭpĕt|īnnūp|tāē dōn(um)|ēxĭtĭālĕ Mĭ|nērvāē

The **-um** of **dōnum** elides before the **e** of **exitiăle**.

In reading Latin verse the elided vowel or syllable should be lightly sounded.

The metres

Iambics

We start with iambics, because they are the simplest of the metres. An iambic metron (= unit of measurement) consists of two iambic feet:

˘ – ˘ –

Catullus 4 is written in pure iambic trimeters, that is to say lines consisting of three iambic metra. The rhythm goes:

te tum te tum te tum te tum te tum te tum

or more technically (counting in feet):

$$\overset{1}{˘-}|\overset{2}{˘-}|\overset{3}{˘\underset{\wedge}{-}}|\overset{4}{˘\underset{\wedge}{-}}|\overset{5}{˘-}|\overset{6}{˘\bar{˘}}|$$

There is a rhythmical pause between words (called a caesura) half way through the third or fourth foot. So the opening lines of Catullus 4 scan as follows:

phăsē|lŭs īl|lĕ ˄quēm | vĭdēt|lĭs, hōs|pĭtēs,

ăīt | fŭīs|sĕ ˄nā|vĭūm | cĕlēr|rĭmŭs.

Note that the last syllable may be heavy or light.

(It is a very difficult feat to write in pure iambics and poets usually allowed a spondee (- -) in the first, third and fifth feet.)

Limping iambics

These scan exactly like iambic trimeters except that the last foot is a spondee (- -). This has a peculiar effect on the rhythm, making the line drag or limp at the end. Catullus 8 is written in this metre:

mĭsēr | Cătūl|lĕ, ∧dē|sĭnās | ĭnēp|tīrĕ

ēt quōd| vĭdēs| pĕrīs|sĕ ∧pēr|dĭtūm | dūcās.

Dactylic hexameters

The dactylic hexameter consists of six dactylic metra (-⌣⌣). A spondee (- -) may be substituted for a dactyl in any of the first four feet; the fifth foot is nearly always a dactyl and the sixth is always a spondee or -⌣. There is usually a strong caesura (a break between words after the first long syllable of the foot) in the middle of the third foot:

ārmă vĭ|rūmquĕ că|nō, ∧Trōī|ae quī | prīmŭs ăb | ōrīs
(3rd foot strong caesura)

If there is a weak caesura (a break between words after -⌣) or no caesura in the third foot there are usually strong caesuras in the second and fourth feet:

quīdvĕ dŏ|lēns ∧rē|gīnă dĕ|lūm ∧tōt | vōlvĕrĕ | cāsūs
(3rd foot weak caesura;
strong caesuras in 2nd and 4th feet)

īndĕ tŏ|rō ∧pătĕr | Aenē|ās ∧sīc| ōrsŭs ăb | āltō
(no 3rd foot caesura;
strong caesuras in 2nd and 4th feet)

This is the metre used by Homer and all subsequent epic poets. Virgil uses it in his *Eclogues*, *Georgics* and *Aeneid*. Horace uses it in all the *Satires* and *Epistles*.

Elegiac couplets

These consist of a dactylic hexameter followed by the first half of the same (up to the third foot strong caesura) repeated.

$$- \smile\smile | - \smile\smile | - \wedge - \smile\smile | - \smile\smile | - \smile$$
$$- \smile\smile | - \smile\smile | - \wedge - \smile\smile | - \smile\smile | - \smile$$

Elegiac couplets were used for epigrams early in the Greek tradition and soon developed into longer poems; they were the first Greek metre to be used in Latin verse. Catullus was the first Roman poet to use them for longer poems (e.g. 76 and 68 – the latter 160 lines long) besides epigram. They were Ovid's favourite metre; he uses them in the *Amores*, *Ars Amatoria*, *Tristia* etc.

Lyric metres

There is a wide variety of lyric metres which first appear in the poems of Sappho and Alcaeus, who wrote in the Aeolic dialect about 600 BC. Horace claims to have been the first to adapt these metres to Latin poetry (Odes 3.30.13–14):

> dicar ...
> princeps Aeolium carmen ad Italos
> deduxisse modos.

But Catullus had in fact led the way in the previous generation.

In these metres, which are dance rhythms, we cannot speak of feet or metra; the unit is the line and many systems are constructed in four-line stanzas.

Hendecasyllables (i.e. lines of eleven syllables)

This is Catullus' favourite metre, used in thirteen of the twenty-six poems in our selection. Its rhythm goes:

> tum tum tum te te tum te tum te tum tum

or, more technically:

$$- \overset{\smile}{-} - \smile\smile - \smile - \smile - \overset{\smile}{-}$$

The second syllable may be light or heavy (usually heavy). As usual the last syllable can be light or heavy.

cuī dōnō lĕpĭdūm nŏvūm lībēllūm

ārĭdā mŏdŏ pūmĭc(e) ēxpŏlītŭm?

Cōrnēlī, tĭbĭ: nāmquĕ tū sŏlēbās ...

Sapphics

This was the favourite metre of the Greek lyric poetess Sappho, who lived in Lesbos in the sixth century BC. Catullus uses it in the first and last of his poems to Lesbia (51 and 11).

Unlike the other metres you have studied, it is composed in four-line stanzas. The first three lines follow the same pattern:

tum te tum tum tum te te tum te tum tum

or, more technically:

– ˘ – – – – ˘ ˘ – ˘ ˘̆

The last line goes:

tum te te tum tum: – ˘ ˘ – ˘̆

The last syllable, as usual, can be light or heavy.

īllĕ mī pār ēssĕ dĕō vĭdētŭr,

īllĕ, sī fās ēst, sŭpĕrārĕ dīvōs,

quī sĕdēns ādvērsŭs ĭdēntĭdēm tē

spēctăt ĕt āudĭt.

General vocabulary

This list contains all but the very commonest words.

ā/ab + abl. from, by
abdō, -ere, -didī, -ditum I put away; I hide
abrumpō, -ere, -rūpī, -ruptum I break off
abs = ab
absēns, absentis absent
absistō, -ere, -stitī I desist from, leave off
absolvō, -ere, -solvī, -solūtum I acquit
abstinentia, -ae, *f.* abstinence, moderation
absum, abesse, āfuī I am away from, absent
abūtor, -ī, ūsus sum + abl. I misuse, abuse
ac and
accēdō, -ere, -cessī, -cessum I approach; I am added to
accendō, -ere, -cendī, -cēnsum I set on fire; I excite
accidit, -ere, accidit it happens
accipiō, -ere, -cēpī, -ceptum I receive; I hear
acclāmātiō, -ōnis, *f.* shout, catcall
accubō, -āre, -cubuī, -cubitum I recline (at table)
accūsātor, -is, *m.* accuser, prosecutor
accūsō (1) I accuse
ācer, -ris, -re keen, fierce
acētum, -ī, *n.* vinegar
aciēs, -ēī, *f.* line of battle; pupil (of the eye)
acquiēscō, -ere, -quiēvī I rest
āctor, -is, *m.* doer, advocate, actor
acūtus, -a, -um sharp
ad + acc. to
addō, -dere, -didī, -ditum I add
addūcō, -ere, -dūxi, -ductum I lead to, bring
adeō, -īre, -iī, -itum I approach
adeō (adverb) so, to such an extent
adflīctō (1) I damage
adflīgō, -ere, -flīxī, -flīctum I strike, dash
adhaereō, -ēre, -haesī, -haesum I stick to
adhūc still
adiciō, -icere, -iēcī, -iectum I add
adigō, -ere, -ēgī, -āctum I drive to, bring to
adimō, -ere, -ēmī, -ēmptum I take away
adipīscor, -ī, adeptus I reach, get, obtain, win
aditus, -ūs, *m.* approach
adiungō, -ere, -iūnxī, -iūnctum I join to
adiūtor, -is, *m.* helper
adiuvō, -āre, -iūvī, -iūtum I help

administrātiō, -ōnis, *f.* management
administrō (1) I manage, govern
admīrābilis, -e admirable
admīror (1) admire, wonder at
admittō, -ere, -mīsī, -missum I let in; I commit
admodum (adverb) extremely
admoneō (2) I warn
admoveō, -ēre, -mōvī, -mōtum I move to, move up
adolēscō, -ere, -olēvī I grow up
adorior, -īrī, -ortus I attack
adscēnsus, -ūs, *m.* ascent
adsequor, -ī, secūtus I follow; I catch
adsum, -esse, -fuī I am present
adulēscēns, -tis, *m.* young man
adulēscentia, -ae, *f.* youth, adolescence
adulter, -ī, *m.* adulterer
adveniō, -īre, -vēnī, -ventum I arrive
adventus, -ūs, *m.* arrival
adversārius, -a, -um opposed (to)
adversārius, -ī, *m.* opponent
adversor (1) I oppose
adversus, -a, -um opposite
advolō (1) I fly to; I swoop upon
aedificium, -ī, *n.* building
aedificō (1) I build
aeger, -ra, -rum sick, ill
aegrē with difficulty, unwillingly; scarcely
aequō (1) I equal, level
aequor, -is, *n.* sea
aequus, -a, -um equal, level, fair
  aequē ac as much as
  aequō animō calmly
āēr, āeris, *n.* air, mist
aes, aeris, *n.* bronze, money
aestās, -ātis, *f.* summer
aestimō (1) I value
aestus, -ūs, *m.* tide, heat
aetās, -ātis, *f.* age
aeternus, -a, -um eternal
aevum, -ī, *n.* age
afferō, -ferre, attulī, adlātum I bring to; I report
afficiō, -ere, -fēcī, -fectum I affect
ager, agrī, *m.* field
agger, -eris, *m.* mound, rampart
aggredior, -gredī, -gressus I attack
agmen, -minis, *n.* column

agna, -ae, *f.* lamb
agō, -ere, ēgī, āctum I drive; I do
  agō dē I discuss
agricola, -ae, *m.* farmer
āiō (imperfect **āiēbam**) I say
āit he/she said
alacritās, -ātis, *f.* eagerness
  alacriter eagerly
albus, -a, -um white
aliēnus, -a, -um belonging to another
aliquamdiū for some time
aliquantus, -a, -um a certain amount of
aliquis, aliquid someone, something
aliquot (indecl.) several
aliquotiēns several times
aliter otherwise
alius, -a, -ud other
  alius ac different from
alloquor, -ī, -locūtus sum I speak to, address
alter, -era, -erum one *or* the other
altitūdō, -inis, *f.* height, depth
altus, -a, -um high, deep
  altum, -ī, *n.* the deep (sea)
amābilis, -e lovable, amiable
amāns, -tis loving, lover
amātor, -is, *m.* lover
ambiguus, -a, -um doubtful, ambiguous
ambō, -ae, -ō both
ambulō (1) I walk
āmēns, āmentis mad
amīcitia, -ae, *f.* friendship
amīcus, -ī, *m.* friend
āmittō, -ere, -mīsī, -missum I let slip, lose
amnis, -is, *m.* river
amō (1) I love
amoenitās, -ātis, *f.* pleasantness, loveliness
amoenus, -a, -um pleasant, lovely
amor, -is, *m.* love
amplus, -a, -um large
  amplius (adverb) more, longer
an? or
animal, -is, *n.* animal
ancora, -ae, *f.* anchor
angustiae, -ārum, *f. pl.* narrows, pass
angustus, -a, -um narrow
anima, -ae, *f.* soul, life
animadvertō, -ere, -vertī, -versum I notice, perceive
animus, -ī, *m.* mind, spirit
annōna, -ae, *f.* corn supply; price of food
annus, -ī, *m.* year
annuus, -a, -um annual
ante + acc. before

anteā (adverb) before
anteferō, -ferre, -tulī, -latum I carry before; I prefer
antequam (conjunction) before
antīquus, -a, -um old
aperiō, -īre, -uī, -tum I open
apertus, -a, -um open
apis, -is, *f.* bee
appāreō (2) I appear; I am clear
appellō (1) I call
appellō, -ere, -pulī, -pulsum I drive to
appetō, -ere, -iī, -ītum I attack
approbō (1) I approve
appropinquō (1) + dat. I approach
aptus, -a, -um suitable, fit
apud + acc. at, with
aqua, -ae, *f.* water
aquila, -ae, *f.* eagle, legionary standard
Aquilō, -ōnis, *m.* North wind
āra, -ae, *f.* altar
arātrum, -ī, *n.* plough
arbitror (1) I think
arbor, -is, *f.* tree
arceō (2) I keep at a distance, keep off
arcessō, -ēre, -īvī, -ītum I summon
ārdēns, -tis burning, passionate
ārdeō, -ere, ārsī I am on fire, burn, glow
ārdor, -is, *m.* passion
argentum, -ī, *n.* silver, money
āridus, -a, -um dry
  āridum, -ī, *n.* dry land
arma, -ōrum, *n. pl.* arms
armāmenta, -ōrum, *n. pl.* equipment, tackle
armātus, -a, -um armed
armō (1) I arm
ars, artis, *f.* art, skill
artus, -ūs, *m.* limb
arvum, -ī, *n.* field
arx, arcis, *f.* citadel
ascendō, -ere, -scendī, -scēnsum I climb
ascēnsus = adscēnsus
aspectus, -ūs, *m.* sight, view
asper, -a, -um rough, harsh, dangerous
aspiciō, -ere, aspexī, aspectum I look at
assequor = adsequor
astō, -āre, astitī I stand near
astrum, -ī, *n.* star, constellation
at but
atque and
ātrium, -ī, *n.* hall
attingō, -ere, -tigī, -tāctum I touch, arrive at, concern
attollō, -ere I raise, lift up
attonitus, -a, -um astonished

attribuō, -ere, -tribuī, -tribūtum I assign
auctor, -is, *m.* author, adviser
auctōritātis, *f.* authority, influence
audācia, -ae, *f.* boldness, rashness
audāx, -ācis bold, rash
audeō, audēre, ausus I dare
audiō (4) I hear, listen to
auferō, auferre, abstulī, ablātum I carry away
augeō, -ēre, auxī, auctum I increase, enlarge
aura, -ae, *f.* air, breeze
auris, -is, *f.* ear
aurum, -ī, *n.* gold
aut ... aut ... either ... or ...
autem but
auxilior, -ārī + dat. I assist
auxilium, -ī, *n.* help
   auxilia, -ōrum, *n. pl.* reinforcements
avārus, -a, -um greedy, miserly
āvertō, -ere, -vertī, -versum I turn away, turn aside
avis, -is, *f.* bird
avus, -ī, *m.* grandfather

baculum, -ī, *n.* stick
balineum, -ī, *n.* bath
balneum = balineum
barba, -ae, *f.* beard
barbarus, -a, -um barbarian
bellum, -ī, *n.* war
bellus, -a, -um pretty, charming
beātus, -a, -um blessed, happy
bene well
benefactum, -ī, *n.* good deed
beneficium, -ī, *n.* kindness, favour
benignē kindly
bibō, -ere, bibī I drink
biduum, -ī, *n.* a period of two days
biennium, -ī, *n.* a period of two years
bonus, -a, -um good
   bona, -ōrum, *n. pl.* goods
Boreās, Boreae, *m.* North wind
bōs, bovis, *c.* ox, bull, cow
brevis, -e short
brevitās, -ātis, *f.* shortness, brevity

cacūmen, -inis, *n.* top, roof
cadō, -ere, cecidī, cāsum I fall
caecus, -a, -um blind; dark; hidden
caedēs, -is, *f.* slaughter
caedō, -ere, cedīdī, caesum I cut, beat; I kill
caelum, -ī, *n.* sky, heaven, climate
caespes, -itis, *m.* turf
calamitās, -ātis, *f.* disaster

calor, -is, *m.* heat, warmth
campester, -ris, -re flat, level
campus, -ī, *m.* plain; battlefield
candidus, -a, -um bright, white, beautiful
canis, -is, *m.* dog
cānitiēs, -ēī, *f.* grey hair
canō, -ere, cecinī, cantum I sing
cantō (1) I sing
capillus, -ī, *m.* hair
capiō, -ere, cēpī, captum I capture, take, seize
capra, -ae, *f.* she-goat
captīvus, -a, -um captive
caput, -itis, *n.* head; capital
carcer, -is, *m.* prison, starting gate (of races)
careō (2) + abl. I lack, am short of
carmen, -inis, *n.* song, poem
cārus, -a, -um dear, expensive
casa, -ae, *f.* cottage, hut
castellum, -ī, *n.* fort, fortified village
castra, -ōrum, *n. pl.* camp
castus, -a, -um chaste
cāsus, -ūs, *m.* fall; chance; eventuality
   cāsū by chance
caterva, -ae, *f.* crowd, company
causa, -ae, *f.* cause, reason; lawcase
   causā + gen. for the sake of
cautus, -a, -um cautious
caveō, -ēre, cāvī, cautum I beware (of)
cēdō, -ere, cessī, cessum I yield, give way, go
celeber, -ris, -re crowded, famous
celebrō (1) I celebrate
celer, -is, -e quick
celeritās, -ātis, *f.* speed
celerō (1) I quicken
cēlō (1) I hide
celsus, -a, -um high
cēna, -ae, *f.* dinner
cēnō (1) I dine
cēnseō, -ēre, cēnsuī, cēnsum I vote, decide, think
cernō, -ere, crēvī, crētum I perceive, see, decide
certāmen, -inis, *n.* struggle, fight
certē certainly, at least
certō (1) I contend, fight
certus, -a, -um certain, sure, reliable
   certiōrem faciō I inform
   prō certō habeō I am certain
cervīx, -īcis, *f.* neck
cessō (1) I linger, idle
cēterī, -ae, -a the rest
cibus, -ī, *m.* food
cingō, -ere, -xī, -ctum I surround
cinis, -eris, *m.* ash

circā (adv. & prep.) + acc. around, round about
circiter about
circum + acc. around
circumdō, -dare, -dedī, -datum I surround
circumdūcō, -ere, -dūxī, -ductum I lead around
circu(m)eō, -īre, -iī, -itum I go around
circumfundō, -ere, -fūdī, -fūsum I pour around
circummittō, -ere, -mīsī, -missum I send around
circumsistō, -ere, -stitī I stand around
circumspectō (1) I look around
circumstō, -stāre, -stetī I stand around, encircle
circumveniō, -īre, -vēnī, -ventum I surround
citrā + acc. on this side of
cīvīlis, -e civil
cīvis, -is, c. citizen
cīvitās, -ātis, f. state
clādēs, -is, f. disaster
clam secretly
clāmitō (1) I keep shouting
clāmō (1) I shout
clārus, -a, -um bright; famous
classis, -is, f. fleet
claudō, -ere, clausī, clausum I shut
clēmentia, -ae, f. mercy
cliēns, -tis, c. client
clīvus, -ī, m. slope, hill
coepī, coepisse I begin
cōgitātiō, -onis, f. reflection, thought
cōgitō (1) I think, reflect
cognōscō, -ere, -nōvī, -nitum I learn, get to know
cōgō, -ere, coēgī, coāctum I drive together, collect; I force, compel
cohors, -tis, f. cohort
cohortor (1) I encourage, exhort, cheer up
cōiciō = cōniciō
collaudō (1) I praise
colligō, -ere, -lēgī, -lēctum I collect
collis, -is, m. hill
collocō (1) I place, position
colloquium, -ī, n. talk, parley
colloquor, -ī, -locūtus I talk with
collum, -ī, n. neck
colō, -ere, coluī, cultum I till; I worship; I revere; I inhabit
color, -is, m. colour
columba, -ae, f. dove
coma, -ae, f. hair, foliage
comes, -itis, c. companion
cōmis, -e courteous, kind
comitātus, -ūs, m. company
comitia, -ōrum, n. pl. elections
comitor (1) I accompany

commeātus, -ūs, m. supplies
commemorō (1) I mention, recount
commendātiō, -ōnis, f. recommendation
commendō (1) I recommend
comminus (adverb) at close quarters
committō, -ere, -mīsī, -missum I entrust; I join (battle)
commodum, -ī, n. profit, advantage
commodus, -a, -um convenient, advantageous
commoror (1) I delay, linger
commoveō, -ēre, -mōvī, -mōtum I move deeply, excite
commūniō (4) I fortify
commūnis, -e common, shared
commūtātiō, -ōnis, f. change
commūtō (1) I change
comparō (1) I prepare, get; I compare
compellō, -ere, -pulī, -pulsum I drive together, I compel
comperiō, -īre, -perī, -pertum I find out
complector, -ī, complexus I embrace
compleō, -ēre, -plēvī, -plētum I fill
complexus, -ūs, m. embrace
complūrēs, -a several
compōnō, -ere, -posuī, -positum I put together, compose, arrange
comportō (1) I carry together
comprehendō, -ere, -hendī, -hēnsum I seize, grasp
comprobō (1) I thoroughly approve
concēdō, -ere, -cessī, -cessum I retire, retreat, yield
concidō -ere, cidī I fall, collapse
conciliō (1) I unite, win over
concitō (1) I rouse, urge on
conclāmō (1) I shout
concordia, -ae, f. concord, harmony, agreement
concrēscō, -ere, -crēvī, -crētum I grow together, congeal
concupīscō, -ere, -cupīvī, -cupitum I desire
concurrō, -ere, -currī, -cursum I run together
concursō (1) I run this way and that, run together
concursus, -ūs, m. gathering, crowd
condemnō (1) I condemn
condiciō, -ōnis, f. condition
condō, -ere, -didī, -ditum I hide; I store; I found
condūcō, -ere, -dūxī, -ductum I lead together; I hire
cōnferō, -ferre, -tulī, collātum I bring together; I compare
cōnfertus, -a, -um close-packed, filled
cōnfestim speedily, without delay
cōnficiō, -ere, -fēcī, -fectum I finish
cōnfīdō, -ere, -fīsus + dat. I trust in, rely on
cōnfīgō, -ere, -fīxī, -fīxum I pierce

cōnfirmō (1) I strengthen, encourage

cōnfiteor, -ērī, -fessus sum I confess

cōnflagrō (1) I am burnt down, I am on fire

cōnflictō (1) I bang together

cōnflīgō, -ere, -flīxī, -flīctum I fight

cōnfugiō, -ere, -fūgī I flee for refuge

cōniciō, -ere, -iēcī, -iectum I throw together; I hurl

coniectus, -ūs, m. throwing; hail

coniugium, -ī, n. marriage

coniūnctiō, -ōnis, f. union

coniūnctus, -a, -um adjoining, allied, united

coniungō, -ere, -iūnxī, -iūnctum I join together

coniūnx, -iugis, c. wife or husband

coniūrātiō, -ōnis, f. conspiracy

coniūrātus, -ī, m. conspirator

coniūrō (1) I conspire

conlocō = collocō

cōnor (1) I try

cōnscendō, -ere, -scendī, -scēnsum I climb; I board

cōnscrībō, -ere, -scrīpsī, -scriptum I write

cōnsedeō, -ēre, -sēdī, -sessum I sit down, take up

cōnsensus, -ūs, m. agreement, consensus

cōnsentiō, -īre, -sēnsī, -sēnsum I agree

cōnsequor, -ī, -secūtus I catch up, overtake

cōnservō (1) I save, preserve

cōnsīderō (1) I consider

cōnsīdō, -ere, -sēdī, -sessum I sit down, settle, station myself

cōnsilium, -ī, n. plan, advice

cōnsistō, -ere, -stitī I halt, stand still

cōnsōlātiō, -ōnis, f. consolation, comfort

cōnsolor (1) I console, comfort

cōnsopiō, -īre, —, -ītum I lull to sleep

cōnspectus, -ūs, m. sight

cōnspiciō, -ere, -spexī, -spectum I catch sight of, look at, observe

cōnspicor (1) I catch sight of

cōnstantia, -ae, f. constancy, steadiness

cōnstat, -stāre, -stitit it is agreed, well known

cōnstituō, -ere, -stituī, -stitūtum I decide; I position

cōnsuēscō, -ere, -suēvī I am accustomed

cōnsuētūdō, -inis, f. custom

cōnsul, -is, m. consul

cōnsulātus, -ūs, m. consulship

cōnsulō, -ere, -suluī, -sultum I consider, consult
  mihi cōnsulō I consult my own interests

cōnsultō (adverb) on purpose, deliberately

cōnsūmō, -ere, -sūmpsī, -sūmptum I use up, consume

cōnsurgō, -ere, -surrēxī, -surrēctum I rise, stand up

contemnō, -ere, -tempsī, -temptum I despise

contemptiō, -ōnis, f. contempt

contendō, -ere, -tendī, -tentum I stretch, strain, strive, march, hasten, fight

contentiō, -ōnis, f. struggle, fight, combat, effort

contentus, -a, -um content

contestor (1) I call to witness

continēns, -tis, m. continent

contineō, -ere, -tinuī, -tentum I contain, bound, hold back

contingō, -ere, -tigī, -tāctum I touch, border on
  contingit, -ere, -tigit + dat. it happens

continuō immediately, straight away

continuus, -a, -um continual, on end

contiō, -ōnis, f. public meeting, speech

contrā + acc. against, opposite

contrā (adverb) on the other hand

contrahō, -ere, -trāxī, -tractum I draw together, contract

contrōversia, -ae, f. argument, debate

conubium, -ī, n. marriage

convalēscō, -ere, -valuī I recover, grow well

convallis, -is, f. valley

convectō (1) I carry together, gather

conveniō, -īre, -vēnī, -ventum I come together, gather

conventus, -ūs, m. gathering, meeting

convertō, -ere, -vertī, -versum I turn

convīcium, -ī, n. insult

convīvium, -ī, n. dinner party

coorior, -īrī, -ortus I arise

cōpia, -ae, f. plenty
  cōpiae, -ārum, f. pl. forces

cōpiōsus, -a, -um plentiful

cor, cordis, n. heart

cōram (adverb) face to face

corpus, -oris, n. body

corrigō, -ere, -rēxī, -rēctum I correct

corripiō, -ere, -ripuī, -reptum I seize, snatch up

corrumpō, -ere, -rūpī, -ruptum I spoil, corrupt

cotīdiē/cottīdiē every day

crās tomorrow

creber, -ra, -rum close, frequent

crēdō, -ere, crēdidī, crēditum + dat. I believe, trust

cremō (1) I burn

creō (1) I make, elect

crēscō, -ere, crēvī I increase, grow

crīmen, -inis, n. charge (judicial)

crinis, crinis, m. lock of hair; pl. hair

crūdēlis, -e cruel

crūdēlitās, -ātis, f. cruelty

crūs, crūris, n. leg

culmen, -inis, n. top, roof

culpa, -ae, f. fault, blame

culpō (1) I blame

cultus, -a, -um cultivated, elegant

cultus, -ūs, *m.* worship, culture, elegance, habitation

cum (conjunction) when; since, although

cum + abl. with

cūnctor (1) I delay

cupiditās, -ātis, *f.* greed, lust

cupīdō, -inis, *f.* desire

cupidus, -a, -um desirous of, eager

cupiō, -ere, cupīvī, cupītum I desire

cūr? why?

cūra, -ae, *f.* care, anxiety

cūria, -ae, *f.* senate house

cūrō (1) **ut** I care for; I take care that

currō, -ere, cucurrī, cursum I run

currus, -ūs, *m.* chariot

cursus, -ūs, *m.* run, course, race; career

curvus, -a, -um curved

custōdia, -ae, *f.* custody, guard

custōdiō (4) I guard

custōs, -dis, *m.* guard

damnō (1) I condemn

damnum, -ī, *n.* loss, destruction

dapēs, -um, *f. pl.* feast

dea, -ae, *f.* goddess

dē + abl. down from; about

dēbeō (2) I ought; I owe

dēcēdō, -ere, -cessī, -cessum I withdraw, retire, depart from

dēcernō, -ere, -crēvī, -crētum I decide, decree

decet (mē) it suits (me)

dēcipiō, -ere, -cēpī, -ceptum I deceive

dēclārō (1) I make clear, declare

dēcurrō, -ere, -currī, -cursum I run down

decus, -oris, *n.* glory, beauty, honour

dēdecus, -oris, *n.* disgrace

dēdicō (1) I dedicate

dēditiō, -ōnis, *f.* surrender

dēdō, -ere, -didī, -ditum I give up, surrender

dēdūcō, -ere, -dūxī, -ductum I lead down, launch

dēfectiō, -ōnis, *f.* defection, revolt

dēfendō, -ere, -fendī, -fēnsum I defend

dēferō, -ferre, -tulī, -lātum I carry down, report

dēfessus, -a, -um tired

dēficiō, -ere, -fēcī, -fectum I fail; I revolt

dēgredior, -ī, -gressus I go down; I come down

dēiciō, -ere, -iēcī, -iectum I throw down

dein, deinde then; next

deinceps (adverb) in succession

dēlectō (1) I delight, please

dēleō, -ēre, -ēvī, -ētum I destroy

dēliciae, -ārum, *f. pl.* darling, sweetheart

dēligō (1) I bind fast

dēligō, -ere, lēgī, -lēctum I choose, pick out

dēlitēscō, -ere, delituī I hide

dēlūbrum, -ī, *n.* shrine

dēmēns, -tis mad

dēmittō, -ere, -mīsī, -missum I send down, let down

dēmō, -ere, dēmpsī, dēmptum I take away, remove

dēmōnstrō (1) I show, point out

dēmum (adverb) at last

dēnique finally

dēnsus, -a, -um dense, thick

dēplōrō (1) I lament, bewail

dēpōnō, -ere, -posuī, -positum I put down, give up

dēpopulor (1) I lay waste

dēprehendō, -ere, -dī, -sum I catch

dēripiō, -ere, -ripuī, -reptum I tear off, snatch away

dēscendō, -ere, -scendī, -scēnsum I go down

dēserō, -ere, -seruī, -sertum I desert, abandon

dēsinō, -ere, -sīvī/-siī, situm I cease

dēsīderium, -ī, *n.* desire, longing

dēsīderō (1) I desire, long for, miss

dēsiliō, -īre, -siluī I jump down

dēsinō, -ere, -siī/-sīvī I cease

dēsistō, -ere, -stitī I cease

dēspērātiō, -ōnis, *f.* desperation, hopelessness

dēspērō (1) I despair

dēsum, -esse, -fuī + dat. I fail

dēsuper (adverb) down from above

dēterreō (2) I frighten off, deter

detrimentum, -ī, *n.* loss, damage

dēturbō (1) I dislodge

deus, -ī, *m.* god

dēvehō, -ere, -vēxī, -vectum I carry down, carry away

dēveniō, -īre, -vēnī, -ventum I arrive at

dēvolō (1) I fly down

dēvolvō, -ere, -volvī, -volūtum I roll down

dēvorō (1) I devour

dexter, dextera, dexterum/dexter, dextra, dextrum right

    dextrā on the right (hand)

dīcō, -ere, dīxī, dictum I say

dictum, -ī, *n.* saying, word

dīdūcō, -ere, -dūxī, -ductum I divide, lead apart

diēs, -ēī, *m.* day

differō, differre, distulī, dīlātum I carry in different directions, scatter; I differ; I postpone

difficilis, -e difficult

difficultās, -ātis, *f.* difficulty

diffugiō, -ere, -fūgī I flee away

digitus, -ī, *m.* finger

dignitās, -ātis, *f.* worth, dignity, importance
dignus, -a, -um + abl. worthy (of), deserving
dīgredior, -ī, -gressus I go away
dīlābor, -ī, -lāpsus I slip away
dīligēns, -tis careful, diligent
dīligentia, -ae, *f.* care, diligence
dīligō, -ere, -lēxī, lēctum I love, am fond of
dīmicō (1) I fight, struggle
dīmittō, -ere, -mīsī, -missum I send away, dismiss
dīripiō, -ere, -ripuī, -reptum I plunder
dīrus, -a, -um terrible
discēdō, -ere, -cessī, -cessum I go away, depart
disciplīna, -ae, *f.* learning, discipline
discipulus, -ī, *m.* pupil
discō, -ere, didicī I learn
discordia, -ae, *f.* discord, disagreement
disertus, -a, -um eloquent
dispersus, -a, -um scattered
disputātiō, -ōnis, *f.* discussion, argument
dissēnsiō, -ōnis, *f.* disagreement
dissimilis, -e unlike
dissimulō (1) I dissemble, disguise
dissonus, -a, -um dissonant, discordant
dissuādeō, -ēre, -suāsī, -suāsum I dissuade
distribuō, -ere, -tribuī, -tribūtum I distribute
diū for a long time
diiūdicō (1) I judge, decide
diūturnus, -a, -um long-lasting
dīversus, -a, -um contrary, different
dives, -itis rich
dīvī, -um, *m. pl.* the gods
dīvidō, -ere, -vīsī, -vīsum I separate, divide
dīvīnus, -a, -um divine
dīvitiae, -ārum, *f. pl.* riches
dīvus, -a, -um divine
dō, dare, dedī, datum I give
doceō, -ere, -docuī, doctum I teach
    doctus, -a, -um learned
doleō (2) I grieve, feel pain
dolor, -is, *m.* grief, pain
dominor (1) + dat. I rule, dominate
dominus, -ī *m.* master, lord
domus, -ūs, *f.* home
    domī at home
dōnec until
dōnō (1) I give, present with
dōnum, -ī, *n.* gift
dormiō (4) I sleep
dubitātiō, -ōnis, *f.* doubt, hesitation
dubitō (1) I doubt, hesitate
dubius, -a, -um doubtful
dūcō, -ere, dūxī, ductum I lead; I marry

dulcis, -e sweet
dum while, until
duplicō (1) I double
dūrō (1) I last, endure
dūrus, -a, -um hard
dux, ducis, *m.* leader

ē/ex + abl. out of, from, according to
ecce! look!
ēdō, -ere, -didī, -ditum I give out
edō, ēsse, ēdī, ēsum I eat
ēdoceō, -ēre, -docuī, -doctum I teach, inform
ēducō (1) I educate
ēdūcō, -ere, -dūxī, -ductum I lead out, lead forth
efficiō, -ere, -fēcī, -fectum I accomplish, effect, cause
effodiō, -ere, -fōdī, -fossum I dig up, dig out
effugiō, -fugere, -fūgī I escape
ēgredior, -ī, -gressus I go out
ēgregius, -a, -um remarkable, excellent, peerless
ēiciō, -ere, -iēcī, -iectum I throw out, eject
ēlābor, -ī, -lāpsus I slip out, escape
ēliciō, -ere, -licuī, -licitum I entice, coax
ēligō, -ere, -lēgī, -lēctum I pick out, choose
ēloquentia, -ae, *f.* eloquence
ēloquium, -ī, *n.* the art of public speaking
ēlūdō, -ere, -lūsī, -lūsum I elude
ēmineō (2) I project, stand out, excel
emō, emere, ēmī, ēmptum I buy
emptiō, -ōnis, *f.* purchase
ēn! look! behold!
enim for
ēnsis, -is, *m.* sword
ēnumerō (1) I count
eō, īre, iī, itum I go
eō (adverb) thither, to there
epistola/epistula, -ae, *f.* letter
eques, equitis, *m.* horseman
    equitēs, -um, *m. pl.* cavalry
equester, -ris, -re equestrian, of cavalry
equidem I for my part
equitātus, -ūs, *m.* cavalry
equus, ī, *m.* horse
ergō and so, therefore
ēripiō, -ere, -ripuī, -reptum I snatch away, rescue
errō (1) I wander; I am wrong
error, -is, *m.* wandering, mistake
ērudiō (4) I teach
ērudītus, -a, -um learned
ērumpō, -ere, -rūpī, -ruptum I burst out
ēruptiō, -ōnis, *f.* (military) sally, breakout
essedārius, -ī, *m.* charioteer
essedum, -ī, *n.* war chariot

ēvādō, -ere, -vāsī I escape, get out of
etiam also; even, yet
etsī even if, although
ēveniō, -īre, -vēnī, -ventum I turn out
ēventus, -ūs, *m.* outcome, result
ēvertō, -ere, -vertī, -versum I overturn
ēvolō (1) I fly out
exanimātus, -a, -um deprived of mind; dead; in a faint
exardescō, exardescere, exarsī I blaze, flare up
exaudiō (4) I hear
excēdō, -ere, -cessī I go out, depart
excellō, -ere, -celuī I excel
excīdō, -ere, -cīdī, -cīsum I cut out, cut off
excitō (1) I rouse
exclūdō, -ere, -clūsī, -clūsum I shut out, exclude
exemplum, -ī, *n.* example
exeō, -īre, -iī, -itum I go out
exerceō (2) I exercise, train; I harass
exercitus, -ūs, *m.* army
exhauriō, -īre, -hausī, -haustum I drain out, empty
exiguitās, -ātis, *f.* tininess, smallness
exiguus, -a, -um tiny
exīstimātiō, -ōnis, *f.* judgement, opinion
exīstimō (1) I think
exitus, -ūs, *m.* way out, ending
expedītiō, -ōnis, *f* expedition, campaign
expedītus, -a, -um unencumbered, lightly armed
expellō, -ere, -pulī, -pulsum I drive out
experior, -īrī, -pertus I try, test
explicō (1) I unfold, set forth
explōrātor, -is, *m.* scout
explōrō (1) I search, investigate
expōnō, -ere, -posuī, -positum I put out, explain, disembark
exposcō, -ere, -poposcī I ask earnestly, demand
expugnātiō, -ōnis, *f.* storming, sack
expugnō (1) I take by storm
exsiliō, -īre, -uī I jump out
exsilium, -ī, *n.* exile
exsistō, -ere, -stitī, -stitum I step out, appear, exist
exsolvō, -ere, -solvī, -solūtum I loose, free, release
exspectātiō, -ōnis, *f.* waiting, expectation
exspectō (1) I wait for
exstīnctiō, -ōnis, *f.* exstinction
exstō, -stare, -stitī, -stitum I stand out
exstruō, -ere, -strūxī, -strūctum I build up
ex(s)ul, -is, *m.* exile
extemplō (adverb) straightaway
extendō, -ere, -tendī, -tentum I stretch out, extend
externus, -a, -um external, foreign
exterreō, -ēre, -terruī, -territum I terrify
extrā + acc. outside

extrēmus, -a, -um furthest, remote; last, final
exuō, -ere, -uī, -ūtum I take off, strip

faber, -rī, *m.* workman, artisan
fabricō (1) I make, construct
fābula, -ae, *f.* story
facētus, -a, -um witty
faciēs, -ēī, *f.* face, appearance
facilis, -e easy
facile easily
faciō, -ere, fēcī, factum I make, do
factum, -ī, *n.* deed
facultās, -ātis, *f.* opportunity
fallō, -ere, fefellī, falsum I deceive, cheat
falsus, -a, -um false
fāma, -ae, *f.* rumour, report, fame
famēs, -is, *f.* hunger, starvation
familia, -ae, *f.* family, household
familiāris, -is, *c.* friend
fās, *n.* (indecl.) right
fateor, -ērī, fassus I confess
fatīgō (1) I tire out, harass
fātum, -ī, *n.* fate
faveō, -ēre, fāvī, fautum + dat. I favour, support
favor, -is, *m.* favour, support
fēlīx, -īcis lucky
fēmina, -ae, *f.* woman
femur, -oris, *n.* thigh
fenestra, -ae, *f.* window
ferē/fermē nearly, about, almost
feriō, -īre, percussī, ictum I strike, beat
feritās, -ātis, *f.* savagery
ferme (adverb) almost, about
ferō, ferre, tulī, lātum I carry, bring; I propose (a law)
ferōx, -ōcis fierce
ferrum, -ī, *n.* iron; sword
fertilis, -e fertile, productive
ferus, -a, -um wild, savage
fessus, -a, -um tired
festīnātiō, -ōnis, *f.* haste
festīnō (1) I hasten
fidēlis, -e loyal
fidēs, -ēī, *f.* loyalty, trust, faith, promise
fīgō, -ere, fīxī, fīxum I fix, transfix
figūra, -ae, *f.* shape, figure
fīlia, -ae, *f.* daughter
fīliola, -ae, *f.* little daughter
fīlius, -ī, *m.* son
findō, -ere, fīdī, fissum I split
fingō, -ere, fīnxī, fictum I make up, invent
fīniō (4) I limit, bound
fīnis, -is, *m.* end

fīnēs, -ium, *m. pl.* bounds; territory, country
fīnitimus, -a, -um neighbouring
fīō, fierī, factus I become, am made
firmus, -a, -um strong, firm, reliable
flamma, -ae, *f.* flame
flēbilis, -e lamentable, tearful
fleō, -ēre, flēvī, flētum I weep
flētus, -ūs, *m.* weeping
flōrēns, florentis flourishing
flōreō (2) I flower, flourish
flōreus, -a, -um flowery
flōs, flōris, *m.* flower
fluctus, -ūs, *m.* wave
flūmen, -inis, *n.* river
fluō, -ere, -xī I flow
fluvius, -ī, *m.* river
foedus, -eris, *n.* treaty; agreement, pact
for, fārī, fātus I speak
fōrma, -ae, *f.* shape, beauty
formīca, -ae, *f.* ant
formīdō, -inis, *f.* fear
fōrmōsus, -a, -um beautiful
fors, fortis, *f.* chance
fortasse perhaps
forte by chance
fortis, -e brave, strong
fortūna, -ae, *f.* fortune
forum, -ī, *n.* forum; public life
fossa, -ae, *f.* ditch
foveō, -ēre, fōvī, fōtum I nourish, nurture, warm,
   foster, respect
fragilis, -e breakable, brittle
frangō, -ere, frēgī, frāctum I break
frāter, -ris, *m.* brother
fraus, fraudis, *f.* deceit, cheating
fremitus, -ūs, *m.* groan, roar
fremō, -ere I roar, clamour
frequēns, -ntis crowded, in crowds, frequent
frequentia, -ae, *f.* crowd, throng
frīgidus, -a, -um cold
frīgus, -oris, *n.* cold
frōns, frontis, *f.* forehead; front
   ā fronte from the front
frōns, frondis, *f.* foliage, leaves
frūctus, -ūs, *m.* fruit, profit
frūmentārius, -a, -um of corn
   rēs frūmentāria corn supply
frūmentor (1) I forage for corn
frūmentum, -ī, *n.* corn, grain
fruor, fruī, frūctus + abl. I enjoy
frūstrā in vain
fuga, -ae, *f.* flight

fugāx, -ācis fleeting
fugiō, -ere, fūgī, fugitum I flee
fulgeō, -ēre, fulsī I shine
fulvus, -a, -um tawny
fūmus, -ī, *m.* smoke
funda, -ae, *f.* sling
fundō, -ere, fūdī, fūsum I pour; I rout, cause to flee
fundus, -ī, *m.* estate, farm
fūnis, -is, *m.* rope
fūnus, -eris, *n.* funeral, death
furō, -ere I rage, rave, am mad
fūror (1) I steal
furor, -is, *m.* fury, madness
fūrtim furtively, secretly
fustis, -is, *m.* club

gaudeō, -ēre, gāvīsus I rejoice, rejoice in
gaudium, -ī, *n.* joy
gelidus, -a, -um icy, cold
gelū, -ūs, *n.* frost, ice
geminus, -ī, *m.* twin, double
gemitus, -ūs, *m.* groan, groaning
gemō, -ere, gemuī I groan
gena, -ae, *f.* cheek
gēns, gentis, *f.* race, people
genū, -ūs, *n.* knee
genus, -eris, *n.* race, family; kind
germānus, -a, -um genuine, true
gerō, -ere, gessī, gestum I carry, wear; I do; I wage
   mē gerō I behave
glaciēs, -ēī, *f.* ice
gladius, -ī, *m.* sword
gradior, -ī, gressus I step, walk, go
gradus, -ūs, *m.* step
Graecus/Graeus, -a, -um Greek
grātia, -ae, *f.* thanks, favour, influence
   grātiās agō I thank
grātulātiō, -ōnis, *f.* congratulations
grātulor (1) + dat. I congratulate
grātus, -a, -um pleasing, thankful, popular
gravis, -e heavy; serious
gravitās, -ātis, *f.* weight; seriousness
gubernātor, -is, *m.* helmsman

habeō (2) I have; I consider
habitābilis, -e habitable
habitō (1) I live in, inhabit
haereō, -ēre, haesī, haesum I stick
hasta, -ae, *f.* spear
haud not
hauriō, -īre, hausī, haustum I drain, drink down
herba, -ae, *f.* grass

hērēs, -ēdis, *c.* heir
hībernus, -a, -um (of) winter
   hīberna, -ōrum, *n. pl.* winter quarters
hīc here
hiemō (1) I spend the winter
hiems, hiemis, *f.* winter
hinc hence, from here
hodiē today
homō, -inis, *c.* man, human being
honestus, -a, -um honourable
honor, -is, *m.* honour; public office
hōra, -ae, *f.* hour
horreō, -ēre, horruī I bristle, shudder at, stand in awe of
horridus, -a, -um horrid
hortor (1) I encourage
hortus, -ī, *m.* garden
hospes, -itis, *c.* guest, host; stranger
hosticus, -a, -um of the enemy, hostile
hostis, -is, *c.* enemy
hūc hither, to here
hūmānus, -a, -um humane, civilized
humus, -ī, *f.* ground, earth
   humī on the ground

iaceō (2) I lie
iaciō, -ere, iēcī, iactum I throw
iactātiō, -ōnis, *f.* tossing
iactō (1) I toss, throw about
   mē iactō I boast
iaculum, -ī, *n.* spear, javelin
iam now, already
iamdūdum now for a long time
ibi there
ictus, -a, -um struck
identidem again and again
idōneus, -a, -um suitable
igitur therefore, and so
ignārus, -a, -um ignorant (of)
ignāvus, -a, -um cowardly, lazy
igneus, -a, -um fiery
ignis, -is, *m.* fire
ignōrō (1) I am ignorant, do not know
ignōscō, -ere, nōvī + dat. I pardon
ignōtus, -a, -um unknown
illīc there
illinc from there
illūc to that place
illūstris, -e bright, famous
imāgō, -inis, *f.* image, likeness, ghost
imbellis, -e unwarlike
imber, -ris, *m.* rain

immānis, -e monstrous, inhuman, huge
immātūrus, -a, -um untimely
immemor, -oris forgetful
immineō, -ēre I hang over, project over; I threaten
immittō, -ere, -mīsī, -missum I send into, throw against
immortālis, -e immortal
immortālitās, -ātis, *f.* immortality
immōtus, -a, -um unmoved, immoveable
impedīmenta, -ōrum, *n. pl.* baggage
impediō (4) I hinder
impellō, -ere, -pulī, -pulsum I drive against
impendeō, -ēre I hang over; I threaten
imperātor, -is, *m.* general; emperor
imperātum, -ī, *n.* order
imperitō (1) I govern, command
imperītus, -a, -um unskilled
imperium, -ī, *n.* order, command, empire
imperō (1) + dat. I order
impetrō (1) I effect, get (by entreaty)
impetus, -ūs, *m.* attack; violence, dash
impius, -a, -um impious; undutiful
improbus, -a, -um wicked, cruel
imprōvīsus, -a, -um unforeseen, unexpected
   dē imprōvīsō unexpectedly
imprūdēns, -tis imprudent, silly, ignorant
imprūdentia, -ae, *f.* imprudence, folly
impudentia, -ae, *f.* shamelessness
īmus, -a, -um lowest
inamābilis, -e unlovely
inānis, -e empty
inaudītus, -a, -um unheard of
incautus, -a, -um off one's guard
incēdō, -ere, -cessī, -cessum I go, advance
incendium, -ī, *n.* fire
incendō, -ere, -cendī, -cēnsum I set on fire, burn
incertus, -a, -um uncertain, doubtful
incidō, -ere, -cidī I fall into, light on
incipiō, -ere, -cēpī, -ceptum I begin
incitō (1) I urge on
inclūdō, -ere, -clūsī, -clūsum I shut in
incognitus, -a, -um unknown
incolō, -ere, -coluī, -cultum I live in, inhabit
incolumis, -e safe
incommodum, -ī, *n.* inconvenience, misfortune, set-back
incrēdibilis, -e incredible
incubō, -āre, -cubuī, -cubitum I lie on, sit on
incultus, -a, -um uncultivated; barbarous
incursō (1) I run against, attack
incustōditus, -a, -um unguarded
inde from there; then

indignor (1) I am indignant
indignus, -a, -um unworthy (of); undeserved
indūcō, -dūcere, -dūxī, -ductum I bring into
induō, -ere, -ī, -tum I put on
industria, -ae, *f.* industry, hard work
ineō, -īre, -iī, -itum I enter; I begin
inermis, -e unarmed, defenceless
inexpertus, -a, -um untried
infamis, -e disreputable, infamous
īnfēlīx, -īcis unlucky
inferior, -is lower, inferior
īnferō, -ferre, -tulī, illātum I bring into, carry against
īnfestus, -a, -um hostile, dangerous; endangered, disordered
īnfidēlitās, -ātis, *f.* infidelity, treachery
infimus, -a, -um lowest
infirmitās, -ātis, *f.* weakness
īnfirmus, -a, -um weak
īnflammō (1) I set on fire, burn
infrā + acc. below
ingemō, -ere, -gemuī I groan
ingenium, -ī, *n.* talents, character
ingēns, -tis huge
ingrātus, -a, -um ungrateful
ingredior, -gredī, -gressus I go into, enter
inhūmānus, -a, -um inhuman, cruel
inhumātus, -a, -um unburied
īniciō, -ere, īecī, -iectum I throw into
inimīcus, -ī, *m.* enemy
iniquitās, -ātis, *f.* inequality, unevenness, unfairness
inīquus, -a, -um unequal, unjust, unfavourable
initium, -ī, *n.* beginning
iniūria, -ae, *f.* injury, wrong
iniussū without orders
inligō (1) I tie to
innumerābilis, -e innumerable
inopia, -ae, *f.* scarcity, shortage
inquam, inquit, inquiunt I, he/she, they say/said
īnscius, -a, -um not knowing, ignorant
īnsequor, -ī, -secūtus I pursue; I follow after
īnsideō, -ēre, -sēdī, -sessum I sit upon, occupy
īnsidiae, -ārum, *f. pl.* ambush, plot, treachery
īnsīdō, -ere, -sēdī, -sessum I settle down, sit upon, occupy
īnsignis, -e distinguished
īnsistō, -ere, -stitī I stand on, press on
īnsōns, -tis innocent
īnspectō (1) I look at, observe
īnspiciō, -ere, -spexī, -spectum I look at, observe
īnstō, -āre, stitī, -statum I stand on, press hard, threaten
īnstruō, -ere, -struxī, -structum I draw up

īnsula, -ae, *f.* island
īnsum, -esse, -fuī + dat. I am in, on, among
intellegō, -ere, -lēxī, -lēctum I understand
intendō, -ere, -tendī, -tentum I intend, aim
intentus, -a, -um eager
inter + acc. among, between
intercēdō, -cēdere, -cessī, -cessum I come between
intercipiō, -ere, -cēpī, -ceptum I intercept, cut off
interclūdō, -ere, -clūsī, -clūsum I cut off, blockade
interdiū in the day time
interdum (adverb) from time to time
intereā meanwhile
intereō, -īre, -iī I perish, die
interest, -esse, -fuit it is important
interficiō, -ere, -fēcī, -fectum I kill
interim meanwhile
interior, -is inner
interitus, -ūs, *m.* death
intermittō, -ere, -mīsī, -missum I leave off, let pass
interpellō (1) I interrupt
interpōnō, -ere, -posuī, -positum I put between, interpose
interpres, -etis, *c.* interpreter
interrogō (1) I question, ask
intersum, -esse, -fuī I take part in
intestīna, -ōrum, *n. pl.* intestines
intrā + acc. inside, within
intrō (1) I enter
introeō, -īre I enter
introitus, -ūs, *m.* entrance
intueor (2) I gaze at
intus (adverb) within
inultus, -a, -um unavenged
inūsitātus, -a, -um unusual
inūtilis, -e useless
invādō, -ere, -vāsī, -vāsum I attack
invehō, -ere, -vēxī, -vectum I carry to, carry against
invehor, -ī, -vectus (in) I attack (verbally)
inveniō, -īre, -vēnī, -ventum I find
invideō, -ēre, -vīdī, -vīsum + dat. I am jealous of, envy
invidia, -ae, *f.* envy, malice
invidiōsus, -a, -um hateful, hated
invīsō, -ere, -vīsī I visit
invītō (1) I invite, entice
invītus, -a, -um unwilling
invius, -a, -um impassable, trackless
iocor (1) I joke
iocus, -ī, *m.* joke, jest
iocōsus, -a, -um funny, humorous
ipse, -a, -um himself, herself, itself
īra, -ae, *f.* anger

īrāscor, -ī, īrātus I am angry
īrātus, -a, -um angry
irrumpō, -ere, -rūpī, -ruptum I burst into
iste, -a, -ud that
istīc there
ita thus, so
itaque and so
item in the same way
iter, itineris, *n.* journey, march
iterum again; a second time
iubeō, -ēre, iussī, iussum I order
iūcundus, -a, -um pleasant, delightful
iūdex, -icis, *c.* judge; juryman
iūdicium, -ī, *n.* judgement; lawcourt, trial
iūdicō (1) I judge
iugum, -ī, *n.* yoke; mountain pass, ridge
iūmentum, -ī, *n.* beast of burden
iungō, -ere, iūnxī, iūnctum I join
iūrō (1) I swear
iūs, iūris, *n.* right, law, oath
iussū by order
iūstitia, -ae, *f.* justice
iūstus, -a, -um just
iuvenīlis/iuvenālis, -e youthful
iuvenis, -is, *m.* young man
iuventūs, -ūtis, *f.* youth
iuvō, -āre, iūvī, iūtum I help; I please

lābor, -ī, lāpsus I slip
labor, -is, *m.* labour, toil
labōriōsus, -a, -um laborious
labōrō (1) I work, suffer
lacertus, -ī, *m.* arm
lacessō, -ere, -īvī, -ītum I provoke, challenge
lacrima, -ae, *f.* tear
lacus, -ūs, *m.* lake
laedō, -ere, laesī, laesum I hurt, offend
laetitia, -ae, *f.* joy, happiness
laetus, -a, -um joyful, happy
laniō (1) I tear apart
lapis, -idis, *m.* stone
lāpsus, -ūs, *m.* falling, slide
Lar, -ris, *m.* household god
lassus, -a, -um tired
lātē far and wide
lateō (2) I lie hidden
latus, -eris, *n.* side; lung
lātus, -a, -um wide
laudābilis, -e praiseworthy
laudō (1) I praise
laus, laudis, *f.* praise
lautus, -a, -um washed, smart

lavō, -āre, lāvī, lautum I wash
lectīca, -ae, *f.* litter
lectus, -ī, *m.* couch, bed
lēgātus, -ī, *m.* deputy, ambassador
    lēgātus legiōnis legionary commander
legiō, -ōnis, *f.* legion
legō, -ere, lēgī, lēctum I choose; I read
leō, leōnis, *m.* lion
lētālis, -e deadly
lētum, -ī, *n.* death
levis, -e light
levō (1) I lighten, relieve, lift
lēx, lēgis, *f.* law
libellus, -ī, *m.* little book
liber, librī, *m.* book
līber, lībera, līberum free
līberālis, -e gracious, generous
līberī, -ōrum, *m. pl.* children
līberō (1) I free
lībertās, -ātis, *f.* freedom
licet (mihi) it is lawful for me; I am allowed
lignātio, -ōnis, *f.* wood collecting
lignātor, -ōris, *m.* wood collector
ligō (1) I bind
līmen, -inis, *n.* threshold
lingua, -ae, *f.* tongue, language
linquō, -ere, līquī I leave
liquidus, -a, -um liquid, pure
lītorālis, -e of the shore
littera, -ae, *f.* letter (of the alphabet)
    litterae, -ārum, *f. pl.* a letter, literature
lītus, -oris, *n.* shore
locō (1) I place, position
locuplēs, -ētis rich
locus, -ī, *m.* place; *pl.* **loca, -orum,** *n.*
longē far off, at a distance; by far
longinquus, -a, -um far off, distant
longitūdō, -inis, *f.* length
longus, -a, -um long
loquāx, -ācis talkative, garrulous
loquor, -ī, locūtus I speak, say
lōra, -ōrum, *n. pl.* reins
luctor (1) I struggle
lūctus, -ūs, *m.* grief
lūdō, -ere, lūsī, lūsum I play
lūdus, -ī, *m.* school; play, game
lūgeō, -ēre, lūxī, luctum I grieve, mourn
lūmen, -inis, *n.* light, eye
lūna, -ae, *f.* moon
lupus, -ī, *m.* wolf
lūsor, -is, *m.* playful poet
lūx, lūcis, *f.* light

mactō (1) I sacrifice, kill
maereō (2) I mourn
maeror, -is, *m.* grief
maestus, -a, -um sad
magis more
magister, -rī, *m.* master
magistrātus, -ūs, *m.* magistrate
magnitūdō, -inis, *f.* size
magnopere greatly
magnus, -a, -um great
māiōrēs, -um, *m. pl.* ancestors
maledictum, -ī, *n.* abuse
mālō, mālle, māluī I prefer
malus, -a, -um evil, bad
    mala, -ōrum, *n. pl.* evils, troubles
mandātum, -ī, *n.* instruction, order
mandō (1) I instruct, entrust to
māne (adverb) early
maneō, -ere, mānsī, mānsum I wait, wait for
manifestus, -a, -um clear, evident
manus, -ūs, *f.* hand, band
mare, -is, *n.* sea
maritimus, -a, -um sea
marmor, -is, *n.* marble
māter, -ris, *f.* mother
māteria, -ae, *f.* material
māternus, -a, -um maternal
mātrōna, -ae, *f.* married woman, wife
mātūrē in good time
mātūrus, -a, -um timely, early, ripe
medicīna, -ae, *f.* medicine, cure
medicus, -ī, *m.* doctor
mediocris, -e moderate
medius, -a, -um middle
mehercle by Hercules!
membrum, -ī, *n.* limb
meminī, meminisse I remember
memor, -is mindful of, remembering, recalling
memorābilis, -e memorable, remarkable
memoria, -ae, *f.* memory, recollection
memorō (1) I mention, narrate
mēns, mentis, *f.* mind
mēnsis, -is, *m.* month
mercātor, -is, *m.* merchant
mereō/mereor (2) I deserve, merit; I serve
meretrix, -icis, *f.* whore
meritum, -ī, *n.* desert, reward
meritus, -a, -um deserved
merīdiēs, -ēī, *m.* midday
merīdiānus, -a, -um of midday
mēta, -ae, *f.* turning post
metō, -ere, messuī, messum I reap

metuō, -ere, -uī I fear
metus, -ūs, *m.* fear
meus, -a, -um my
migrō (1) I remove, depart
mīles, -itis, *m.* soldier
mīliēns a thousand times
mīlitāris, -e military
mīlitia, -ae, *f.* military service
mīlitō (1) I serve as a soldier, campaign
mina, -ae, *f.* threat
mināx, -ācis threatening
minor (1) I threaten
minuō, -ere, -ī, -tum I lessen
mīrandus, -a, -um wonderful
mīrifīcus, -a, -um amazing, wonderful
mīror (1) I wonder at, admire
mīrus, -a, -um wonderful
misceō, -ere, miscuī, mixtum I mix, mingle, confuse
miser, -a, -um unhappy, wretched
misereor, -ērī, miseritus I pity
miseria, -ae, *f.* misery
misericordia, -ae, *f.* compassion
miseror (1) I pity
mittō, -ere, mīsī, missum I send
modo (adverb) only, recently
modo ... modo now ... now
modus, -ī, *m.* way; limit; metre
moenia, -um, *n. pl.* walls, fortifications
mōlēs, -is, *f.* heavy mass, difficulty, labour
molestiae, -ārum, *f. pl.* annoyance, vexation
molestus, -a, -um annoying, troublesome
    molestē ferō I bear with annoyance, am vexed by
mollis, -e soft
mōmentum, -ī, *n.* importance; moment
moneō (2) I warn, advise
monitus, -ūs, *m.* warning
mōns, montis, *m.* mountain
mōnstrō (1) I show
montānus, -a, -um mountain
monumentum, -ī, *n.* monument
mora, -ae, *f.* delay
morbus, -ī, *m.* disease
morior, morī, mortuus I die
moror (1) I delay
mors, mortis, *f.* death
mortālis, -e mortal
mōs, mōris, *m.* custom
mōtus, -ūs, *m.* movement
moveō, -ēre, mōvī, mōtum I move
mox soon
mulier, -is, *f.* woman
multitūdō, -inis, *f.* multitude, crowd

multus, -a, -um much, many
mūniō (4) I fortify
mūnītiō, -ōnis, *f.* fortification
mūnus, -eris, *n.* gift; duty
murmur, -is, *n.* murmur, roaring
mūrus, -ī, *m.* wall
mūtus, -a, -um dumb

nactus, -a, -um having obtained
nam for
nancīscor, -ī, nactus I get, obtain
nārrō (1) I narrate, tell
nāscor, -ī, nātus I am born
nātālis, -is, *m.* birthday
nātiō, -ōnis, *f.* tribe
nātūra, -ae, *f.* nature
nātūrālis, -e natural
nātus, -a, -um born, old
nauta, -ae, *m.* sailor
nāvālis, -e naval
nāvigātiō, -ōnis, *f.* sailing, navigation
nāvigō (1) I sail
nāvis, -is, *f.* ship
nē lest
nē ... quidem not even
necessārius, -a, -um necessary
necesse (indecl.) necessary, inevitable
necessitūdō, -inis, *f.* (close) friendship
necō (1) I kill, butcher
nefārius, -a, -um wicked
neglegō, -ere, -lēxī, -lēctum I neglect
negō (1) I deny
negōtium, -ī, *n.* business
nēmō, nēminis no one
nemus, -oris, *n.* grove, wood
nēquāquam not in the least
nequeō, -īre, -iī I cannot
nēquīquam in vain
nesciō (4) I do not know
nescioquis, -quid someone, something or other
nescius, -a, -um unknowing, unaware
nī = nisi
nihil (indecl.) nothing
nihilōminus nevertheless
nīl (indecl.) nothing
nimbus, -ī, *m.* rain cloud
nimis too much
nimium too much
nisi unless; except
niteō, -ēre, nituī I shine
nītor, -ī, nīxus/nīsus I lean on, strive, struggle
nix, nivis, *f.* snow

nōbilis, -e noble, famous
noceō, -ēre, nocuī + dat. I harm
noctū by night
nocturnus, -a, -um of the night
nōlō, nōlle, nōluī I am unwilling, do not wish
nōmen, -inis, *n.* name
nōminō (1) I name, call by name
nōndum not yet
nōnnūllī, -ae, -a some
nōnnunquam sometimes
nōscō, -ere, nōvī, nōtum I get to know, learn
noster, -ra, -rum our
notō (1) I mark, note
nōtus, -a, -um known
novitās, -ātis, *f.* novelty, newness, strangeness
novus, -a, -um new
nox, noctis, *f.* night
nūb -ēs, -is, *f.* cloud
nūbō, -ere, nūpsī, nuptum + dat. I marry
nūdus, -a, -um bare, nude
nūgae, -ārum, *f. pl.* trifles, nonsense
nūllus, -a, -um no
nūmen, -inis, *n.* divine power
numerus, -ī, *m.* number, metre, verse
numquam never
nunc now
nūntiō (1) I announce
nūntius, -ī, *m.* message, messenger
nūper lately
nusquam nowhere

ob + acc. on account of
obdormīscō, -ere I fall asleep
obeō, -īre, -iī, -itum I go to meet, I die
obitus, -ūs, *m.* death
obīvīscor, -ī, oblītus + gen. I forget
obruō, -ere, -ī I rush over, overwhelm
obscēnus, -a, -um obscene
obscūrus, -a, -um dark, dim
obses, -sidis, *c.* hostage
obsideō, -ēre, -sēdī, -sessum I besiege, block, guard
obsidiō, -ōnis, *f.* siege
obstō, -stāre, -stitī I stand in the way of; I block
obstruō, -ere, -strūxī, -strūctum I block up, obstruct
obtemperō (1) + dat. I obey
obtineō, -ēre, -tinuī, -tentum I hold, possess, occupy, keep
obviam eō + dat. I go to meet
obvius, -a, -um meeting, to meet
occāsiō, -ōnis, *f.* opportunity
occāsus, -ūs (sōlis) *m.* sunset
occupō (1) I seize, occupy

occīdō, -ere, -cīdī, -cīsum I beat; I kill
occidō, -ere, -cidī I fall; I set; I die
occultō (1) I hide
occultus, -a, -um hidden, secret
occupātus, -a, -um occupied, busy
occupō (1) I seize
occurrō, -ere, -currī + dat. I meet
occursō (1) I run to meet, I charge
ocellus, -ī, *m.* (little) eye
oculus, -ī, *m.* eye
ōdī, ōdisse I hate
odium, ī, *n.* hatred
offendō, -ere, -fendī, -fēnsum I offend
offēnsus, -a, -um offensive, odious
offerō, -ferre, obtulī, oblātum I offer
officium, -ī, *n.* duty
olēns, -tis fragrant
ōlim once; at some time
ōmen, -inis, *n.* omen
omnīnō altogether; at all
omnipotēns, -tis all-powerful
omnis, -e all
onerāria (nāvis) merchant ship, transport vessel
onerō (1) I burden, load
onus, -eris, *n.* burden
opera, -ae, *f.* pains, care; member of a gang
operiō, -īre, -uī, -tum I cover, hide
opēs, -um, *f. pl.* riches, wealth; resources
opīniō, -ōnis, *f.* opinion, report
opīnor (1) I think
oportet mē (2) I ought
oppidum, -ī, *n.* town
opportūnus, -a, -um opportune, at the right time, convenient, advantageous
opprimō, -ere, -pressī, -pressum I press on, crush, overwhelm
oppugnātiō, -ōnis, *f.* attack
oppugnō (1) I attack
ops, opis, *f.* aid, help
   opēs, opum, *f. pl.* wealth, resources
optābilis, -e desirable
optō (1) I wish for, pray for, choose
opus, operis, *n.* work; siege work
   opus est mihi + abl. I have need of
ōra, -ae, *f.* coast
ōrātiō, -ōnis, *f.* speech
ōrātor, -is, *m.* speaker
orbis, -is, *m.* circle, globe
   orbis terrārum, the world
ōrdior, -īrī, ōrsus I begin
ōrdō, -inis, *m.* rank, class, line
orīgō, -inis, *f.* origin

orior, orīrī, ortus I arise
ornātus, -ūs, *m.* adornment
ōrnō (1) I adorn, equip
ōrō (1) I beg, pray
ōs, ōris, *n.* mouth, face
os, ossis, *n.* bone
ostendō, -ere, -tendī, -tentum I show
ōstia, -ōrum, *n. pl.* (river) mouth
ōtiōsus, -a, -um at leisure
ōtium, -ī, *n.* leisure

pābulātor, -ōris, *m.* forager
pābulor (1) I forage
pacō (1) I pacify
palam openly
palma, -ae, *f.* palm (of victory)
palūs, -ūdis, *f.* marsh
pār, paris equal
parātus, -ūs, *m.* preparation
parcō, -ere, pepercī + dat. I spare
parēns, -tis, *c.* parent
pāreō + dat. I obey
pariō, -ere, peperī, partum I bring forth, produce, obtain
parō (1) I prepare; I acquire
pars, partis, *f.* part
   partēs, -ium, *f. pl.* party
parumper for a little
parvulus, -a, -um poor little
parvus, -a, -um small
pāscō, -ere, pāvī, pāstum I feed, pasture
pāscuum, -ī, *n.* pasture
passim here and there, hither and thither
passus, -ūs, *m.* pace
   mille passūs one mile
pāstor, -is, *m.* shepherd
patefaciō, -ere, -fēcī, -factum I open
pateō (2) I lie open, I am revealed
pater, -ris, *m.* father
patientia, -ae, *f.* patience
patior, -ī, passus I suffer; I allow
patria, -ae, *f.* native land
patrius, -a, -um of one's father, native
patrōnus, -ī, *m.* patron
paucī, -ae, -a few
paucitās, -ātis, *f.* fewness, scarcity
paulātim little by little
paulīsper for a little time
paul(l)um (adverb) a little
   paul(l)ō (by) a little
pauper, -is poor
paveō, -ēre I tremble, am afraid

pāx, pācis, *f.* peace
peccō (1) I do wrong, sin
pectus, -oris, *n.* breast
pecūnia, -ae, *f.* money
pecus, -oris, *n.* herd, flock, cattle
pedester, -ris, -re on foot
peditātus, -ūs, *m.* infantry
peditēs, -um, *m. pl.* infantry
pelagus, -ī, *n.* sea
pellō, -ere, pepulī, pulsum I drive
penātēs, -ium, *m. pl.* household gods, home
pendeō, -ēre, pependī I hang
pendō, -ere, pependī, pēnsum I weigh; I pay
penetrō (1) I penetrate
per + acc. through
peraeque equally
percussus, -a, -um struck
perdō, -ere, -didī, -ditum I lose, waste, destroy
pereō, -īre, -iī, -itum I perish, die
perferō, -ferre, -tulī, -lātum I carry through, report, endure
perficiō, -ere, -fēcī, -fectum I complete
perfidia, -ae, *f.* treachery
perfidus, -a, -um treacherous
perfuga, -ae, *m.* deserter
perfugiō, -ere, -fūgī, -fugitum I flee (for refuge)
pergō, -ere, perrēxī, perrēctum I proceed, go on
perīculum, -ī, *n.* danger
perimō, -ere, -ēmī, -ēmptum I destroy
perītus, -a, -um skilled
perlegō, -ere, -lēgī, -lēctum I read through
permaneō, -ēre, -mānsī, -mānsum I remain, persist
permittō, -ere, -mīsī, -missum I permit, allow
permoveō, -ēre, -mōvī, -mōtum I move deeply
perniciēs, -ēī, *f.* destruction, ruin
perōrō (1) I complete a speech
perpetuus, -a, -um perpetual
   in perpetuum for ever
perrumpō, -ere, -rūpī, -ruptum I break through
perscrībō, -ere, -scrīpsī, -scrīptum I write in full
persequor, -ī, -secūtus I pursue
persevērō (1) I persist, persevere in
persōna, -ae, *f.* character
perspiciō, -ere, -spexī, -spectum I look at, perceive
persuādeō, -ēre, -suāsī, -suāsum + dat. I persuade
perterreō (2) I terrify
pertinācia, -ae, *f.* persistence, obstinacy
pertineō (2) + **ad** I pertain to, concern
perturbātiō, -ōnis, *f.* confusion
perturbō (1) I throw into confusion
perūrō, -ere, -ussī, -ustum I burn up, scorch

pervincō, -ere, -vīcī, -victum I conquer completely
pēs, pedis, *m.* foot
pestis, pestis, *f.* plague, ruin
petitiō, -ōnis, *f.* request, petition, candidature
petō, -ere, petīvī, petītum I seek, ask, attack
petulanter impudently, wantonly
pharetra, -ae, *f.* quiver
pietās, -ātis, *f.* loyalty, devotion, piety
pīlum, -ī, *n.* javelin
piscis, -is, *m.* fish
pius, -a, -um loyal, pious
placeō (2) + dat. I please
   placet mihi it pleases me; I decide
placidus, -a, -um calm, peaceful
placō (1) I placate
plānē plainly, clearly
plānus, -a, -um flat
plausus, -ūs, *m.* applause
plēbs, plēbis, *f.* common people
plēnus, -a, -um full, abundant
plērīque, plēraeque, plēraque most
plērumque commonly, generally
plōrātus, -ūs, *m.* lamentation
plōrō (1) I lament
plūs, plūris more
pluvia, -ae, *f.* rain
poēma, -atis, *n.* poem
poena, -ae, *f.* punishment, penalty
   poenās dō I pay the penalty
Poenī, -ōrum, *m. pl.* Carthaginians
poēta, -ae, *m.* poet
polliceor (2) I promise
pondus, -eris, *n.* weight
pōnō, -ere, posuī, positum I place, put
pōns, pontis, *m.* bridge
pontus, -ī, *m.* sea
populāris, -e popular
   populārēs, -ium, *m. pl.* the popular party
populus, -ī, *m.* people
porta, -ae, *f.* gate
porticus, -ūs, *f.* portico, colonnade
portō (1) I carry
portus, -ūs, *m.* harbour
poscō, -ere, poposcī I demand
possideō, -ēre, -sēdī, -sessum I possess, have
possum, posse, potuī I am able; I can
post + acc. after, behind
post (adverb) later
posteā afterwards
posteritās, -ātis, *f.* posterity
posterus, -a, -um the next

posthāc after this
postis, -is, *m.* door-post; door
postquam (conjunction) after
postrīdiē the next day
postulō (1) I demand
potēns, -tis powerful
potentia, -ae, *f.* power
potestās, -ātis, *f.* power, permission
potis, -e possible
potissimum most
potius rather
prae + abl. before, in front of
praebeō (2) I offer, provide, show
praeceps, -cipitis headlong, precipitous, hasty
praeceptor, -is, *m.* teacher
praeceptum, -ī, *n.* precept, teaching, order
praecipiō, -ere, -cēpī, -ceptum I teach, order;
   I take in advance
praecipuē especially
praeclārus, -a, -um famous
praecō, -ōnis, *m.* herald
praecurrō, -ere, -currī, -cursum I run ahead
praeda, -ae, *f.* booty
praedīcō, -ere, -dīxī, -dictum I foretell, proclaim
praedō, -ōnis, *m.* pirate
praedor (1) I plunder
praefectūra, -a, *f.* prefecture
praeficiō, -ere, -fēcī, -fectum I put in charge of
praegredior, -ī, -gressus I go ahead, precede
praemium, -ī, *n.* reward
praemittō, -ere, -mīsī, -missum I sent ahead
praeparō (1) I prepare
praesēns, -tis present
praesentia, -ae, *f.* presence
praesertim especially
praesidium, -ī, *n.* garrison
praestō, -āre, -stitī, -stitum I excel; I show (qualities)
praesum, -esse, -fuī + dat. I am in charge of
praeter + acc. past, beyond, except for, beside, along
praetereā moreover
praetereō, -īre, -iī, -itum I pass by, overtake
praetermittō, -ere, -mīsī, -missum I pass over, omit
praevideō, -ēre, -vīdī, -vīsum I foresee
prātum, -ī, *n.* meadow
precēs, -um, *f. pl.* prayers
precor (1) I pray
premō, -ere, pressī, pressum I press, overwhelm; I
   darken
pretium, -ī, *n.* price
prīdiē the day before
prīmus, -a, -um first

prīmum (adverb) first
in prīmīs especially
prīnceps, -cipis, *m.* chief, leading man; first
prīncipium, -ī, *n.* beginning
prior, prius former
priscus, -a, -um former, ancient
prīstinus, -a, -um former
priusquam before
prīvātus, -a, -um private
prō + abl. in front of, on behalf of, instead of, in return
   for
probō (1) I approve of
probus, -a, -um good, honest
prōcēdō, -ere, -cessī, -cessum I go forward, proceed,
   advance
procul far, at a distance
prōcurrō, -ere, -currī, -cursum I run forward
prōditiō, -ōnis, *f.* betrayal
prōdō, -ere, -didī, -ditum I betray
prōducō, -ere, -dūxī, -ductum I lead forward, prolong
proelium, -ī, *n.* battle
prōfectiō, -ōnis, *f.* setting out, departure
prōficiō, -ere, fēcī, -fectum I make progress
proficīscor, -ī, -fectus I set out
prōfugiō, -ere, -fūgī, -fugitum I flee, run away from
prōgredior, -ī, -gressus I advance
prohibeō (2) I prevent
prōiciō, -ere, -iēcī, -iectum I throw down, away
proinde accordingly
prōlābor, -ī, -lāpsus I fall down, slip forward
prōmissum, -ī, *n.* promise
prōmittō, -ere, -mīsī, -missum I promise
prōnuntiō (1) I proclaim
prope + acc. near
prōpediem (adverb) soon
prōpellō, -ere, -pulī, -pulsum I drive forward
properō (1) I hasten
propinquus, -a, -um near
propinquus, -ī, *m.* kinsman
prōpōnō, -ere, -posuī, -positum I put forward,
   propose
prōpositum, -ī, *n.* intention, purpose
propter + acc. on account of
prōsequor, -ī, -secūtus I escort, pursue
prōspectus, -ūs, *m.* view
prōspiciō, -ere, -spexī, -spectum I see in front,
   foresee
prōtegō, -ere, -texī, -tectum I cover, protect
prōtinus (adverb) straight away
prosperē successfully
prōsum, prōdesse, prōfuī + dat. I benefit, help

prōvehō, -ere, -vēxī, -vectum I carry forward
prōvehor, -ī, -vectus I ride, sail forwards
prōvideō, -ēre, -vīdī, -vīsum I foresee, provide
prōvincia, -ae, *f.* province
proximus, -a, -um nearest, next
prūdēns, -tis sensible, wise
prūdentia, -ae, *f.* good sense
pudet (mē) I am ashamed
pudīcus, -a, -um chaste, virtuous
pudor, -is, *m.* shame, modesty
puella, -ae, *f.* girl
puer, -ī, *m.* boy
pueritia, -ae, *f.* boyhood
pugna, -ae, *f.* battle
pugnō (1) I fight
pulcher, pulchra, pulchrum beautiful
pulchritūdō, -inis, *f.* beauty
pulsō (1) I strike, beat
pulvis, -eris, *m.* dust
pūniō (4) I punish
puppis, -is, *f.* stern, ship
pūriter purely, cleanly
pūrus, -a, -um pure
putō (1) I think, consider

quā where
quaerō, -ere, quaesīvī, quaesītum I seek, ask
quaesō, -ere, -īvī I ask (for)
quaestūra, -ae, *f.* quaestorship
quālis, -e what sort of? what?
quam than; how; as
quamquam although
quamvīs however much, although
quandō? when?
quandoquidem since
quantus, -a, -um? how great?
quārē? for what reason?, why?
quārē and so, for this reason
quasi as if
quassō (1) I shake, batter
quatiō, -ere, —, quassum I shake
-que and
-que ... -que both ... and
queō, quīre, quīvī I can
querēla, -ae, *f.* complaint
queror, -ī, questus I complain
quia because
quīcumque, quaecumque, quodcumque whoever, whatever
quid? = why?
quīdam, quaedam, quoddam a, a certain
quidem indeed (emphasizes preceding word)

quiēs, -ētis, *f.* rest
quīlibet, quaelibet, quodlibet any you please
quis? quid? who? what?
quis, quid anyone, anything
quisquam, quicquam anyone, anything
quisque, quaeque, quodque each
quisquis, quidquid whoever
quīvīs, quaevīs, quodvīs any, anyone, anything
quō? whither? where to?
quoad until
quōcumque wherever
quod because
quōmodo? how?
quondam once, formerly; at some future time
quoniam since
quoque also
quot? (indecl. adj.) how many? as many
quotiēns how often, as often as, every time that

rapidus, -a, -um swift, rapid
rapiō, -ere, rapuī, raptum I snatch
raptim hastily
rārō (adverb) rarely
rārus, -a, -um rare, scanty
ratiō, -ōnis, *f.* reason, plan, method, way
    ratiōnēs, *f. pl.* accounts
ratis, -is, *f.* raft, ship
rebelliō, -ōnis, *f.* rebellion
recēdō, -ere, cessī, -cessum I retire, retreat, go away
recēns, -entis recent, fresh
recessus, -ūs, *m.* retreat
recipiō, -ere, -cēpī, -ceptum I take back
    mē recipiō I retire, retreat
recitō (1) I read aloud
reconciliō (1) I reconcile
recordor (1) I remember
recreō (1) I restore, revive
redeō, -īre, -iī, -itum I return
reditus, -ūs, *m.* return
referō, referre, rettulī, relātum I carry back; I report
    pedem referō I retreat
refert, -ferre, -tulit it matters
reficiō, -ere, -fēcī, -fectum I repair
refugiō, -ere, -fūgī I flee back
rēgīna, -ae, *f.* queen
regiō, -ōnis, *f.* region, district
rēgius, -a, -um royal
rēgnātor, -is, *m.* ruler, king
rēgnō (1) I rule as king
rēgnum, -ī, *n.* kingdom, power
regō, -ere, rēxī, rēctum I rule
regredior, -ī, -gressus I return

religiō, -ōnis, *f.* religion
relinquō, -ere, -līquī, -lictum I leave behind
reliquiae, -ārum, *f. pl.* remnants, remains
reliquus, -a, -um remaining, the rest
remaneō, -ēre, -mānsī, -mānsum I stay behind, persist
rēmigō (1) I row
remigrō (1) I return
remittō, -ere, -mīsī, -missum I send back; I slacken
removeō, -ēre, -mōvī, -mōtum I remove
remūneror (1) I pay back
rēmus, -ī, *m.* oar
renovō (1) I renew, refresh
renūntiō (1) I report
reor, rērī, ratus I think
repellō, -ere, -pulī, -pulsum I drive back, I reject
repente suddenly
repentīnus, -a, -um sudden
reperiō, -īre, repperī, repertum I find
repetō, -ere, -petiī, -petītum I seek again, demand back, recall
repleō, -ēre, -plēvī, -plētum I fill up, replenish
repōnō, -ere, -posuī, -positum I put back
reportō (1) I carry back
reposcō, -ere I demand back
reprehendō, -ere, -prehendī, -prehēnsum I blame
repudiō (1) I reject, divorce
repugnō (1) I fight back
repulsa, -ae, *f.* rejection
requiēs, -tis, *f.* rest
requiēscō, -ere, -quiēvī I rest
requīrō, -ere, -quīsiī, -quīsītum I look for, ask for
rēs, rēī, *f.* thing, matter
rescrībō, -ere, -scrīpsī, -scrīptum I write back, reply
reservō (1) I keep back, reserve
resīdō, -ere, -sēdī I sit down, settle
resistō, -ere, -stitī, -stitum + dat. I resist
resolvō, -ere, -solvī, -solūtum I loosen, melt
resonō (1) I resound, echo
respectō (1) I look back
respiciō, -ere, -spexī, -spectum I look back
respondeō, -ēre, -spondī, -spōnsum I reply, answer
rēspūblica, rēīpūblicae, *f.* the republic, public affairs
restituō, -ere, -stituī, -stitūtum I restore, put back
restō (1) I remain, am left
retegō, -ere, -texī, -tectum I uncover
revertor, -ī, -versus I return
revellō, -ere, -vellī, -vulsum I pluck out, undo
revīsō, -ere, -vīsī I revisit
revīvīscō, -ere I come to life again
rēx, rēgis, *m.* king
rhētoricus, -a, -um rhetorical

rīdeō, -ēre, rīsī, rīsum I laugh (at)
rigidus, -a, -um stiff, hard
rīpa, -ae, *f.* bank
rivus, -ī, *m.* stream
rixa, -ae, *f.* quarrel
rōbur, -oris strength, flower, oak
rogō (1) I ask, I ask for
rogus, -ī, *m.* funeral pyre
rōstra, -ōrum, *n. pl.* speaker's platform
rota, -ae, *f.* wheel
rubeō (2) I am red, become red
rūmor, -is, *m.* rumour, report
rumpō, -ere, -rūpī, -ruptum I break
ruō, -ere, ruī I rush
rūpēs, -is, *f.* crag, rock, cliff
rūrsus (adverb) again
rūs, rūris, *n.* countryside

sacer, sacra, sacrum sacred; cursed
sacerdōs, -ōtis, *m.* priest
sacrificō (1) I sacrifice
saeculum, -ī, *n.* generation, age
saepe often
saevus, -a, -um savage
sagitta, -ae, *f.* arrow
saltem at least
saltus, -ūs, *m.* defile, pass, glade
salūber, -ris, -re healthy
salūbritās, -ātis, *f.* healthiness
salūs, -ūtis, *f.* health, safety, greetings
salūtō (1) I greet
salvus, -a, -um safe
sānctus, -a, -um holy
sānē certainly, truly
sanguis, -inis, *m.* blood
sapiēns, -tis wise
sapientia, -ae, *f.* wisdom
sarcina, -ae, *f.* pack
satis enough
saucius, -a, -um wounded
saxum, -ī, *n.* rock
scāla, -ae, *f.* ladder
scelus, -eris, *n.* crime
scientia, -ae, *f.* knowledge
scindō, -ere, scidī, scissum I cut, break
sciō (4) I know
scrība, -ae, *m.* secretary
scrībō, -ere, scrīpsī, scrīptum I write
scūtum, -ī, *n.* shield
sēcēdō, -ere, -cessī, -cessum I retire
secō, -āre, secuī, sectum I cut
secundus, -a, -um second, favourable

sedeō, -ēre, sēdī, sessum I sit
sēdēs, -is, *f.* seat
segnis, -e slack, lazy
semel once
sēmimortuus, -a, -um half-dead
sēmita, -ae, *f.* path
semper always
sempiternus, -a, -um everlasting
senex, senis, *m.* old man
senior, -is older
sēnsus, -ūs, *m.* feeling
sententia, -ae, *f.* opinion, vote
sentiō, -īre, sēnsī, sēnsum I feel, perceive
sequor, -ī, secūtus I follow
sermō, -ōnis, *m.* conversation, talk, speech
sērō late
servō (1) I save, preserve; I observe
servus, -ī, *m.* slave
sēstertius, -ī, *m.* sesterce
seu ... seu ... whether ... or ...
sevērus, -a, -um severe
sī if
sīc thus
siccus, -a, -um dry
sīcut, sīcutī just as, just as if
sīdus, -eris, *n.* constellation, star
significō (1) I signify
signum, -ī, *n.* sign, standard, signal
silentium, -ī, *n.* silence
sileō (2) I am silent
silēscō, -ere I fall silent
silva, -ae, *f.* wood, forest
silvestris, -e wooded, silvan
similis, -e like
simul together
    simul ac/atque at the same time as
simulātiō, -ōnis, *f.* pretence
simulō (1) I pretend
simultās, -ātis, *f.* quarrel
sīn but if
sincērus, -a, -um genuine, faithful
sine + abl. without
singulāris, -e single, remarkable, unique
sinister, sinistra, sinistrum left
    sinistrā on the left
sinō, sinere, sīvī, situm I allow
sinus, -ūs, *m.* curve, fold of a toga, embrace
sistō, -ere, stitī, statum I stand
situs, -ūs, *m.* site, position
situs, -a, -um sited
sīve ... sīve ... whether ... or ...

socius, -ī, *m.* ally, partner
sōl, sōlis, *m.* sun
soleō, -ēre, solitus I am accustomed
sōlitūdō, -inis, *f.* solitude, loneliness
solitus, -a, -um customary
sollicitō (1) I harass, worry
sollicitūdō, -inis, *f.* anxiety
sollicitus, -a, -um anxious
sōlor (1) I console
sōlum (adverb) only
sōlus, -a, -um alone
solvō, -ere, solvī, solūtum I loose, cast off
somnus, -ī, *m.* sleep
sonō, -āre, -uī, -itum I sound, make a noise
sonus, -ī, *m.* sound
sordēs, -ium, *f. pl.* filth, squalor, low condition
sordidus, -a, -um dirty, mean
soror, -ōris, *f.* sister
sors, sortis, *f.* chance, lot; *pl.* oracle
spatium, -ī, *n.* space (of time or distance)
speciēs, -ēī, *f.* appearance; pretence
speciō, -ere, spexī I look at
spectāculum, -ī, *n.* sight, show
spectātor, -is, *m.* spectator
spectō (1) I watch
spēlunca, -ae, *f.* cave
spernō, -ere, sprēvī, sprētum I despise
spērō (1) I hope, expect
spēs, spēī, *f.* hope
spīritus, -ūs, *m.* breath
spondeō, -ēre, spopondī, spōnsum I guarantee
sponte (meā) of (my) own accord
statim at once
statiō, -ōnis, *f.* post
status, -ūs, *m.* state (of affairs)
stella, -ae, *f.* star
stīpendium, -ī, *n.* pay, year of military service, tax
stīpō (1) I press, crowd together; I surround
stirps, -is, *f.* stock, family
stō, stāre, stetī, statum I stand
strāgēs, -is, *f.* slaughter
strēnuus, -a, -um strenuous, active, vigorous
strepitus, -ūs, *m.* noise
stringō, -ere, strīnxī, strictum I draw (a sword), I graze
studeō (2) + dat. I am keen on
studiōsus, -a, -um eager, studious
studium, -ī, *n.* eagerness, effort, study
stupeō (2) I am amazed, am stunned
suādeō, -ēre, suāsī, suāsum + dat. I persuade, advise
sub + abl. under

subdūcō, -ere, -dūxī, -ductum I lead down; I beach; I remove, steal

subeō, -īre, -iī, -itum I approach; come into one's mind

subiciō, -ere, -iēcī, -iectum I throw under, subject

subiectus, -a, -um lying under

subigō, -ere, -ēgī, -āctum I subdue

subitō (adverb) suddenly

sublātus (past participle passive of **tollō**) uplifted, excited, destroyed

sublevō (1) I lift, lighten

subsequor, -ī, -secūtus I follow closely

subsidium, -ī, *n.* help, support

subsīdō, -ere, -sēdī, -sessum I sit down, sink

subsistō, -ere, -stitī I stand firm

subveniō, -īre, -vēnī, -ventum + dative I come to help

subvolvō, -ere, -volvī, -volūtum I roll uphill

succendō, -ere, -cendī, -cēnsum I set alight, inflame

successus, -ūs, *m.* success

succīdō, -ere, -īdī, -cīsum I cut down

sudis, -is, *f.* stake

summa, -ae, *f.* sum, main point, total

summātim in sum, in brief

summittō, -ere, -mīsī, -missum I send help

summoveō, -ēre, -mōvī, -mōtum I remove, dislodge

summus, -a, -um highest, greatest

sūmō, -ere, sūmpsī, sumptum I take, take up

sūmptus, -ūs, *m.* expense

super + acc. above

superbus, -a, -um proud

superī, -ōrum, *m. pl.* the gods above

superior, -us higher, earlier, superior

superō (1) I overcome

supersum, -esse, -fuī I am left over, I survive

supplex, -icis, *c.* suppliant

supplicium, -ī, *n.* punishment, death penalty

suppōnō, -ere, -posuī, -positum I place beneath

suprā + acc. above

suprēmus, -a, -um highest, last

surgō, -ere, surrēxī, surrēctum I rise, get up

surripiō, -ere, -ripuī, -reptum I snatch away, steal

suscipiō, -ere, -cēpī, -ceptum I undertake

suspīciō, -ōnis, *f.* suspicion

suspiciō, -ere, -spexī, -spectum I suspect

suspicor (1) I suspect

sustentō (1) I support, hold up

sustineō, -ēre, -tinuī I sustain, bear up, support

sustulī see **tollō**

taceō (2) I am silent

tacitus, -a, -um silent

taedet (mē) I am tired of

taedium, -ī, *n.* weariness

tālis, -e such

tam so

tamen but, however

tametsī although

tamquam (sī) as if

tandem at length

tangō, -ere, tetigī, tāctum I touch

tantulus, -a, -um so small

tantum only

tantus, -a, -um so great

tardus, -a, -um slow, late

tēctum, -ī, *n.* roof, house

tegō, -ere, tēxī, tēctum I cover

tellūs, -ūris, *f.* the earth, land

tēlum, -ī, *n.* missile

temerē rashly

temeritās, -ātis, *f.* recklessness

tempestās, -ātis, *f.* storm, weather

templum, -ī, *n.* temple

temptō (1) I try, attempt

tempus, -oris, *n.* time

tenāx, -ācis firm

tendō, -ere, tetendī, tentum I stretch, pull, strive

tenebrae, -ārum, *f. pl.* darkness

teneō, -ēre, tenuī, tentum I hold

tener, tenera, tenerum tender

tenuis, -e thin, weak

tepeō (2) I am warm

tergum, -ī, *n.* back

   ā tergō from behind

terra, -ae, *f.* earth; land

terreō (2) I terrify

terror, -is, *m.* terror

testimōnium, -ī, *n.* evidence

testis, -is, *c.* witness

theātrum, -ī, *n.* theatre

thymum, -ī, *n.* thyme

timeō (2) I fear

timiditās, -ātis, *f.* fear, nervousness

timidus, -a, -um timid

timor, -is, *m.* fear

toga, -ae, *f.* toga

tolerō (1) I endure

tollō, -ere, sustulī, sublātum I raise, remove, destroy

torqueō, -ēre, torsī, tortum I twist, turn

torreō (2) I scorch

torum, -ī, *n.* couch

tot (indecl.) so many

totiēns so often

tōtus, -a, -um whole

trādō, -ere, -didī, -ditum I hand over, hand down

trādūcō, -ere, -dūxī, -ductum I lead across

trāgula, -ae, *f.* javelin
trahō, -ere, trāxī, tractum I draw, drag
trāiciō, -ere, -iēcī, -iectum I throw across, send across; I cross
trāiectus, -ūs, *m.* crossing
trāns + acc. across
trānscendō, -ere, -scendī, -scēnsum I climb across
trānseō, -īre, -iī, -itum I cross
trānsfīgō, -ere, -fīxī, -fīxum I pierce
trānsgredior, -ī, -gressus I cross
trānsiliō, -īre, -siluī I jump across
trānsitus, -ūs, *m.* crossing
trānsportō (1) I transport
trepidō (1) I panic
trepidus, -a, -um alarmed, trembling
tribūnātus, -ūs, *m.* tribunate
tribūnus plēbis tribune of the people
trīclīnium, -ī, *n.* dining room
trīduum, -ī, *n.* a period of three days
trīstis, -e sad
triumphō (1) I triumph
triumphus, -ī, *m.* triumph
trūdō, -ere, trūsī, trūsum I push, shove
tueor (2) I gaze at, observe; I protect
tum then
tumidus, -a, -um swollen
tumultuōsus, -a, -um turbulent, violent
tumultus, -ūs, *m.* commotion, uproar; rebellion
tumulus, -ī, *m.* tomb; hillock
tunc then
turba, -ae, *f.* crowd
turbidus, -a, -um confused, disordered
turbō (1) I disturb, confuse, trouble
turpis, -e disgraceful
turris, -is, *f.* tower
tūtus, -a, -um safe

ūber, -is fertile
ubi when
ubi? where?
ubīque everywhere
ulcīscor, -ī, ultus I avenge
ūllus, -a, -um any
ulterior, -us further
ultimus, -a, -um furthest, last
ultor, -oris, *m.* avenger
ultrā + acc. beyond
ultrā (adverb) beyond
ultrō (adverb) of one's own accord
umbra, -ae, *f.* shadow
umerus, -ī, *m.* shoulder
umquam ever

ūnā together (with)
unda, -ae, *f.* wave
unde? whence?
undique from all sides
ūnicus, -a, -um one and only, unique
ūniversī, -ae, -a altogether
unquam ever
urbānus, -a, -um of the city
urbs, urbis, *f.* city
urgeō, -ēre I push, press
ūrō, -ere, ussī, ustum I burn up
usquam anywhere
usque continually
    usque ad right up to
ūsus, -ūs, *m.* use
ut prīmum as soon as
uter, utra, utrum? which of two?
uterque, utraque, utrumque each of two
utī = ut
ūtilis, -e useful
ūtor, -ī, ūsus + abl. I use
utrimque from both sides
utrum ... an ... whether ... or ...
uxor, -is, *f.* wife

vacō (1) I am empty, vacant
vacuus, -a, -um empty
vada, -ōrum, *n. pl.* waters (of the sea)
vāgīna, -ae, *f.* sheath
vagor (1) I wander
valdē very
valeō (2) I am well; I am strong; I am able
    valē farewell
valētūdō, -inis, *f.* health
validus, -a, -um strong
vallēs, vallis, *f.* valley
vāllum, -ī, *n.* rampart
vānus, -a, -um vain, empty
varius, -a, -um various, different
vāstō (1) I lay waste
vātēs, -is, *m.* prophet, poet
-ve or
vehemēns, -tis violent
vehō, -ere, vēxī, vectum I carry
vel or
vel ... vel either ... or
vēlāmen, -inis, *n.* covering
velut like; just as (if)
vendō, -ere, vendidī, venditum I sell
venēnum, -ī, *n.* poison
venia, -ae, *f.* pardon
veniō, -īre, vēnī, ventum I come

vēnor (1) I hunt
venter, -ris, *m.* belly, stomach
ventitō (1) I come and go
ventus, -ī, *m.* wind
venustus, -a, -um beautiful
vēr, vēris, *n.* spring
verbum, -ī, *n.* word
verbus, -eris, *n.* lash
vereor (2) I fear
vērō in fact, certainly; but
versō (1) I keep turning, turn over
versor (1) I come and go, I take part in
versus, -ūs, *m.* verse
vertex, -icis, *m.* top, head
vertō, -ere, vertī, versum I turn
vērum (conj.) but
vērus, -a, -um true
vesper, -is, *m.* evening
vester, -ra, -rum your
vestīgium, -ī, *n.* footprint, track, trace
vestiō (4) I clothe
vestis, -is, *f.* clothing
vetō, -āre, vetuī, vetitum I forbid
vetus, -eris old
vexō (1) I harass, annoy
via, -ae, *f.* road, way
vīcīnia, -ae, *f.* neighbourhood
vīcīnus, -a, -um neighbouring
victor, -is, *m.* conqueror
victōria, -ae, *f.* victory
vīcus, -ī, *m.* village
videō, -ēre, vīdī, vīsum I see
videor, -ērī, vīsus I seem, appear
viduus, -a, -um bereft, mateless
vigilia, -ae, *f.* watch, wakefulness
vigilō (1) I am awake

vigor, -is, *m.* vigour, energy
vīlis, -e cheap, worthless
vīlla, -ae, *f.* country house
vinciō, -īre, vīnxī, vīnctum I bind
vincō, -ere, vīcī, victum I conquer
vinculum, -ī, n. chain
vīnum, -ī, *n.* wine
violō (1) I violate
vir, -ī, *m.* man
viridis, -e green
virtūs, -ūtis, *f.* manliness, courage
vīs, vim, vī, *f.* force
vīrēs, -ium, *f. pl.* strength
vīsō, -ere, vīsī I visit, go to see
vīta, -ae, *f.* life
vitium, -ī, *n.* fault, vice
vītō (1) I avoid
vituperō (1) I abuse
vīvō, -ere, vīxī, victum I live
vīvus, -a, -um alive
vix scarcely
vocō (1) I call
volātilis, -e flying
volō (1) I fly
volō, velle, voluī I wish, am willing
volucer, -ris, -re winged, flying
voluntās, -ātis, *f.* will, good will
voluptās, -ātis, *f.* pleasure
volvō, -ere, volvī, volūtum I roll
vōtum, -ī, *n.* prayer, vow
vōx, vōcis, *f.* voice
vulgus, -ī, *m.* the people
vulnerō (1) I wound
vulnus, -eris, *n.* wound
vultus, -ūs, *m.* face, expression

Index of names

A few names, which only occur once, are omitted.
Reference is to page numbers.